WHO'S YOUR IDEAL LOVER?

- A sociable life-of-the-party type who enjoys being the center of attention—or a quietly caring spouse who's content to be the mainstay of your life?
- A creative dynamo who can conjure up big, new ideas—or a rational thinker who can zero in on the facts?
- A sensitive lover who never goes to bed angry—or an intense and dynamic paramour who'll stay up and fight?

To understand the type of relationship you want, you must first learn which type of lover you are! In this engaging guide to knowing yourself and others you will discover:

- Whether you are a gregarious Extravert or a reflective Introvert;
- Why Sensors prefer to get straight to the facts while iNtuitive types are in search of the big picture;
- If you are a Thinker who charts an analytical course to love or a Feeler who'll do anything to make someone else happy;
- Whether your tendency to schedule everything (including love-making!) means that you're a Judger—or if you're really a Perceiver, with an unquenchable passion for exploring the unknown. . . .

16 WAYS TO LOVE YOUR LOVER

16 WAYS TO LOVE YOUR LOVER

Understanding the 16
Personality Types
So You Can Create a Love
That Lasts Forever

OTTO KROEGER · JANET M. THUESEN

A Tilden Press Book

◆

A Dell Trade Paperback

In honor of our marriage:
Through our commitment to celebrating
differences, it continues to grow and flourish—
and, above all, is never boring.

Contents

—— III ——

PUTTING
TYPE TALK
TO WORK

Acknowledgments

This is a book about relationships. It is the product of thousands of personal and professional relationships we have enjoyed over the years. We have been blessed by an endless fount of stories about intimate relationships—both the agony and the ecstasy—from friends, staff, and neighbors as well as couples' workshops and marital counseling. Their stories can be found throughout these pages (mercifully, with identities changed). So we must begin by thanking all of those who shared so openly with us, knowing that their tales might someday be enshrined in a book.

In addition, there are those who deserve special recognition and thanks.

First and foremost we must extend thanks to our staff, which we consider extended family: Pat Hutson, Connie Ridge, Kim Crawford, and Nikki Binford, who freed us from daily office life sufficiently to spend time on this book. Special thanks to Emily King, who provided editorial help beyond the call of duty. As usual, our associates—Vic Cocowitch, Eleanor Corlett, Jill M. Esbeck, Mike Esnard, Gloria C. Fauth, Joyce S. Kaser, Catherine Lilly, Anthony Moore, Don Mulvihill, Janet Newberg-Gilbert, Harry Noel, Judith Noel, Chum Robert, and Joan Wofford—continue to provide professional feedback and encouragement.

This book, like its two predecessors, would not have happened without the efforts of our friend and colleague Joel Makower. He is an unending resource who has a talent for crafting our rambling thoughts into the readable and intelligible work that follows. Sometimes encouraging, sometimes confronting and directing, yet always pursuing excellence, Joel has been the driving force behind this project.

Our friends at Dell Publishing continue to provide support and enthusiasm that any authors would envy. Isabel Geffner has been an inspiring and insightful editor who has pushed us in positive and affirming ways. Carole Baron has been our faithful supporter and guiding light at every stage of this project.

Several individuals graciously submitted anecdotes and vignettes that we have used in this book: Lisa Y. Beldon, Jonathan K. Burns, Marjorie D. K. Cameron, Ron and Janet Carr, Terry Cohen, Laura J. Emerson, Molly Gibbs, George G. Mack, Tom and Rita Osborn, Diane Rauschenfels, Damien F. Renella, Tina Rolen, Trisha Svehla, Phil Wendel—as well as several modest souls who identified themselves only as "Bill," "Joy," "Maureen," and "Patti."

Others who provided inspiration, friendship, and support include Susan Scanlon and *The Type Reporter*; Randy Rosenberg and Shayna P. Rosenberg, for their cheerful hospitality; our children, E. Scott Esbeck, Jill M. Esbeck, Karen M. Esbeck, Stephen O. Kroeger, Susan E. Kroeger, and Amy Jane Kroeger; Sandy Falvey, Vincent Guss, Donald and Shirley Kroeger, Robert and Shirley Kroeger, Donald and Alice Imig, Frank and Jean Lee, and James A. and Carmella Kroeger; our friends at Peace Lutheran Church; and last but by no means least, the Every-Other-Friday-Night Lake Barcroft Hard-Core-Attitude-Adjustment Group, an ongoing source of joy.

—O.K. and J.M.T.
Falls Church, Virginia

How to Read This Book

All of us do things a bit differently. That's what makes each of us unique and special. Even something as simple as reading a book can be done in a number of ways. None of them is the "right" or "wrong" way. They're just different.

Consider the book you're now reading. It is divided into three main sections. Part I introduces the basics of Type-watching and can help you determine your personality preferences and explain how this self-awareness can help you in every aspect of your life. In Part II we show you how to apply that knowledge and insight in the four most significant parts of any intimate relationship. Finally, in Part III, we offer thumbnail sketches of the sixteen personality types, revealing their strengths and weaknesses in various parts of life.

Here are some suggestions on how to take advantage of all this information in a way that will satisfy your individual style and needs:

- If you're the kind of person who likes to share what you read with others, and who learns best by talking things through, we encourage you to do so. In fact, we recommend sharing some of the boxed material immediately with your friends and significant others. It will make for some lively discussions.

+ However, if you're the kind of person who likes to reflect on what you've read, that's perfectly legit. We encourage you to find some quiet, reflective place and time in which you can contemplate parts of the book and integrate them into your thinking.

+ If you're the kind of person who likes to take things from beginning to end, with as few detours as possible, read on. We have presented this material in a format whose orderly progression should be to your liking.

+ However, if you're the kind of person who enjoys scanning, occasionally jumping in when something catches your eye, then letting your imagination run wild, you will find plenty of possibilities on almost any page. Your scanning will be most effective if you lay a foundation by reading the first three chapters of Part I.

+ If you're a natural skeptic, particularly when it comes to psychology, you're not alone. This book is not going to "psych you out," and the theory upon which it is based has nearly fifty years of research behind it. As you'll see, the theory even encourages healthy skepticism.

+ However, if you're the kind of person who likes psychology or other motivational materials that help people feel good about themselves and their accomplishments, you will find much to your liking here. But don't get carried away simply with the notion that happiness is its own reward. There's life to live, and the principal goal of this book is to harness personality differences to get through it with as little interpersonal conflict as possible.

+ If you're the kind of person who likes things organized and according to a rigid plan, we recommend that you schedule a fixed time each day to read a section of the book. You will find that we have organized this book into bite-sized chunks so that even ten minutes' reading will offer a complete thought.

+ However, if you're the kind of person who resists plans and prefers to do things on the spur of the moment, don't worry if you're not able to read the entire book in a few sittings. Even if you put the book down for a few weeks or even months, you can apply what you've already read to your everyday life. But it is our sincere hope that you eventually get through the entire book.

As you can see, there are very different ways of doing something as simple as reading a book. And yet each way is valid. The process may be different, but the result is the same.

That's a central theme to this book: Our individual differences, when understood and appreciated, make any relationship more successful and enjoyable.

So read on—however you choose to do it.

I

HOW TO
TYPE TALK

1

LEARNING TO DANCE

"She should know I love her. I'm always around."

There are no easy relationships. For too long we have labored under the myth that marriages are made in heaven and that friendships are forever. Of course, we know such statements are simply not true. It takes a great deal of hard work to maintain a healthy, growing relationship. And not just with marriage and significant others: neighbors, parents, children, colleagues, employees, bosses—any relationship that is more than a casual acquaintance requires some effort in order to understand each party's individual styles and differences.

We liken the process to learning to dance. You can never take your partner for granted, lest you end up stepping on each other's toes. There are few natural-born Fred Astaires and Ginger Rogers in the world. Indeed, even Fred and Ginger labored daily to achieve that dancing-on-air appearance. So, too, with friends, lovers, and others with whom we relate. Behind even the most enviable marriage or friendship inevitably lies a great deal of learning to "dance": fitting into each other's space, knowing when to lead and when to follow, adapting to constantly changing conditions, and ensuring that we interact with grace and style.

3

Those of us who do not have a regular dance partner face additional challenges. As we scan the great ballroom of life searching for potential partners, we must be aware of our own needs, desires, competencies, and limitations. Without such knowledge it is difficult even to venture onto the dance floor, let alone move with ease and grace with a partner. That, too, takes some effort and persistence. You can talk about the tango endlessly, but until you get out there and do it—and then do it some more—you'll never be light on your feet.

This book is about the dances of life: the delicate footwork, graceful teamwork, and even the wild intensity we face in our everyday encounters and relationships. It is about how to pick the right partner or move more gracefully with the one you already have. It is how to be in touch with your own moves and your partner's, and how to communicate—verbally and nonverbally—in order to get to where you want to go next.

Dancing and relating with others are two very different things, of course. We may only dance with a handful of partners in life, and usually with only one partner at a time. And you can get through life just fine without ever dancing a step. But most of us relate every day with a wide range of individuals, both alone and in groups. There is simply no way to escape it. And just when you think you've mastered the challenges of the moment, along comes another "partner" or a new "song" that trips you up and reminds you that there are new and different steps to learn.

We could tell you endless stories about how people trip themselves up every day by not understanding some relatively simple concepts about human behavior. We can do this because for more than three decades we have been in the business of helping people learn to relate better—with themselves, their spouses, bosses, children, parents, friends, and many others. We know firsthand that for the vast majority of people there isn't a problem that can't be solved or prevented by better communication and understanding. You name the dilemma, from flirtatious spouses to friends who don't return things they borrow, from hurt feelings to unexpressed gratitudes, from mangled finances to messy rooms, from the ridiculous to the sublime. We've worked with them all, and we know some of the secrets to success.

We'll get to many of the stories later in this book. For now, let's focus in on intimate relationships and begin to illustrate some of the pitfalls and promises of getting along.

◆

"Do You Love Me?"

Those four simple words are at the heart and soul of many meaningful relationships. Though it may seem a simple question, it often begs more than a simple answer. Merely posing it can mask a host of frustrations and problems lurking in a relationship. More often than not those words—and the behavior that can go with them—represent the tip of an iceberg, often obscuring many complex issues hiding beneath the surface.

In the case of Julie and Mark, her asking that question repeatedly without receiving a satisfactory answer symbolized the beginning of what seemed to be the end of an eight-year marriage.

It hadn't always been that way, of course. During the early years of dating and mating Mark thought Julie's constant query to be cute—an endearing invitation to a variety of intimate exchanges between them. Sometimes Mark would "answer" with a hug, or perhaps venture a Gary Cooper "Yup!" Other times the mere asking of the question would quickly lead to a passionate moment—or an all-night marathon.

But as Julie's questions persisted over the years, Mark's willingness to offer even these indirect responses waned.

"Why do I have to keep stating the obvious?" he told us sometime later. "She should know I love her. I'm always around. I'm a great father to our two kids. I bring home a handsome paycheck every two weeks. I've never cheated, or flirted in her company. What else do I have to do to prove myself?"

Besides, Mark went on, "Talk is cheap. Why do I have to state the obvious when I express my love in so many more meaningful ways every day?"

It wasn't that Julie didn't appreciate Mark being her Rock of Gibraltar. But she wanted more. "What's wrong with saying, 'I love you'?" she asked us. "I want our relationship to be fun. I want it to be new and romantic every day, just like in the beginning. There will be plenty of time in later years to take each other for granted and deal with more serious things."

All of this was more than a simple dispute over a few well-chosen words. Mark's growing reluctance to give Julie the verbal expression she needed had become a thorn in the side of their marriage. In Julie's eyes Mark's nonresponsiveness told her she was no longer seen as attractive—physically or otherwise—to her husband. That tapped into her own deep feelings of insecurity, self-doubt, and anxiety about whether she could ever please any of the men in her life—her husband, her father, her boss, even her young son. Her frustration with Mark was slowly but surely taking the form of resentment. She found herself less willing to do some of the little things she knew pleased him—give him backrubs at the end of a long day, cook his favorite meal, allow him time to tinker in his workshop on weekends. *After all,* she figured, *why bend over backward to meet his needs, when he's not meeting mine?*

Mark was well aware of the way Julie seemed to be changing. Believing he was doing all the right things, he couldn't understand how he could be part of her problem. "It must be a phase she's going through," he figured. "Just leave her alone. She'll work things through on her own. I just need to provide a strong foundation by continuing to be a good and responsible husband so she knows the marriage is secure."

It doesn't take a master's degree in psychology to see where this marriage was headed. Yesterday's excitements and turn-ons had slipped away, eroded by life's changing roles and responsibilities—careers, child rearing, finances, and all the rest. Both Mark and Julie tended to avoid the obvious misunderstandings in the hopes that they would go away by themselves. After all, these seemed relatively minor issues—it wasn't as if one party was having an affair or had threatened to leave the other—which would be resolved if only they weren't blown out of proportion. Love, they believed, would conquer all.

We first encountered them when they joined a couples' workshop we were conducting. One of the first big insights for Mark and Julie was that their differences were much bigger than they had realized and that it might take some time to explore at a deeper level what were becoming some serious relationship problems. That alone was both a surprise and a breakthrough, though Mark was reluctant and embarrassed about declaring publicly (at least within the group) that a real problem existed. Part of him continued to say, "It's basically Julie's problem. After all, like so many women, she seems to make mountains out of molehills. Even worse, she insists on airing our dirty linen in public."

Mark also owned up to the fact that like most men, he was brought up to believe that turning to professionals for help with normal personal problems was a sign of weakness. That, too, was a breakthrough, but it didn't solve the problem; it only opened the door for further discussion. In fact, the discussions themselves seemed to be creating even more problems. Mark at one point exclaimed sadly, "The more we talk, the more we seem to be hopelessly different on everything. She thinks human frailties are a sign of strength. I've always thought them to be signs of weaknesses." And, finally, the ultimate question: "Can this marriage be saved?"

Little by little, as the weekend wore on, Mark and Julie came to some realizations. One was that the things that were causing so many problems were the same things that a few years ago seemed so exciting to them. Another insight was that while each of them was trying to accomplish the nearly impossible task of "redoing" each other's personality, that wasn't even a worthy goal. After all, if they had somehow succeeded in changing the other, the spark that had been their original attraction would most likely be lost.

In the end Mark and Julie came to a startling revelation: Keeping their marriage together didn't mean changing each other's—or even their own—personalities. Instead, it meant accepting their differences and giving each other the time and space to be themselves. Over time they hoped that would allow them to rediscover the things in each other that had initially brought them together.

Of course, we knew all along that there was some negotiable common ground between Mark and Julie—there always is—but helping them find it was the challenge. And even after they renewed their pledge to work through the issues, a great deal of time, hard work, and patience would still be required.

Their commitment to continue the discussion opened during the weekend inevitably would lead to a long list of tough questions. For example: Could Mark come to appreciate that public expressions of his love for Julie and the kids were not always out of place? Could he continue to be serious in his role as a parent and yet still occasionally be fun and lighthearted?

As for Julie, could she appreciate and respond genuinely to the more subtle expressions of Mark's affection and still be secure in her role as wife, mother, and lover? Could she appreciate Mark's need for structure, timeliness, and appropriateness in a way that was a challenge rather than drudgery to her? Would Julie be able to see her spontaneity and adaptability as a strength to the marriage and enjoy that part of herself, rather than beat up on herself when things went somewhat differently than planned?

Finding the answers to these and other questions could take a lifetime. And that's perfectly natural: At least some part of our need to be in relationships is because they are opportunities for unending personal growth. In Mark and Julie's case the breakthrough came in the acknowledgment of their differences and the recognition that those differences were both attractive and the source of their stress. From there it was a matter of both parties learning to live with themselves and their partner in a way that would bring out each of their strengths.

And that's probably a recipe for a long and happy relationship.

◆
"Is There Really a Mr. Right for Me?"

We greeted Leah, our vivacious and attractive dental hygienist, in the usual way—"How's your love life?"—knowing full well that this single woman always had a tale to tell about life in the relationship trenches. And with precious little encouragement (and without much chance for rebuttal from the dental chair) Leah indulged us:

"Sometimes I wonder," she began. "Is there really a Mr. Right for me? If he comes along will I know it, and will he even come along at the right time? It seems they are either married or they're about to move to a new city, and I'm not ready for either type of relationship. If they're single and living here, they're either unemployed or want too much too soon, which turns me off. And it seems that when I'm ready, any male who has potential is just coming off a bad relationship or is otherwise unavailable. And whenever someone seems both reasonable and ready, it always seems to be a bad time for me."

"Is there any hope?" she went on. "Will the timing ever be right? I'm thirty-seven and I'm getting impatient. Even worse, I wonder whether any one man could ever meet all my needs and desires. For example, I have so many male friends— just friends—that seem to pose a threat to anyone I ever get serious with. I don't want that. I want my friends and a special person too. Likewise, I'm so active and love so many things that many men feel uncomfortable. I *love* to go fishing, and I go often, usually with a group of men friends. I love football, especially the Redskins, and I love to go to tailgate parties and games, the more the merrier. I love to do so many different things that I have groups of male and female friends that I engage for the different events, because not all enjoy the same things. I figure that since I'm only passing this way once, I don't want to miss out on anything.

"But, see, that's part of the problem," she continued. "I had this guy. It was okay, even a little better. He had one child, and even the kid and I were doing pretty well. But he was in a hurry to find a wife—and his child a new mother. He wanted me to give up my interests, my job, and my friends just to be a wife and mother. I told him that as nice as it was with him, it wasn't *that* nice, and so I told him good-bye. He couldn't believe I could say good-bye that easily. I don't know if it was easy or not. I just wasn't ready for what he wanted."

The more we talked with Leah, the more it became clear that there were several things going on here causing her to be her own worst enemy. For example, while her enthusiasm was refreshing, it also could be tiring to others. Her social gregariousness made her easy to meet, but it also made her intimidating to some men.

Leah's "problem" was that she embodied the notion of "too much of a good thing." With so many interests, and so little direction, she came off as flighty and unsettled. She found it difficult to make decisions and stick with them— from how she wanted to spend her time to whom she wanted to spend it with. Given her free-spiritedness, it seemed to us that Leah needed to focus herself a bit. We tried to help her look at a few things: What did she really want in life? How much was she willing to negotiate to achieve her goals? What was not negotiable?

In asking and answering these questions, we in no way wanted to lose Leah's lovely spirit and zest for life. We did not want to make her less enthusiastic or gregarious, or less interested in outdoor activities or anything else. It was really a matter of helping her focus so that she could direct her energies toward specific goals.

When we last heard from Leah, she was still single, but more happily so. She seemed committed to seeing more things (and people) through to their logical conclusions, rather than jumping around from one thing (or person) to another. She decided to put a few of her interests aside for the time being, directing her energies in just a couple of extracurricular activities. Understanding that her dilemma stemmed from an overabundance of strengths, and not any serious weaknesses, provided Leah with some peace of mind that allowed her to continue her search—and her life—with more self-confidence and resolve.

♦

"Are You My Type?"

Joyce had been divorced for almost seven years and was somewhat resigned to the likelihood of spending the rest of her life alone. At age thirty-six she had even convinced herself that living alone had its own rewards. After all, she didn't have to be a substitute "mom" to any man—one of the issues that had sunk her first marriage. And she was her own boss, able to spend her own time and money the way she wanted. Besides, as she told us, "All of the men out there worth having are either already married, too young, or gay."

Being somewhat shy, Joyce was not one to frequent bars or singles' events. That made her feel even more limited in her ability to find a partner.

One night on a whim she decided to drop in at a local pub because they were having some live music she enjoyed. *What the heck,* she thought, *at least I won't sit around watching TV again.*

The bar was noisy and crowded, and her first impulse was to turn around and leave. Somehow, she convinced herself to stay, found a seat at a table in a corner, and ordered a glass of wine.

Within a few minutes she heard a male voice saying, "I know I know you. You're in my Wednesday-night bowling league."

Joyce's first reaction was to laugh. She hadn't bowled in over twenty years. "That's an old line," she responded with a smile. He introduced himself. His name was Russ.

He insisted he recognized her, though as they talked Russ came to realize it was a classic case of mistaken identity. "As long as we're talking," he said after a few mintues, "would you like to dance?"

She agreed, and three or four dances later she found herself excited but confused. Russ's world as an auto mechanic and part-time race-car driver was a world far away from her career as a well-credentialed computer trainer. As they talked into the evening, she found herself increasingly attracted to him, but concerned that his high-risk life-style and obvious self-confidence were so different from her reserved and mundane existence.

Her heart was saying, *Just do it,* but her head was saying, *We are worlds apart. It will never work.*

Nearly a year into the relationship Joyce hasn't changed her tune. She still finds Russ extremely exciting and his fast-paced, earthy life-style more erotic than she could have imagined.

But she is still plagued with doubts. *Will I tire of him?* she wonders. *Will his inability to plan for the future drive me nuts? Can I learn to live with his constant partying, or will it wear me out?* With each question she seems to get fewer and fewer answers, yet she feels her blood rush at the very mention of his name.

We've been talking with her about these issues for months, trying to help her reconcile her head and her heart. We've tried to show her that their differences, though significant, do not mean that they can't have a meaningful and successful relationship. It will take hard work, but if both are commit ted, it could be well worth it.

As of this writing they are still together, Joyce is still questioning things, but the sound of wedding bells can be heard off in the distance.

As varied and different as these stories may seem, they have at least one key thing in common: they have less to do with who's right and who's wrong than with personality differences—diverging perspectives on the nature and cause of a problem, or whether a problem even exists. Things get bad in relationships when we quickly turn those differences into value judgments and personalize them. Instead of building bridges to solve a problem, we build walls that only make matters worse. And in the process we label people, call them names, and otherwise say or think things that we later regret. All because we failed to understand some basic personality differences between ourselves and others.

The good news is that the simple act of understanding our own and others' personality types can go a long way to bringing people together in creative and positive ways. We call the process Typewatching.

Typewatching is based on the notion that as long as we're going to label one another, we might as well do it as skillfully, objectively, and constructively as possible. When we "Type Talk," we are using an organized, scientifically validated system that has been used for many years by individuals and organizations that want to communicate better. The model can be used by anyone at any time in any situation and can be applied to a wide range of life's challenges and circumstances, from finding a date to living with a mate, from relating to one's children to better understanding one's parents, from choosing or changing a career to smoothing the transition into retirement. Almost literally, from the cradle to the grave.

Indeed, Typewatching can be as varied and as useful as the people you encounter every day: friends, lovers, spouses, parents, children, neighbors, and veritable strangers. In our counseling, training, and seminars, we have helped people make career changes, settle old scores with their parents (or children), straighten out their finances, even gain control of their eating habits. We apply Typewatching to everything, including friends, associates, children, pets, and the plans for our own wedding. Above all, we find that Typewatching is most powerful when helping lovers get close, stay close, or regain their former closeness.

In fact, we've found that there is a reasonable possibility that the more you Type Talk, the better you will get at it and the more ways you will find to use it. In fact, some people find it mildly addicting, though such an addiction isn't something to be concerned about. One of the great advantages of Typewatching, as we've learned over the years, is that it is a judgment-free psychological system, a way of explaining "normal" rather than abnormal behavior. There are no good or bad "types" in Typewatching; there are only differences. Typewatching celebrates those differences, using them constructively rather than to create strife. It enables us to view objectively actions that we might otherwise take personally. When you Type Talk, the tendency for someone who has trouble saying the words *I love you* might be viewed as a typological characteristic rather than a personal affront or a character defect. Someone for whom flourishing in social situations doesn't come naturally can be viewed in a more positive, constructive light.

In short, Typewatching elevates name-calling from a negative "put-down" tactic that mainly produces distance and distrust, to a positive, healthy exercise with the potential for producing not just harmony, but synergy between lovers and mates.

And that can make the tangoes, twists, and tap dances of relationships glide smoothly across the dance floor of life.

2

THE ABCS OF TYPE

*"I meant to return your phone call,
but I'm an Introvert."*

Do you prefer people who are the same as you, or people who are different? If you're like most people, you are initially attracted to people who are different, but over time you find that those differences don't wear well. In fact, whether with a spouse, lover, or friend, after the initial attraction has subsided, you may find yourself quite intolerant of the differences. If you are in a position to do so, you might even demand that these differences simply be eliminated: "Shape up or ship out." If you are not in a position to make such demands, you may simply become distant and alienated.

It is interesting that we think we prefer differences, yet in reality few of us make much allowance for them. Though we may say, and truly believe, "different strokes for different folks," we are nonetheless resistant to those who choose to "do their own thing." In a friendship or family such nonconformity may be viewed as disloyal at best, dangerous or destructive at worst. With Typewatching you will gain the insight to understand the attractiveness of some of those differences and will develop the patience to allow them to exist for the benefit of everyone involved.

◆
The Birth of a Type

Typewatching allows you to identify your personal preferences and how you are similar to and different from those with whom you relate on a daily basis. You can identify where those similarities and differences make for harmony and where they cause discord.

With that in mind, let's take a look at how your preferences are formed and what they mean for your life. Such self insight is the key to Typewatching.

The theory behind Typewatching comes from the work of C. G. Jung, a Swiss-born psychiatrist who died in 1961, and two of his disciples, Katharine Briggs and her daughter, Isabel Briggs Myers. Together, these two women expanded significantly Jung's theory of psychological type. The product of their work, the Myers-Briggs Type Indicator® instrument, is a scientifically validated self-reporting questionnaire that is now one of the most widely used psychological tools of its kind. Its principal goal is to increase self-understanding, whether in business, social settings, or personal relationships of any kind. (For more information, contact Consulting Psychologists Press, Inc., 3803 E. Bayshore Road, Palo Alto, CA 94303, the exclusive publisher of the MBTI® questionnaire.)

According to type theory, each of us is born with a predisposition for certain personality preferences. The work of the two women suggests there are four pairs of alternatives. You are either

Extraverted (E)*	or	Introverted (I)
Sensing (S)	or	iNtuitive (N)**
Thinking (T)	or	Feeling (F)
Judging (J)	or	Perceiving (P)

*While the preferred dictionary spelling of this word is *extroverted*, Jung preferred *extraverted*, which is the way it is spelled throughout his writings—and throughout typological literature, including this book.
**The letter N is used to designate iNtuition because the letter I is already used for Introversion.

When you choose one preference from each pair, you end up with four personality characteristics—say, Extraverted, Sensing, Thinking, and Judging. There are sixteen possible combinations of preferences, which means there are sixteen different personality types. None of them is better or worse than the others. They are simply different.

Keep in mind that these eight labels reflect degrees of *preferences*. By way of analogy, think of left- versus right-handedness. If you are right-handed, it doesn't mean that you never use your left hand. It simply means you *prefer* the right. And you may prefer it strongly, in which case you make relatively little use of your left hand, or you may use both with ease, in which case you border on being ambidextrous. The same is true for the preference pairs listed on page 17. You may prefer one characteristic a great deal, and another only slightly. As we further examine the preferences by describing the two poles of each pair, you may find that you identify with both—for example, Extraversion and Introversion. Within each pair, however, there is one that you prefer—that you rely upon and to which you more naturally gravitate.

Each of us develops a preference early in life and sticks with it. And the more we practice those preferences—intentionally or unintentionally—the more we rely on them with confidence and strength. That doesn't mean we're incapable of using our nonpreferences from time to time. In fact, the more we mature, the more our nonpreferences add richness and dimension to our lives. However, they never take the place of our original preferences. So, Extraverts never become Introverts, and vice versa. (Back to the left-hand, right-hand analogy. Right-handers do not become left-handers, and vice versa. The longer they live, the more they learn to use effectively their nonpreferred hand. But no matter how long a right-hander lives, he or she will never become a left-hander.)

Perhaps another way to view this is to liken an individual's type development to a house. Your type is like the foundation of a house: it doesn't really experience many radical changes through life. The rest of the house, and especially that part readily seen by others, can be likened to your behavior, the outward appearances of your type. Over time the house experiences many changes—an added room, a coat of paint, landscaping, interior renovations, and all the rest. The house, after twenty years of living, is changed significantly from what it was when it was built—but the foundation is still intact. So, too, with our personalities and behavior. Over the years we experience many changes and may appear to be considerably different to a friend we haven't seen in years. But like the house's foundation, our personalities remain pretty much intact and the changes are, for the most part, merely behavioral.

This is not to rule out real change, growth, and development, or to imply that we are all hopelessly rigid. It does mean that change comes slowly to our more basic selves and that to effect change and growth in the malleable parts of our lives is a full-time job, day in, day out. Just to manage yourself and your own growth constitute a busy day—never mind trying to "psych out" the rest of the world.

◆

The Eight Preferences

What exactly are the eight preferences? Let's take a brief look at each of them. In the following chapter you will have a chance to take stock of your personality preferences by agreeing or disagreeing with a series of statements. For now, we'll provide a brief overview of each preference's principal characteristics. Throughout the rest of the chapter we have italicized some of the key words that illustrate each preference.

EXTRAVERSION VERSUS INTROVERSION

The first letter—Extraversion (E) or Introversion (I)—refers to your preferred source of energy:

• Do you conduct much of your life in the *outer* world of other people? Do you tend to open your mouth and then engage your brain? Are you energized when you are around other *people* and surrounded by a lot of *action*? Do you become tired and drained if you must spend too much time inside yourself being quiet and reflective? Would you rather *talk* than listen? Do you tend to leave social situations saying, "Will I ever learn to keep my mouth shut?" If so, you are probably an Extravert, designated by the letter *E*. Extraverts prefer words like *lively* or *popular* rather than *calm* or *private*.

• On the other hand, would you rather keep your observations and decisions *inside*, sharing them only rarely? Are you energized by *thoughts* and *ideas* but drained by intense discussions? Would you rather *listen* than talk? Do you often leave a meeting thinking, *Why didn't I speak up and say . . . ?* If so, you are likely an Introvert, designated by the letter *I*. Introverts find it necessary to "recharge"—to be alone with their thoughts—after spending a few hours with several people.

◆ **JUST SAY KNOW**
_____

If you don't know it from an Extravert, you haven't been listening.
If you don't know it from an Introvert, you haven't asked.

Of all the preferences, the division between Extraversion and Introversion may be the most important distinction between people, because it describes the source, direction, and focus for one's energy. Understanding and making allowances for those differences certainly can make or break a relationship.

Extraverts, as we said, are energized by the outer world, and as a result, all those activities that Es find exhilarating, uplifting, and exciting can drain Introverts. And the reverse is equally true: the reflection, introspection, and solitude that produce energy, focus, and attention for Introverts can be a drain on the energy of Extraverts. So, your success at home, school, or work is usually linked in part to the degree to which you are allowed to indulge in your preferred source of energy—your preference.

In American society, Introverts are outnumbered by Extraverts by about three to one. As a result, Introverts must develop extra coping skills early in life because there will be an inordinate amount of pressure on them to "shape up," to act like the rest of the world. Introverts are pressured daily, almost from the moment of awakening, to respond and conform to the outer world: from classroom teachers who announce that "one third of your grade is based on classroom participation" to life in general, where the "squeaky wheel"—the individual most likely to speak up—gets the "grease."

Introverts and Extraverts cause each other no end of suffering. Extraverts can invade nearly everybody's space with seemingly empty words—thinking out loud, providing a running commentary on life, or simply repeating the same thoughts over and over. And Introverts can be so uncommunicative as to be maddening, even to other Introverts. Trying to get them to answer a simple question with more than a monosyllabic yes or no can be like pulling teeth.

There are more Introvert-Extravert frustrations than you can imagine. Es, for example, typically need a great many more overt "strokes" than Introverts. Introverts, in turn, tend to be suspicious of those same overt strokes. True, both need affirmation, but too much affirmation makes the Introvert wonder why so much is needed, while to the Extravert "too much affirmation" is a contradiction in terms. As a result an Extravert tends to overpraise his or her partner; the Extraverted partner loves it, but an Introvert begins to wonder if such praise isn't superficial, unnecessary, or maybe even phony. This, in turn, can make the praisers feel uneasy and wonder whether it's worth it to proffer such praise—though their natural tendency would be to pile it on. Conversely, Introverted lovers often refrain from giving strokes, even when they know that their partners would like it, because they feel like phonies doing it. This, in turn, can make an Extravert feel rejected or, at best, unappreciated. Both are being true to their respective types while sending the wrong signals to the other.

What's important to remember is that both kinds of behavior are prefectly normal, depending on who's doing the behaving. It is from their respective behaviors that Introverts and Extraverts draw their energies and strength. We need both types—Extraverts to communicate openly to the world, and Introverts to provide good listening and inner strength.

◆ A HARD ACT TO FOLLOW

One constant complaint by Introverts is that Extraverts don't delineate between public and private lives. With little encouragement Es won't hesitate to reveal the most personal aspects of themselves and their relationships. And that drives their Introverted mates up the wall.

We sometimes conduct workshops in which Otto, the Extravert, appears on the first day, and Janet, the Introvert, joins him on the second. Janet often begins her presentation by saying, "Having spent a day with Otto, you probably already know more about me than I want you to know. . . ."

SENSING VERSUS INTUITION

The second letter—Sensing (S) or iNtuition (N)—describes how you prefer to gather information about the world around you:

   • As you perceive, observe, or collect data about your world, do you prefer to be quite *literal* about it all? Do you prefer to be *practical* and *realistic* and enjoy the *tactile* side of life? Are you more interested in the *experience*, in the *hands-on, tangible, here-and-now* parts of a situation? If so, you have a preference toward Sensing, designated by the letter *S*. Sensors like things presented in an *exact* and *precise* manner and have come to rely primarily on their five *senses* as a means of gathering information—they are most certain of and trust those things they can see, hear, touch, taste, and smell. Sensors prefer to focus on *facts* and *details* of something and have less need to interpret what they mean.

   • Or do you prefer to gather information by *translating* and *interpreting* it, looking at things in a more *figurative* way? As you gather information from your five senses, do you immediately look for *possibilities*, *meanings*, and the *relationships* between and among various things? Do you prefer to look at the *grand scheme*, the *big picture*, the *holistic* perspective? Do you like fitting things into some *theoretical framework*? If so, you have a preference for iNtuition, designated by the letter *N*.

The difference between Sensors and iNtuitives is crucial because the way each of us gathers information is the starting point for most human interactions. Sensors are literal: they ask a specific question, for which they want a specific answer. In contrast iNtuitives may find a hundred ways to provide an answer, none of which may be the one the Sensor was looking for.

For iNtuitives everything is relational: it must have meaning. If an iNtuitive isn't looking for something in particular, he or she may walk right by it, never recognizing its existence. A sexy new outfit may be ignored, a lovingly set dinner table never seen. Sensors find that very difficult to comprehend. For them something is real, it exists, it is there—how can you not see it?

So many of our communication difficulties begin with S-N misperceptions: one person sees a forest, the other sees trees. In relationships these misperceptions can become the basis of countless problems, as two people try to communicate on a daily basis using commonly understood words, but with very different meanings.

◆ Sensing vs. iNtuitive Directions

At an informal church service, an iNtuitive clergyman said, "Let's sing two stanzas of hymn number 236" (which had five stanzas).
    A Sensor from the congregation shouted out, "Which two?" The iNtuitive pastor replied, "Any two you want!"

THINKING VERSUS FEELING
The third letter—Thinking (T) or Feeling (F)—describes how you prefer to make decisions:
    ◆ Are you among those who, in the decision-making process, prefer to be very *logical, detached, analytical,* and driven by *objective* values as you come to conclusions? Do you tend not to let interpersonal issues get involved in a decision and prefer that the *consequences of the action* be the driving force wherever possible? Do you strive for *justice* and *clarity* and often get called *firm minded?* If so, you prefer Thinking, designated by the letter *T.*

♦ Or, is your decision-making process guided by how it is going to impact on the people involved? Are you driven by your own *subjective* values? Words like *harmony, mercy,* and *tenderhearted* come to mind for people who prefer Feeling as their judging process.

Understanding this preference may have profound effects on how you and your partner function within a relationship. Unfortunately, the terms—Thinking and Feeling—are a little misleading. In our society the former denotes intellect and the latter emotion. So, there is often a misunderstanding about the meanings of these preferences.

It is important to remember that Thinking types feel, and Feeling types think. What we're talking about is the objective (T) or subjective (F) process one *prefers* in making a decision. At their worst Thinking types *think* that Feeling types are fuzzy headed and Feeling types *feel* that Thinkers have ice for blood. At their best Thinkers bring objectivity to any decision-making situation and Feelers bring an awareness of how that decision will be received by those whom it affects. Too frequently, in the more intimate issues of life, Ts and Fs pass like ships in the night, often with negative feelings, resulting in unresolved issues and much interpersonal dissatisfaction.

It's also important to keep in mind that this preference doesn't describe how easy or difficult it is for an individual to come to a decision. (That has to do with the final letter—*J* or *P*; more on that in a moment.) Individual Thinkers or Feelers can be very decisive or very indecisive. The issue here is the process each goes through in making a decision. We like to say that in making a decision, the Thinker starts with the head and moves to the heart and finally goes back to the head ("What do I understand about this decision? What feelings do I have about it? Now that I *know* how I feel, I can decide.") Meanwhile, the Feeler starts with the heart and moves to the head and then goes back to the heart. ("How do I feel about what's involved? What knowledge do I have that impacts on my feeling? Now that my *understanding* is clear, I am ready to decide based on my experience.")

Of the four pairs of preferences, this is the only one that conforms to a gender bias: roughly two thirds of Thinkers are males, while roughly two thirds of Feelers are females. Over the short term men and women may be charmed by this difference between them: opposites usually do attract—for a while. Over the long haul this factor becomes a major source of interpersonal problems. Further, when a female who prefers to make Thinking decisions behaves in ways that would seem perfectly natural and acceptable if she were a man, she is called a variety of unflattering names. The same is true of a male who prefers Feeling decisions. "Real men," as conventional wisdom has it, don't show their emotions. "Real women," it would follow, can't make the tough decisions, those that require that personal feelings be put aside. Both statements, of course, are simply untrue.

We believe the T-F distinction to be the one most closely related to how intimacy is defined: an F wants to *experience* intimacy, a T wants to *understand* it. Given the gender difference on this set of preferences, it is easy to see how this sets many couples up for some serious relationship struggles.

◆ HEAD VERSUS HEART

Thinkers and Feelers approach emotionally charged issues very differently. When there is an eruption, the Thinker immediately races to his/her head to analyze the problem, understand it, and get clarity.

The Feeler immediately experiences the turmoil viscerally, is engulfed by the emotion, and physically feels the impact of the dynamics.

JUDGING VERSUS PERCEIVING

The fourth and final of the letters that describe our type we believe to be the most significant source of interpersonal tension. They deal with which process—gathering information or making decisions—you most naturally use as you relate to the outer world.

Once again there are two preferences:

• If the environment you have created around you is *structured, scheduled, ordered, planned,* and *controlled,* and if you are *decisive, deliberate,* and able to make *decisions* with a minimum of stress, chances are you prefer to use your decision-making abilities as you relate to life. If so, you are a Judger, designated by the letter J. Judgers *plan their work* and *work their plan.* Even playtime can be organized. For Js there's usually a "right" way and a "wrong" way to do anything.

• If, however, you seek an environment that allows you to be *flexible, spontaneous, adaptive,* and *responsive* to a variety of situations, if making and sticking to decisions causes anxiety, if other people often have trouble understanding where you stand on a particular issue, you are more likely to rely on your information-gathering abilities as you relate to life. That makes you a Perceiver, designated by the letter P. Perceivers prefer to take a *wait-and-see* attitude on most things—what chores need to be done, how to resolve a conflict, what to do today.

Put another way, Perceivers prefer to perceive—to keep collecting new information—rather than to draw conclusions (judgments) on any subject. Judgers, in contrast, have a tendency to judge—to make decisions—rather than to respond to new information, even (or perhaps especially) if that information might change their decision. At their respective extremes Perceivers are virtually incapable of making decisions while Judgers find it virtually impossible to change theirs. Such extremes, however, are not the rule.

We find the J-P preference to be the source of the greatest amount of tension in relationships. One reason is that unlike any of the other three sets of preferences (Extraversion vs. Introversion, Sensing vs. iNtuition, Thinking vs. Feeling), the Judging-Perceiving preference is difficult to hide on a day-to-day basis. An Introvert could, for example, develop sufficient skills to fool you into thinking he or she was an Extravert. You could, at times, mistake a Sensor who was theorizing about something as an iNtuitive, or mistake a schmaltzy-talking Thinker for a Feeler. But the J-P preference is the one you will find easiest to detect as you begin Typewatching. That is because this is the preference that most affects how we interact with others.

Take, for example, these three "P" statements:

• I saw *Oprah* today.
• Oprah Winfrey's show sure seems to be popular.
• *Oprah* is on just before the five o'clock news.

You'll notice that in each statement, there's no judgment—you don't know how the speaker feels or thinks about Oprah Winfrey, nor is there any evaluation of her latest show. They are simply statements describing the situation or calling for more data about the situation, with no implied judgment.

Now, here are three "J" statements:

• *Oprah* was great today, although I thought her first guest did all the talking.
• I think Oprah Winfrey should win a prize for the best show on TV.
• I don't like it when Oprah does the same show over and over.

In each statement you are aware of the speaker's opinion of Oprah Winfrey and her television show, and exactly where the speaker stands on the subject. Those three statements have considerably more closure and definition than the first three, insofar as they reveal both something about the speaker's opinion—at least when it comes to *Oprah*—and something about the speaker. (*What* exactly it leads you to think about the speaker will depend on *your* type—and your own feelings about Oprah and her show.)

The above statements about a TV show, of course, are pretty tame compared with the major and minor issues we face each day, particularly in our relationships. Whether at work, play, or home, most of us are faced with a never-ending array of information and decisions that involve other people, from family to friends to strangers on the street. And those data and decisions—regardless of how important or trivial the issue—are a source of constant friction between Ps and Js, who all the while retain a mysterious attraction to one another.

For example, Judgers run Perceivers up the wall with their continued need for closure: to have an opinion, a plan, and a schedule for nearly everything. Perceivers, meanwhile, drive Judgers to drink with their ability to be spontaneous and easygoing about *everything* short of life-and-death issues, and sometimes even about those. Neither Perceivers nor Judgers are right or wrong or more desirable. Indeed, we need both types in our world. Js need Ps to inspire them to relax and not to make a major issue of everything; and Ps need Js to help them become reasonably organized and to follow through on things.

It's hard to describe the extent of the problems resulting from J-P conflicts. Perceivers tend to find Judgers obnoxious, opinionated, and closed minded, while Judgers find Perceivers to be unbelievably flaky and unfocused. In general, Js get things organized so that Ps can foul up the Js' grand schemes.

Both Js and Ps, of course, wonder why the other insists on making the day so difficult.

By now, you should begin to see how Typewatching keeps personality differences in perspective. Rather than viewing those differences as something to be feared or reviled, they are in fact exactly what they are: differences. They are neither good differences nor bad ones. They're just different.

Keeping this in mind can do wonders for a relationship. Instead of driving a wedge between two otherwise committed individuals, they can bring them closer by being a source of laughter, sharing, and growth.

◆ OLDER BUT WISER

As we get older, our personality goes through many modifications. And although we do not change our basic personality type, there is a tendency for each of us to get more in touch with our nonpreferences.

So, a sixty-year-old Extravert can behave very differently from a thirty-year-old Extravert. While both are Es, the older one has come to appreciate and even long for contemplative, reflective moments. The different needs, goals, and drives of the younger E won't even allow the possibility of those things happening.

Such is true with all of our preferences. As they reach their golden years, hard-charging, objective Thinking-Judgers will be more likely than in any time in their life to stop and smell the daisies, or even dabble in painting or some other free-spirited, open-ended endeavor. It doesn't mean they suddenly become transformed into Feeling-Perceivers, nor does it mean that they have had a basic personality change. It more likely reflects a healthy growth pattern that encompasses both their preferences and nonpreferences.

As this book unfolds, we'll show you how understanding personality differences can work in a variety of the trials and tribulations that any relationship encounters. And we'll help you turn these ordeals into positive and creative experiences that can help you deepen your love for each other.

But first, we'll offer you a simple checklist to help you determine your personality preferences.

3

WHAT'S YOUR TYPE?

"Doesn't anyone care about what I want?"

In order to find out whether someone "is your type," it is first necessary to determine your own type. As we said in the previous chapter, Typewatching begins with understanding yourself.

In the chapters that follow, you will learn how an understanding of your preferences, and those of your mate, can become a relationship-saving tool. In the meantime here are some simple ways to translate your everyday behavior into typological terms. As you count how many of the statements in each section you agree with, your own four letters—and perhaps those of your lover or mate—will begin to emerge.

If you are an Extravert (E), you probably:

- Tend to talk first and think later, generally not knowing what you'll say until you hear yourself say it; it's not uncommon for you to berate yourself: "Will I *ever* learn to keep my mouth shut?"
- Know a lot of people, and count many of them among your "close friends"; you like to include them in many of your activities.

* Are approachable and easily engaged by friends and strangers alike, though perhaps somewhat dominating in a conversation.

* Find telephone calls to be welcome interruptions and don't hesitate to call someone whenever you have something to tell them.

* Like going to parties and prefer to talk with many people instead of just a few; your conversations aren't necessarily limited to those you already know, and you aren't beyond revealing relatively personal things to veritable strangers.

* Prefer generating ideas with a group rather than alone; in fact, you may even become drained if you spend too much time in reflective thinking without being able to bounce your ideas off others.

* Find listening more difficult than talking because you like sharing the limelight; you can get bored when you cannot participate in a conversation.

* "Look" with your mouth instead of your eyes—"I lost my glasses. Has anyone seen my glasses? Who knows where my glasses are?"—and, when you lose your train of thought, verbally "find" your way back—"Now, what was I saying? I think it had something to do with last night's dinner."

* Need affirmation from friends and your mate about who you are, what you do, how you look, and just about everything else.

If you are an Introvert (I), you probably:

* Have been called "shy" or "aloof" from time to time; whether or not you agree, you do tend to see yourself as somewhat quiet and reflective and never seem to have enough time to yourself.

* Rehearse things before saying them and wish that others would do the same, and not blurt out whatever they are thinking; when faced with a confrontation, you would prefer to respond with "I'll have to think about that."

- Never seem to have enough peace and quiet; you tend to adapt, however, by developing a high power of concentration that can close out the TV, noisy kids, or nearby conversations.
- Haven't learned how to say no when someone wants to share a thought or a problem; others call you "a great listener," but you know better.
- Wish that you could get your ideas out more forcefully; you particularly resent those who blurt out things you were just about to say.
- Need to "recharge" after you've spent time socializing with a group; the more intense the encounter, the greater the chance you'll feel drained afterward.
- Don't understand why some people jabber away and can't keep their thoughts to themselves; you'd like to tell them to keep quiet, but you rarely do.
- Were often told by your parents to "go outside and play with your friends"; your parents probably worried about you because you liked to be by yourself.
- Believe that "talk is cheap"; you likely get suspicious if someone close to you is too complimentary, or says something that's already been said by someone else.

Remember, what we're dealing with here are *preferences*. It is likely that you will prefer some Extraverted statements and some Introverted ones. Everybody has both, but we're looking for what you generally prefer, the way you are most likely to act in a given situation. Remember, also, that everything is relative. Some people may agree with *every* Extraverted statement and *none* of the Introverted ones. They are likely to be strong Extraverts. Others may agree with half the Extraverted statements and half the Introverted ones; they are somewhere in the middle, although they probably prefer one over the other.

Now, on to the next preference.

If you are a Sensor (S), you probably

• Prefer specific answers to specific questions; when you ask someone the time, you prefer "three fifty-two" over "a little before four."

• Like to concentrate on what you're doing at the moment and generally don't wonder about what's next; moreover, you would rather *do* something than *think* about it.

• Find the most satisfying tasks those that make you work hard and which yield some tangible result; as much as you hate doing so, you would rather clean the house than think about where your career is going.

• Believe that "if it ain't broke, don't fix it"; you don't understand why some people have to try to improve everything.

• Would rather work with facts and figures than ideas and theories; you get frustrated when people don't give you clear instructions.

• Like things specifically instead of generally; it frustrates you when someone says, "Here's the overall plan—we'll take care of the details later."

• Are very literal in your use of words; you also take things literally and find yourself often asking people, "Do you really mean that or are you joking?"

• Find it easier to see the individual trees more than the overall forest; at work you are happy to focus in on your own job, and aren't as interested in how it fits into the entire organization.

• Subscribe to the notion that "seeing is believing"; if someone tells you "the train is here," you know it really isn't true until you can see it on the tracks.

If you are an iNtuitive (N), you probably:

• Believe that time is relative; no matter what the hour, you still have time to do three more things.

• Would rather fantasize about spending your next paycheck than sitting and balancing your checkbook.

+ Tend to give general answers to most questions; you don't understand why so many people can't follow your directions and get irritated when people push you for specifics.
+ Believe that *boring details* is a redundancy.
+ Like figuring out how things work just for the sheer pleasure of doing so.
+ Are prone to puns and word games (you may even do these things standing up—*get it?*)
+ Tend to think about several things at once; you are often accused by friends and colleagues of being absentminded.
+ Find yourself seeking the connections and interrelatedness behind most things rather than accepting them at face value; you're always asking, "What does that *mean?*"
+ Find the future and its possibilities more intriguing than frightening; you are usually more excited about where you're going than where you are.

Again, you probably see yourself as having some of both preferences. That's okay. As we said, nearly everyone has some Sensing characteristics and some iNtuitive ones. Besides, it is natural to perceive things differently at different times. On April 15 even the most iNtuitive person must deal with the realistic, hard facts and figures of taxes.

If you are a Thinker (T), you probably:

+ Enjoy proving a point for the sake of clarity even at the expense of harmony.
+ Pride yourself in your objectivity despite the fact that some people accuse you of being cold and uncaring; this couldn't be farther from the truth.
+ Are more firm minded than gentle hearted; if you disagree with someone, you would rather tell them even at the risk of offending them, rather than say nothing and letting them think they're right.
+ Would rather settle a dispute based on what is right and truthful rather than what is fair and good.

- Think it's more important to be right than liked; you don't believe it is necessary to like someone to work with them and do a good job.
- Don't mind making difficult decisions and don't understand why so many people get upset about things that aren't relevant to the issue at hand.
- Are impressed with and lend more credibility to things that are logical and scientific; you probably are skeptical about Typewatching and what it can do.
- Remember numbers and figures more readily than faces and names.
- Are able to stay cool, calm, and objective in situations when everyone else is upset.

If you are a Feeler (F), you probably:

- Consider "a good decision" one that considers others' feelings.
- Feel that "love" cannot be defined; you take great offense at those who try to do so.
- Enjoy serving others; you'll do almost anything to make people happy, even at the expense of your own comfort.
- Have wondered, *Doesn't anyone care about what I want?* although you may find it difficult actually saying this to anyone.
- Enjoy providing needed services to people; at a party you may find yourself serving others, even though you're not the host.
- Put yourself in other people's moccasins; you are likely the one in a meeting who asks, "How will this affect the people involved?"
- Won't hesitate to take back something you've said that you perceive has offended someone; as a result you may be accused of being wishy-washy.
- Prefer harmony over clarity; you are embarrassed by conflict in groups or family gatherings and will probably either try to avoid it ("Let's change the subject") or smother it with love ("Let's kiss and make up").
- Are often accused of taking things too personally.

You might want to check your self-perceptions with a mate or colleague. Sometimes others see us in ways we can't see ourselves.

If you are a Judger (J), you probably:

• Are always waiting for others, who never seem to be on time.

• Have a place for everything, and aren't satisfied until everything is in its place.

• *Know* that if everyone would simply do what they're supposed to do (and when they're supposed to do it) the world would be a better place to live.

• Wake up in the morning and know what your day is going to look like; you have a schedule and follow it.

• Don't like surprises, and make this well known to everyone.

• Keep lists, and use them; if you do something not on your list, you may even add it to the list just so you can cross it off.

• Thrive on order; you have a special system for keeping the things in your refrigerator, the hangers in your closet, and pictures on your wall.

• Are accused of being angry when you're not; you're only stating your opinion.

• Like to get things done quickly and out of the way, even if it means having to do it over to get it right.

If you are a Perceiver (P), you probably:

• Love to explore the unknown, even if it's something as simple as a new route home from work.

• Don't plan a task, but wait and see what it demands; people accuse you of being disorganized, although you know better.

• Have to resort to last-minute spurts of energy to meet deadlines; you'll probably make the deadline, although you may drive everyone else crazy in the process.

• Don't believe that "neatness counts," even though you would prefer to have things in order; what's important is creativity, spontaneity, and responsiveness.

• Turn most work into play; if it can't be made into fun, it probably isn't worth doing, or, at least, not prolonging.
• Change the subject often in conversations; the new topic can be anything that enters your mind or walks into the room.
• Don't like to be pinned down about most things; you'd rather keep all the options open.
• Tend to put off until tomorrow what isn't absolutely necessary to do today; you'll get things done when they need to be done—maybe.
• Tend to usually make things less than definite from time to time, but not always—it all depends.

As you count the statements with which you agree—and, perhaps, check those perceptions with friends or colleagues—you can get a preliminary reading on your four preferences. You may enter them below:

E or I   S or N   T or F   J or P

———   ———   ———   ———

Now that you have an idea of your own preferences, you might consider going back through the above questions and answering as if you were your mate. Try to answer as your mate really is, not how you would like your mate to be. Above all, answer the questions before you discuss them with your mate. That will keep your thoughts from being unduly influenced. Ideally, have your mate fill out these questions twice, once for himself or herself, and once for you. (If your mate refuses, you've already got the basis for a hearty discussion about your differences.)

After you have zeroed in on your own preferences and have hunches about your mate's, it's time for you to exchange answers and talk about each others' perceptions of yourselves and each other. Chances are, you'll find yourselves quickly caught up in a wide-ranging discussion about issues you've either been overlooking or ignoring.

Keep in mind that these letters—yours or your mate's—shouldn't be carved in stone. As you gain more knowledge of how each of the eight preferences come into play in a variety of life's situations, you'll gain a fuller understanding of your preferences—and how to use them constructively through Typewatching.

◆

The Ten Commandments of Typewatching

You now have a good idea of your four preference letters, which, combined, constitute your "type." It's important to keep in mind that there are no "good" or "bad" types. Each has its own strengths and weaknesses. It literally takes all types to make a world.

Before we proceed to Part II, in which we will describe in depth the way Typewatching can work in relationships, we'd like to offer our own version of the Ten Commandments, to help you use Typewatching in the most productive and constructive manner. They can also prevent you from using Typewatching recklessly, inappropriately, and unethically.

1. Life tends to support our preferences, making us even more distrustful of our nonpreferences. Whatever your type, you will find that the day's events seem to take place according to your preferences. So if you are a Judger, you will be glad at day's end that you had a structured plan, for it likely saved your hindquarters more than once. And if you're a Perceiver, you'll sigh at day's end that you were able to hang loose and cope with the many surprises you encountered. This will be true with each of the eight preferences. In a stressful situation Thinkers will be glad their objectivity helped them to keep cool under fire while in the same situation, Feelers will be equally glad that they were able to be supportive to the people who needed them. And so on.

2. Your strength maximized becomes a liability. It is perfectly natural for us to rely on that part of us with which we feel most comfortable. But by doing so we can further neglect other parts of ourselves that eventually become uncomfortable, underdeveloped, and unskilled. So, while Extraverts, for example, can bring excitement to any situation, they can become poor listeners or overpower others. Introverts, on the other hand, have good listening skills and the power of concentration, but when maximized these strengths can lead to isolation and avoidance of controversial issues in the external world. Thinkers, for their part, bring objectivity and rationality to any situation, but when these qualities are maximized it can lead to their disregarding people's likes and dislikes. Feelers, meanwhile, bring subjectivity and people concerns to a situation, but when these qualities are maximized they can overpersonalize and can carry grudges for years.

3. Typewatching and typology is only a theory; it takes real life to validate it. Once you have a sense of your type preferences—or those of others—it still must be validated against actual behavior, experience, and self-awareness. For many reasons we often see ourselves or others differently from how each of us really is. For example, if you are expected by others in your life to be objective, analytical, and organized, you may behave that way. Over time you may come to believe that these are your preferences. In fact, you may simply be adapting to those around you. You may assume that someone will be outgoing and assertive in a situation because you think of them as an Extravert. If, for whatever reasons, their behavior doesn't match their preference, you have either mistyped them or there are some other extenuating circumstances causing them to behave differently than their preferences would lead them to act. In any case it is essential to validate one's behavior with one's experience before leaping to conclusions or making false assumptions.

4. Typewatching is only an explanation; it's never an excuse. There's nothing more offensive in Typewatching than the neophyte ready to excuse all bad behaviors as the result of their personality preferences. For example, "I meant to return your phone call, but I'm an Introvert, and we don't return phone calls." Or, "I meant to be on time today, but I'm a Perceiver and we're always late." Such excuses may be acceptable in small doses or in special circumstances, but in day-to-day life it's an unacceptable cop-out.

5. The whole is greater than the sum of its parts. No doubt you've heard this before, but nowhere is this more true than with Typewatching. This is both good news and bad news. The good news is that the "parts" of typology—the four pairs of preferences—make Typewatching easy to apply instantly. You may not easily be able to distinguish whether someone is an ENTJ and ESTJ, for example, but you might readily spot their Extraversion (their constant thinking out loud), or even their preference for Extraverted-Judging (their constant complaining about everything). The complexities of putting all four preferences together are immense. The ENTJ, to use the example above, is a big-picture person who wants to improve his or her mate, along with the rest of the world; the ESTJ, in contrast, is a hands-on person who sees a mate and a relationship as another opportunity to apply their administrative skills. So, two people who look so similar can end up with severe disagreements.

6. Typewatching is only one lens through which to view human personality. While facilitating, affirming, and dramatically insightful, the four-letter descriptions of typology are only door openers to understanding the people behind the letters. Gender, ethnicity, values, socioeconomic factors, and many other things combine to make us who we are. One of the dangers of Typewatching is that there's a tendency to take the four letters as gospel. That not only violates some basic ideals of Typewatching, but in the real world often causes more harm than good. There's nothing that can turn off anyone more quickly than being put into a four-letter box as the sum and substance of their humanity.

7. To be effective, Typewatching must begin with yourself before you can apply it to others. The more you know about yourself, the more you will be in a position to be involved and intimate with those who are different. The process must begin with self-understanding before it can become a frame of reference to be applied to others.

8. Typewatching is easier said (or thought about) than done. There's a natural tendency for people to want to stick with what works. If your preference is to always be in control, for example, it will likely be difficult for you to cede that control to others, even when such an action might be in a relationship's best interest. To make the most constructive use of differences involves commitment, personal skill, and an underlying trust that the process will lead to a better end result.

9. Don't blame everything on your opposite type. This is a natural thing to do. It's easy to believe that everyone who doesn't agree with you is your typological opposite. For one thing, some types naturally disagree or are prone to arguing. Arguing for them is a means to sorting things out. Moreover, some types need to see results—where a relationship is leading, for example. In their quest for direction they may continually raise questions that sound like they're questioning your judgment. When things don't go as expected, don't assume that it was sabotaged by someone of another type.

10. Typewatching can't solve everything. Because Typewatching is very positive and because it explains many parts of everyday behavior, there is a tendency on the part of enthusiasts to use it as an explanation for everything. Such a tendency moves us beyond the original intent and may add meanings to behavior that cannot be explained by type. Sometimes, for example, people have physical or psychological problems that are outside the realm of "normal" behavior. Some people have personalities that are so complex—or so simple—as to defy analysis. Typewatching doesn't have all the answers. It is legitimate and even professional for a Typewatcher to occasionally declare, "I can't explain that," or simply, "I don't know."

4

GETTING TO KNOW YOU

*"I loved listening to him, but I was nervous
about what I'd say if he ever stopped talking."*

It's a classic story: Two people meet, they fall in love, and off
they ride into the sunset. And lo and behold, anywhere from
six weeks to six years down the road, they find themselves
seriously at odds. "You're not the person I fell in love with,"
says one. "You've turned on me," charges the other. And
slowly but ever so surely, these two well-meaning individuals
are at each others' throats, and on their way to a breakup.

What happened? Did one or both individuals really
change? Did one party really turn on the other?

Probably neither. It is far more likely that the more time
the two spent intimately with one another, the less the
original attractions seemed important and the sharper their
differences seemed.

The fact is, when it comes to intimate relationships,
opposites attract. That may seem odd to some people, who
spend years searching for a "soul mate," someone with whom
they feel comfortable and "in sync." But it's true. The things
that initially attract us to other people, and them to us, are
the key to what psychologists call "personality integration."
That refers to the need of each of us to be a complete person,
possessing a variety of skills that enable us to cope with and

45

succeed in whatever life throws our way. For example, if you talk with ease, you may not be as good at listening. So someone who is a good listener may be a natural attraction. And that good listener may welcome someone who is ready to take the initiative and carry the ball in a conversation.

That reminds us of the story of our friends Rachel and John. On their first date, sitting in a sushi restaurant, John, the Extravert, spent the evening telling his life story. Barely pausing to eat or breathe, he filled the time with his easygoing and enjoyable tales. Rachel, the Introvert, simply sat, ate, and listened, nervously enjoying it all. Afterward she confided to her friend, "I loved listening to him, but I was nervous about what I'd say if he ever stopped talking." John didn't specifically say so, but he was no doubt pleased to have had an enthusiastic audience.

We hear the stories over and over again. There's the one about the structured, organized, and somewhat rigid individual who attracts and is excited by a more spontaneous, playful type. One looks at the other and says, "At last, someone who will help me loosen up." Simultaneously the other one says, "At last, someone who will help me get my life in order." And then they spend the rest of their lives trying to get each other to "shape up." The structured one complains, "Get your act together!" The spontaneous one replies, "Would you please back off? What's the big deal?"

Then there's the case of the practical, sensible individual being drawn to the free-thinking dreamer. Each sees in the other something they lack: the dreamer sees a means to fulfilling those fantasies; the sensible one sees a world of excitement and titillation with the unknown. Of course, that initial attraction often dissipates, replaced with frustration. The dreamer's dreams never seem to have any practical value, and the practical sensibility is viewed as needless nitpicking.

And so it goes. There's little doubt that in the initial phases of an intimate relationship, there is a deep draw to those who are opposite from our own personality preferences because they hold the key to our completeness. And there's even less doubt that without some basic understanding of personality type, these attractions will become the basis for chronic relationship problems, perhaps even leading to the relationship's demise.

Interestingly, when it comes to nonintimate relationships—friends, neighbors, colleagues, and the like—the opposite holds true: we were drawn to people who share our basic personality styles, values, religions, politics, and other things that make us who we are. We've seen it happen at parties and receptions where we are aware of the four-letter types of a large number of attendees. As we look around the room, we see clusters of type-alike configurations. For example, the NFs find and hang out with other NFs, sharing experiences and generally affirming each other, and the NTs gravitate to a corner where they can have an intense discussion about something. All of this happens quite naturally. Among other things it helps us affirm who we are in our community and our society.

•
Thinking for Ourselves

As you can see, our personality types come into play during the first moments of any encounter. And Typewatching can be a very useful tool to cut through superficiality and move a relationship to the next level of significance, or to move on with a minimum of interpersonal heartburn.

None of this can take place, however, without a basic understanding of our own personality strengths and weaknesses. So we encourage you before going further to have at least a rough idea of your four personality preferences and generally agree with your type's profile in the back of this book. From here on we'll assume that this is the case.

So, what happens during those first few minutes, typologically speaking?

Our first and most natural tendency is to fall back on our strengths, to go with what we know. Hence, Extraverts tend to talk a lot and listen little, and Introverts tend to hang back and listen, perhaps not contributing much to the conversation. Judgers often are quick to proffer an opinion, risking alienating everyone around, while Perceivers' never-ending curiosity may lead them to interrupt with a series of questions, frustrating someone trying to tell a story. (Judgers complain that Perceivers answer one question with another question. To which Perceivers respond, "Is that bad?")

The good news is that going with your strength means that you are being yourself, which always makes for a good, honest start. The bad news is that unknowingly, your strength maximized can become your weakness, and you may be oblivious to the alienating effect your behavior may have on others. So in their nervousness to make a good impression, Extraverts may go way overboard, dominating a conversation, while an Introvert may be so unrevealing as to appear aloof or uninterested.

Things can work somewhat differently in the initial stages of a potentially intimate relationship. A funny thing happens on the way to the bedroom: we downplay or even obscure our personality preferences, saying to ourselves, *If I'm really me, he/she won't like me.* So, an Extravert might purposely act less gregarious and work at listening more intently, so as not to "scare off" the other person by seizing the limelight. A Judger might make an attempt to seem less structured and more spontaneous than would naturally be the case. All of which explains why it is so crucial for two people to spend a sufficient amount of time with each other in the early stages to allow more of the genuine preferences to surface, lest we become attracted to—or turned off by—someone who hasn't yet let the "real" self shine through.

The idea that "opposites attract" goes way beyond mere personality preferences. As any therapist who specializes in relationships can tell you, opposites are clearly drawn to each other for very deep psychological reasons. For starters, your opposite helps bring totality by providing the parts of your personality that are missing. Further, it provides excitement by being drawn to someone so very different, breaking up the propensity for staleness or routine. The differences create a tension that excites the system—a challenge, a dare, perhaps even sexual enticement.

So, someone who is generally fearful of such things as flying or travel might well be attracted to an individual whose principal desire is to see the world. This may not necessarily make the person less fearful, but it creates a vehicle for working through their fears in a supportive way. And the world traveler may be drawn to the homebody, seeing that person as an anchor in an otherwise turbulent and ungrounded life-style. Not that things always work out that way. The traveler may berate the homebody for not being ready, willing, and able to jump on the next flight out of town, leaving the homebody shrouded in guilt and more afraid than ever. And the homebody may see the traveler as an irresponsible, uncaring, part-time partner who not only doesn't respect the homebody's need to take things slowly but may also be avoiding a sense of duty around the home.

So, as we said, the things that initially draw and excite us in a relationship are the very things that can become severe stressors if we are not in touch with the driving forces of our own personality preferences.

We're not saying that the attraction of opposites is either bad or good; it's a fact of life for intimacy. But given this attraction, it is important to be aware that over time, after the physical attraction is balanced with the emotional attraction, the dynamics of the relationship can change dramatically. That means that both you and your partner must be constantly aware of your own true personality strengths and weaknesses, as well as each other's, in order to have the patience and energy necessary to keep the relationship going—and growing.

How do you do that? It might help to keep the following four questions on hand to refer to during the early phases of relationship:

1. What are the things I like most about this person?
2. What are the things I like least about this person?
3. How have I changed since being in this relationship?
4. How has my partner changed since being in this relationship?

In responding to questions 1 and 2, try to make the lists as complete as possible, without being overly complex. (This will be difficult for some types, who will no doubt interpret this assignment as a program to be mastered and continually improved upon, and in the process create an interminable and never definitive list. Of course, this dilutes the purpose of this exercise, which is to get an immediate and relevant gauge of the relationship.) Make sure to include the big, profound issues as well as the seemingly simple and sometimes silly ones. We've seen more relationships begin to splinter and crack over such trivial matters as how and where one squeezes the toothpaste tube (Sensors and Judgers can go ballistic when iNtuitives and Perceivers squeeze from the middle instead of the bottom, or, worse yet, squeeze from any damn place they feel like with no form or order) and what the proper direction is for toilet paper and paper towels to unwind (everyone *knows* there's a right way and a wrong way). From there you can move on to bigger issues, such as where things are kept in the refrigerator, or whether light switches are left in the "proper" position (with "on" pointing up and "off" pointing down).

We don't mean to dwell on these seemingly light matters, although they are illuminating features of where a relationship is going, and where it can lead. Obviously, there are more profound differences that must be considered, lest one or both parties be left in the dark.

Look over the list you made. Are the things you like most about the other person the kinds of things that will wear well over the years, or are they more superficial and fleeting? Are the traits you find attractive things that give you a sense of security and personal worth?

How about the things you said you liked least? Are these likely to become areas that will become difficult later on? Do they represent things that are personally threatening or demeaning, which could lead ultimately to chronic conflict?

Remember: Every relationship has positive and negative aspects. The question is, do the positives outweigh the negatives, and will the differences lead to your mutual growth and intimacy or become a wedge that will drive the two of you apart?

Now, take a look at your answers to questions 3 and 4. The issue here isn't who has changed in what directions so much as how each of you views the changes. In a growing relationship, change is inevitable. However, for each person, it needs to be viewed as something positive, lest one or both of you become resentful. So, it is important that one person isn't "doing all the changing," or at least feeling that way. By answering questions 3 and 4 you stay aware of where each of you stands.

In answering these last two questions it might be helpful to get an outside opinion from a friend or close associate. They often perceive changes more quickly, and often quite differently, than you can yourself. You might find that you are being much more rigid than you had been before the relationship. If so, you'll want to take a look at that, determine why that might be happening, and decide whether you like the change. Or you might find yourself deferring to your partner in social situations when you hadn't done that in the past. By recognizing that, you might get some insight into the overall dynamics of the relationship, and whether the change in you is part of some bigger issue, or simply a phase in your own development. For example, you may defer to your partner because you feel he or she is critical or condescending whenever you speak out. That puts a lid on your natural extraverted tendency. Or, you may defer because you like what your partner says and you appreciate hearing it rather than always being the one who does the talking. In either case recognizing the dynamic is key at this early stage.

Granted, it isn't easy predicting where these early differences will lead. Sometimes they can be very positive, adding new dimensions to the personalities of each partner. Sometimes the result is surprising. For example, the person who appreciates independence, and who encourages a partner to be independent, may not be ready for the results when the previously dependent person develops his or her own life. And the opposite can be true: the person who criticizes the workaholic for never being available may not know what to do with the individual when the workaholic suddenly cuts back on working in order to spend more "quality time."

You've probably been in—or at least know about—many such scenarios:

• You become so engrossed in a new relationship that the two of you spend every moment together, shutting out the rest of the world—including your parents, best friends, and other close individuals.

• You live your partner's life—spending evenings in your mate's favorite bar, attending your mate's business functions and conferences, or adopting your mate's preferred form of attire—even though you realize that such activities are beyond your interests and maybe even your values.

• You abandon your serious pursuits in favor of more amusing pastimes, from watching TV to attending cocktail parties; or, alternatively, give up your playfulness in favor of serious activities and events.

None of these changes is necessarily bad; indeed, they can be quite positive. What's crucial for both parties is to determine whether they are making these changes willingly, whether they like these changes, and whether this is a direction in which they want to be headed.

Answering the four questions on page 50 can be helpful at any point in a relationship, but they are crucial during the first few weeks and months. It is during these early times that we are most blinded and awestruck about the other person— and about ourselves—throwing objectivity, and sometimes common sense, to the wind. It takes some time and effort to conduct this brief survey of your impressions and feelings, but the investment will pay big dividends. Remember: There are no easy relationships. They all take hard work. Answering the questions now could make the effort a little less wearisome down the road.

◆

When You're Expecting

As we said, one of the keys to getting to know someone else is first to understand yourself. As any relationship unfolds, we consciously or unconsciously engage in a pattern of constantly sorting out what's going on. We're always measuring the other person against a series of expectations of the other person and of ourselves. For example, as a female you might expect that on the first few dates the man will pick you up—and will also pick up the check. As a male you might expect that your partner will defer to your judgment about where to go, what to do, and how to get there, and that she will behave appropriately, whatever you define that to mean. Either of you might expect that when things get physical you will proceed slowly, romantically, and seductively—or you may want to get right down to business.

All of these are certainly reasonable things to expect, but

it's important that you stop and take a deeper look: Are these things you always expect of yourself and impose on others? Are they things you never expect of yourself and rely on from others? Or are you simply unclear about the reasons behind your expectations, and therefore give out mixed signals? And how flexible are you on these matters? Is "picking up the check" a nonnegotiable issue, or are you able to bend a little to allow for the other person's needs? If the other person isn't in the mood to take charge, can you allow for that?

We're not suggesting what the "right" answer should be. Obviously there is none. The key is in the questions themselves. Simply asking them heightens the possibility for both people in a relationship to have their needs met, or at least considered, in a constructive way.

A lot of people know what they want. If you read the Personals column in almost any major city's magazine, you'll see how specific some people can be about their needs. It's not unusual for an ad to seek, just to pick one example from a local publication, "a very attractive, slim, 30s, warm, caring professional who likes spicy food, Scrabble, cross-country skiing, Tchaikovsky, and Talking Heads. Smokers, egomaniacs, and Republicans need not apply."

Whatever you may think about the Personals, you can't help but admire these individuals' bravado in establishing their needs, wants, and values at the very front end of a relationship. Obviously, that's much harder to do in a face-to-face social setting. You simply can't or don't bring up such seemingly sensitive matters in the early stages of an encounter.

But that doesn't mean that you shouldn't be prepared with your own list of wants, needs, and values to consider in any relationship, whether it's just starting out or already under way. So, conducting a brief survey of your expectations is a good start. By doing so you'll have a handle on what's important to you and establish some basis for determining how far you want the relationship to go.

Among the questions you might consider asking:

1. What are my expectations about communications? Do I expect others to be free to express their emotions as they unfold, or do I expect them to be strong, silent types? If they show emotion or affection publicly, will I be embarrassed? What are the boundaries about what can be freely discussed, and when and where do those discussions take place?

2. What are my expectations about sex? Does physical contact of any kind wait until we have established a meaningful relationship? What does saying no mean to each party when one makes a move on the other? Will casual flirting and touching automatically lead to sexual intercourse? Does engaging in "the act" imply commitment? How much must the other person reveal about his or her past sexual history?

3. What are my expectations about money? Do I believe in fifty-fifty sharing on everything? Should one party always pay? If so, what obligations does that put on the other one? How open should each party be about their income, debts, and net worth? What value does the other person place on savings, or spontaneous indulgences?

4. What are my expectations about conflict? Is it a creative force that helps a relationship grow, a necessary evil, or something to be avoided at all cost? When things aren't going well, how much should the other person speak up? How much raising of voices or cool, calm discussions is permitted? If no conflicts surface, is something wrong with how the relationship is developing?

5. What are my expectations about neatness? Who is responsible for cleaning up messes and keeping a room or house in order? Does each party take care of his or her own things and space, or is one person principally responsible? How does each person's "job description" read on this issue?

We won't claim that this series of questions is complete, not by a long shot. You'll probably come up with some questions of your own. In any case, spending a bit of time pondering these questions can't help but improve your chances of getting things off on the right foot.

By the way, these questions shouldn't be relegated only to the beginning stages of a relationship. They can provide an ongoing way to gauge where you are at any step of a relationship. In fact, we've encouraged many couples to use the questions as a means of starting a discussion about a specific area that seemed problematic at the time. There's nothing like a few direct questions to get a conversation off and running, or at least to help define what topics are taboo in a relationship.

We can't urge too strongly the importance of asking such questions of yourself, particularly when starting out a relationship, or at any stage when things seem rocky. Post them on the refrigerator, keep them in your desk, carry them in your pocket or purse. Refer to them as often as necessary, but ignore them at your peril.

We could tell you endless tales of how unrequited expectations can make any kind of relationship go awry. For starters there's the case of Eric, a Sensing-Thinking-Judger, who had very clearly defined role expectations for both himself and his girlfriend, Karen. It was very simple: Me Tarzan, you Jane. Tarzan's role was breadwinner; Jane's was to raise a family and have dinner on the table. In dating, Eric took that to mean he had to be in charge of everything, from picking up the dinner tab to being responsible for all conversation, to being sure that all activities were scheduled and under his control. Obviously, such behavior stifled any independence or equality on the part of Karen. Further, once Karen, a Sensing-Thinking-Perceiver, began to understand Eric's style, she turned it into a game. It became far more fun to try to make Eric jump and respond to her whims than to devote any energy in trying to develop a more balanced and equal relationship. At eleven o'clock on some weeknight it wasn't beyond Karen to sigh wistfully, "I have a sweet tooth. It's too bad we don't have any cookies in the house," knowing full well that Eric, after a little grumbling, would dutifully jump in the car and head to some all-night market on her behalf. Karen would even brag to her friends about her subtle powers and her ability to control the relationship.

In the end such one-sided, undiscussed expectations soon led to a one-sided, undiscussed relationship. It was doomed to fail, which it did.

Or there's the tale of Bill, the lovestruck husband, a strong Judger. He liked structure, schedule, an order for everything and everyone, and wouldn't hesitate to berate anyone who wouldn't follow his plan. But his wife, Sarah, had a capacity to sweep him away with her sweetness and love. Contrary to his type, in her presence he seemed far less structured where she was concerned, and even began to try to be a bit more flexible. When Sarah was present, Bill backed off from some of the "shoulds" and demands he believed in, learning to go along with some of her spontaneity.

In his love of Sarah, Bill eased off on his own rigid expectations of his role as a husband. In the process he learned to relax a bit more, and Sarah came to appreciate his structure and need for order. With just the simplest awareness of their personality differences, they were able to be a strength to each other, rather than a burden. By applying Typewatching they made their sharp differences assets to the relationship.

As you can see, the expectations game can be played in all stages of relationships. It's something we do naturally and inescapably throughout our lives.

What causes problems is when we are not clear about what we expect of ourselves and others. It leads quickly to misunderstanding and drives a wedge between any two people who want to relate successfully on any level. So, as a relationship unfolds, it is vital to keep in touch with one's expectations. It is also important to remember that as any relationship grows, develops, and changes, so do our expectations. Sometimes, relationships in their early stages of development fall into the dangerous trap of "taking each other for granted," or "not making waves." Either of which are very poor foundations upon which to build any kind of meaningful relationship.

The process isn't that difficult. It involves such basic communication skills as saying what you mean, checking to make sure that it was heard correctly, then allowing time for a meaningful response. It involves regular, sometimes daily, checking in with each other to assure that each person's needs are being met and whatever is expected of the relationship is being gratified. But be careful: Some types, such as ENFPs, can carry this too far, constantly monitoring and processing every word and movement for some meaning or nuance. Clearly, this can cause more harm than good.

As a relationship begins and grows, here are some tips to help it develop:

- **Stay in touch.** Remember the extra importance of expectations and needs in the early stages of a relationship. Better to overdo it a bit than to ignore this vital communication. If one party feels the other is too hung up on discussing and analyzing every emotional response, the act of keeping in touch will help bring that to light.
- **Be clear with yourself.** The more you know about yourself, the more you'll be capable of being direct in your communications, negotiating your own needs, and collaborating to maximize the relationship's potential.
- **Learn how to give feedback.** For example, make sure the recipient is open to your comments, lest they fall on deaf ears. Try to make your feedback timely, giving it as soon as possible after a specific incident. (But give it enough time to let emotions cool a bit.) Be as specific as possible, avoid personal insults, and limit your comments to behaviors the

other person actually can change; it won't do much good to tell them you don't like the way they laugh. Finally, try to pick a time and place that's conducive to discussion: better to do it while sitting around at home after dinner than in the car on the way to a party.

+ **Be open to the other person's perceptions.** Try to receive them as nondefensively as possible. Respond with more than a few words; it might help to repeat the criticism to make sure you understand what the other person is saying. Though it may seem trivial to you, the mere fact that the other person shared it indicates that it wasn't trivial to them.

+ **Don't give up.** Express yourself, however painful it may be to do this. Feelers should try to hang in there until the air clears, remembering that if you sell out in the early stages in the name of peace and harmony, it will only become more difficult to confront things later on; the world will not end if you speak your mind. Thinkers should remember that your need for clarity may be greater than what is needed to resolve an issue. Both parties should try to focus on a specific topic rather than dumping a whole load of frustrations. Ask yourself whether you are bringing things up in order to foster positive change, or merely to push the other's buttons. Keep in mind that screaming rarely helps.

+ **Stay out of corners.** In all of your communications strive for a win-win outcome whenever possible. Play down such dogmatics as "I said no and that's final," or "Where'd you get such a dumb idea?" or any other phrases that put the other person immediately on the defensive. Such phrases leave the other person in a corner with little way out except to fight or be embarrassed. Relationship dialogues are best when they encourage patterns for continuation, concern, and affirmation.

+ **Sweat the small stuff.** Finally, don't forget the little niceties, especially such basics as "thank you" and, when appropriate, "I'm sorry."

In the end, good, growing, enchancing relationships demand time and energy. They never just happen. If the relationship is worth such energy at the start, then it's worth all the energy you can give it throughout the time you are together. Otherwise, get out of it, and get on with your life.

II

THE FOUR KEYS
TO A
LASTING LOVE

5

COMMUNICATION

"If you didn't want the truth,
why did you ask the question?"

There's a classic story told about a couple visiting a lawyer's office seeking a divorce.

The lawyer begins by asking, "Do you have grounds?"

"We have one and a half acres," responds the man.

"No, no," says the lawyer. "Do you have a grudge?"

"No," the man answers. "But I have an oversized carport."

The lawyer ponders this for a moment and thinks, "I clearly need a different approach." Then he asks, "Does she beat you up?"

To which the man responds, "Nope, I'm up first every morning."

In desperation the lawyer asks, "So why do you want a divorce?"

"I don't," responds the man. "My wife does. She says we have trouble communicating."

Communicating in any relationship brings out the best and the worst of each of our preferences, bringing both similarities and differences into sharper focus. Much like the man and the divorce lawyer, many people think they're communicating clearly when in fact their words and meanings are passing like ships in the night. Communication is at the heart of every human interaction, from the most intimate to the least personal. And yet as soon as one person speaks, personality preferences have everything to do with what is said, meant, heard, and interpreted.

Basic personality differences can wreak havoc on a simple conversation. For example, trouble begins when a Sensor asks "What time is it?" and an iNtuitive responds, "It's late." That frustrates the Sensor because it wasn't the kind of answer he or she had in mind. And the iNtuitive gets frustrated because he or she doesn't understand what was wrong with what seemed to be a perfectly good answer. And then there's the iNtuitive who asks the Sensor, "What's new since I last saw you?" To which the Sensor responds with an hour-by-hour detail-filled recollection. Halfway through, the iNtuitive, eyes glazing over, interrupts with "All I wanted to know was whether everything is okay."

Consider some other common scenarios:

• The Extravert who tells a mate, "You don't tell me you love me enough!" To which the Introvert responds, "Talk is cheap. I've never cheated on you, have I?" Or the Introvert complaining, "If you'd stop talking for a minute and let me think, I'd be able to respond to you." To which the Extravert says, "But if we just talk for a minute more we can clear this whole matter up."

• The Thinker prefacing a remark by saying, "What I'm about to say isn't meant as personal criticism," which is, of course, the only way a Feeler is likely to interpret any personal comment. And the Feeler rationalizing a major decision by saying, "I can't explain it. It just feels right." Such logic is beyond reason to most Thinkers.

• The Judger who insists, "We've got to decide where we're going on vacation this summer." To which a Perceiver responds, "But it's only January. We've got plenty of time to figure things out." Or the Perceiver, trying to settle the matter, says, "How about sometime in July?" which the Judger finds completely dissatisfying, preferring specific dates, if not exact departure and arrival times.

Of course, we can pretty much think what we want with impunity. It's when we open our mouths and share the thought with others that the potential exists for misunderstanding.

When it comes to communication, quality is far more important than quantity. While some folks believe, "If we just talked more, we'd have fewer problems," unfortunately, things just aren't that simple. Even the most well-intended conversations can cause more harm than good if the parties involved are saying one thing and hearing another.

The good news is that Typewatching is an excellent vehicle for avoiding and overcoming communication difficulties. The heightened awareness Typewatching affords provides a frame of reference for detecting miscommunications early on, rather than waiting until things get out of hand. So, Extraverts, aware of their natural proclivity to ramble on and on, can monitor themselves and, when appropriate, modulate their talkativeness and give other parties a chance to speak. And Introverts, aware that they are prone to remaining actively involved in a conversation without saying a word, can similarly monitor themselves and remain aware of the need for verbal, or even nonverbal, feedback in a conversation. The same is true for all eight preferences and all sixteen types.

It might follow that Extraversion and Introversion are the most important preferences when examining communication styles. After all, these preferences determine how public or how private we are in expressing ourselves. E-I differences can also play a role in how people express themselves through their style of dress, how they invade others' space, and how much they are willing to disclose personal information about themselves and others. Each of these can set any relationship up for success or failure.

But we must emphasize strongly that far more than Extraversion and Introversion come into play when examining communication styles. All eight personality preferences play key roles in any conversation, as you will continue to see throughout this book.

◆

Extraverts and Introverts: A Battle of Turfs

Let's focus for a while on Extraverts' and Introverts' communication style, because indeed, this is where so many relationship difficulties begin.

We certainly can attest to that. A few years ago we were invited to make a keynote speech at an international Type conference about E-I communication differences. We decided to title it "When Extraverts and Introverts Meet: A Never-Ending Dilemma." The simple attempt to discuss between ourselves how to best present the subject matter led to one stressful situation after another.

For example, Otto, the Extravert, wanted to play to the crowd, involving the audience to the utmost, with the course of the presentation based on the audience's responses. He didn't want to be tied down to specific words on a manuscript, and resisted Janet's efforts even to sit down and talk about it in advance. Janet, the Introvert, found the notion of "winging it" terrifying. She preferred an outline so she could fall back on it when needed, a process that Otto found confining. Janet also wanted some consensus on the time it would take for the total delivery, as well as on who would be saying what. She wanted us to rehearse the speech so she could pace herself in delivering her portion of the presentation. Otto "knew" that if things were running too short or too long, it was simply a matter of talking louder and faster or slower and softer, as time, need, and audience "vibrations" dictated.

All of this took place before we even determined what we were going to say.

Actually, the speech turned out to be one of our better presentations, and the recording of it remains one of our best-selling tapes.

How did we pull it off? Not without some difficulty and heartache. In fact, the actual resolution didn't take place until the morning of our dinnertime speech. We started by outlining the major points to be covered, then fleshing out the outline on paper. We assigned areas for which each of us would be responsible—who would make which points on the outline—and talked them through in a rehearsal format. After some fine-tuning we agreed that we had an outline we could work with. Then Janet took a couple of hours to write out the thoughts as she planned to deliver them. And Otto went off to socialize with his four hundred closest friends at the conference. We reconvened later in the day and did another rehearsal with the refined material.

And so each of us got what we wanted. Otto was left to his own free-flowing style and quick wit and yet had a firm idea of his major points. Meanwhile, Janet had a thorough sense of what she would cover, and how it would fit in with Otto's portion. That gave her confidence about the material to be covered and freed her up to participate in the repartee that we and our audiences have come to enjoy.

In retrospect the solution to our problem seems like common sense. And perhaps it is. But in the heat of a dilemma common sense can be a rare commodity. Our biggest struggle was the relatively simple act of understanding each other's point of view and genuinely hearing what each of us needed in order to succeed in our mission.

That's a classic struggle between Introverts' and Extraverts' attempts to communicate with one another. The amount of energy that goes into an Extravert's trying to remain quiet and genuinely listen to what the other person (whether an Introvert or another Extravert) is saying—with no interruptions—is difficult to imagine. The reverse is also true: the amount of energy required for an Introvert to listen and sort through the barrage of words coming at her from an Extravert is equally hard to fathom.

For Es and Is it's a constant battle of turfs:

* The Extravert's preferred turf is the *external* world, which is where thoughts, reactions, ideas, and assorted other ramblings are dumped, rehearsed, massaged, and reworked out loud. As a result, if you are an Extravert, you may unload tons of material, with little or no expectation of receiving a response. In fact, you may be shocked, amazed, and perhaps even a little embarrassed that others are even listening.

* For the Introvert it's the opposite. Their favorite turf is the *internal* world. Before any thoughts, reactions, and ideas are verbalized, they are likely to be rehearsed, massaged, and reworked internally. If you are an Introvert, you confront a constant flow of material that needs to be edited. In fact, your thought flow is probably as much and as constant as that of the Extravert, but it all happens inside, and you simply cannot imagine sharing such material until the process is complete. It's too voluminous and it's really nobody else's business. Your slogan might be a version of that classic winery ad slogan: We share no thought before its time.

◆ MIND OVER CHATTER

One quality of Introverts is their ability to carry on entire conversations in their minds, then think that the conversation actually took place. In these inner "conversations" they can even fill in the other person's lines. Later the Introvert might even bring up the alleged conversation as evidence of something the other party said. "You never listen to me," the Introvert might complain. "I told you that a long time ago, and you said . . ."

Sometimes, actively trying to reconstruct such a conversation—when and where it was held—might lead the Introvert to realize that the conversation never really took place—except within the Introvert's head.

So, Extraverts drop great amounts of material in the public arena and hope for help in sorting it all out. A nodded head, an interruption, an opposing point of view, or almost any other sign of life is all an Extravert needs to maintain a verbal stream of consciousness. And Introverts drop precious little, wanting first to sort it out by themselves.

As you can see, this great divergence of styles is an invitation to stress for both parties. Genuine listening and communicating can be replaced with either incessant chatter or zipper-lipped silence. Differences can become exacerbated when an Extravert interprets an Introvert's moment of reflection as an invitation to fill the silence with words. Since "nothing" was happening, the Extravert was ready, willing, and able to come to the rescue of this seemingly awkward moment. (It is not unusual for an Extravert to ask questions out loud, answer them out loud, and then thank whoever is nearby for their help.) Each party is energized by their respective styles: The more Extraverts talk and interact with others, the more excited they become; and the more Introverts reflect, contemplate, or even simply breathe deeply, the more confident and satisfied they become.

Sometimes this simple difference can become a source of major misunderstanding. Our friends Olivia and Jim are a case in point.

One day Jim, the Extravert, came home from work seemingly dead on his feet. He collapsed into a chair, looking forward to an evening of doing nothing more than "vegging out" in front of the TV. Olivia, his Introverted mate, reminded him that they had promised to attend a neighborhood open house that evening. Reluctantly Jim agreed to get out of his chair and attend the event.

Once at the party, it didn't take long for Jim to not only regain his energy but also to find himself very much in his element—laughing, telling jokes, and attracting a small crowd. Olivia watched in astonishment as this previously bedraggled man was transformed into Everybody's Best Friend.

Although she, too, enjoyed the gathering, Jim's gregariousness began to get to her. *Why is he so charged up by everyone
else?* Olivia wondered. *He was exhausted when it was just the
two of us. Is there something wrong between us?*

There was nothing wrong with the relationship, from
Jim's perspective. For him it was simply a matter of the more
the merrier. If it was okay having one person in the room, it
was better with two, and great with three or more. The social
event energized Jim beyond levels even he would have imagined. For Olivia the gathering eventually became tiring.

The problem, of course, had little to do with each person's
capacity to socialize. It had everything to do with Jim and
Olivia understanding each other's needs, including what energized or drained them, and giving them the freedom to
socialize as much or as little as they liked without necessarily
having it reflect on the quality of their own relationship.

In most cases life is a conspiracy of Extraverts. Whether
among Introverts or comfortably ensconced in a crowd of
Extraverted brethren, they dominate the airwaves. Introverts
simply can't understand how Extraverts can talk over, under,
around, and through one another and actually communicate
with any degree of effectiveness. Yet to Introverts' surprise
Extraverts often communicate quite well in such hypercharged
environments. True, there may be much redundancy, and
more than a little exaggeration, a number of key points left
unheard (but certainly not unsaid). But it's all in a day's

◆ AUTO EROTICISM

We know one couple, a strong Introvert and a strong Extravert,
who have discovered one secret to a long, happy relationship:
They drive two cars to some social events. When the Introvert gets
"Extraverted out," he can go home, leaving the Extravert to enjoy
herself for as long as she wants.

words for an Extravert. That puts Introverts at a distinct disadvantage, as they must fight—albeit in their own low-key styles—to even enter the conversation.

While the healthy person spends time both Extraverting and Introverting, too much time spent by either party in his or her nonpreferred turf ultimately becomes an energy drain, leading to a variety of stress-related problems.

Introversion is so unappreciated in our culture that Introverts must learn very early how to succeed in an Extraverted world, or suffer the consequences. From the earliest childhood socialization—schools, Scouts, and all the rest—to the meetings-oriented workplace, Introverts must constantly turn to their nonpreferences to succeed. At work or at home, every time an Introvert engages verbally in a disagreement with an Extravert, the E is given home-field advantage. There is little chance for Introverts to turn the table and put Extraverts at a disadvantage.

As the title of our previously mentioned speech suggests, the dilemma never ends. Serious as their differences sometimes are, Extraverts and Introverts continue to be attracted to one another. And yet without some basic Typewatching skills, in no time the attraction can drive a wedge between them, leaving each with a variety of vulnerabilities. Until you find yourself face-to-face with such a situation, it is difficult to fathom how easy it is for one party to inadvertently stress the other. For example, it isn't that the Introvert deliberately withholds information or is reluctant to participate in a conversation, it is simply that this external "turf" is a foreign one—and, therefore, not a playing field on which they feel comfortable, let alone encouraged to participate.

So, in a mild verbal altercation, the Extravert operates on the assumption that "with just a few more words, the entire situation can be cleared up," while the Introvert, already stressed by the outpouring verbiage, feels that "just a few more words" will be the proverbial backbreaking straw.

When it comes to Introversion and communication, it is

imperative to remember that the Introvert "thinks to speak." That means one must allow time for an Introvert to reflect, contemplate, and formulate a response—all internally. For some Introverts this is done very rapidly, almost seamlessly, to the observer. For others the internal process takes somewhat longer, sometimes excruciatingly so, at least in others' opinions. This doesn't mean the Introvert doesn't enjoy the conversation, or is in any way less capable of "holding their own" in a verbal exchange. Thinking before speaking is not a sign of intelligence any more than is the Extravert's style— speaking before thinking.

♦ YOU MUST REMEMBER THIS

One big difference between Introverts and Extraverts is their capacity to remember specific conversations in detail over long periods of time. Es find themselves continually astounded by Introverts' word-for-word recollections of conversations that the E doesn't even recall having had. If the conversation in question was a promise, a decision, or an argument, the E can be placed at a distinct disadvantage by having dumped and dismissed something weeks, months, or even years earlier. The Introvert, however, was mulling the conversation over internally and developing some framework for discussion at a later time.

We know of one E-I couple in which the Extraverted husband once suggested to his wife that "maybe we should take some time to evaluate and assess where our marriage is going." Getting no response, he dropped the matter and promptly forgot about it.

Three months later the couple found themselves out to dinner to celebrate their anniversary. The evening was splendiferous, replete with a limo, tableside violins, and the best of wines. Halfway through the meal the Introverted wife looked at her husband and said, "Remember when you said you thought we should evaluate our relationship? I'm ready to talk about that now."

◆

Sensors and iNtuitives: What You Say Versus What You Get

Sensors and iNtuitives begin any communication with polar opposite perspectives. Sensors prefer to speak and hear things literally and precisely, while iNtuitives prefer to speak and hear things figuratively. Translated into real life, that can lead to miscommunication that would be funny if it weren't so serious.

Our friend Tim tells of such a situation involving his wife, Rhoda:

"Rhoda and I were in the process of flying home to Denver from Des Moines. If you miss the six-ten out of Denver, you don't get another chance until eleven A.M. the next day. We had left our two preteen kids at home with a sitter who was not prepared to stay the night. Unfortunately, we were running late.

"As I sped down the street to the airport, knowing I was going to have to pull an O. J. Simpson–like dash to return the rental car in order to make the flight, I shouted to Rhoda, 'What kind of car is this?'

"Her reply: 'It's a Ford!'

"Irritated at the reply, I shouted back, 'No, dammit! What kind of car is this?'

" 'It's a Ford Taurus,' she responded, trying to be more helpful.

"I suppose that if I asked her again, she would have responded that it was a *blue* Ford Taurus. What I really wanted to know was whether the car was an Avis, Dollar, or Budget rental car. I wanted to know what lot I needed to head toward and asked the question the only way I knew how. Rhoda answered the only way she knew how."

Rhoda and Tim's tale is an S-N classic: each party genuinely trying to communicate, with both parties coming at the process from opposite directions. It points up a persistent communication problem in many relationships: the difference between what is said, what is meant to be said, and what is heard by the other party.

In Tim's case the gap between what he said and what he meant to say was big enough to drive a Ford Taurus through. As an iNtuitive *he* knew what he meant, and actually thought he was saying it. "What kind of car is this?" obviously referred to the rental company, particularly in the context of the moment. After all, as they raced to the airport, why would he care who manufactured it? For him the question was clear as glass.

That wasn't the way Rhoda heard it. As a Sensor her first inclination is to interpret things literally, and the question, in its most literal translation, referred to the *kind* of car they had. In her effort to be genuinely helpful she responded the best way she could. After all, she could have responded with something like "I don't know, I'm not a car expert" or "I don't know. I didn't rent it; you did," or any number of other nonresponse responses.

In the end Tim and Rhoda made their flight. And the missed communication simply became fodder for one of many funny travel stories we all seem to have. But other couples aren't always so lucky. Sensing-iNtuitive miscommunications can be exasperating, as each party accuses the other of a deliberate put-on because of the gap between "what you said and what I thought you said." With each additional word spoken the miscommunication can become layered and more difficult to follow. Indeed, with some S-N couples, it's probably a miracle that any effective communication ever takes place.

The problem can become severely compounded when you add other preferences. Consider a Sensing-Judger and an iNtuitive-Judger. Both look out the window and see several trees. The SJ picks one specific tree about which to comment, while the NJ shares observations about the entire landscape.

At this point both are convinced they're right—and, in typical J fashion, both are—and so it becomes a head-to-head, right-versus-wrong discussion. What starts off as a difference of perceptions gets reduced to a life-or-death battle of wits. "Don't tell *me* what I saw; I was there!" could be either party's cry. To which the other would likely respond, "What makes you so right? I was there too!"

By the way, the perception battles aren't necessarily limited to typological opposites. Communication can become just as garbled when two people are both Sensors or iNtuitives. Consider, for example, how a Sensor might respond to another Sensor's specific query, "Where did we rent this car?" A strong Sensor might have responded, "At the airport rental counter, silly. You were right there. I'm amazed you don't remember."

"Of course I remember," the Sensor might respond. "What I need to know is what kind of rental it is."

"It's a powder-blue 1993 Ford Taurus with automatic transmission, AM/FM cassette stereo, and a loose jack rattling around in the trunk."

However precise the questions and the answers, these two exact-minded individuals are still bypassing each other at high speeds.

And two iNtuitives might suffer a similar fate:

"What kind of car is this?"

"It seems to be fine."

"No, I mean where is it from?"

"I suppose it was made in Detroit, but I can't tell you without doing some research. Ford imported some of these from overseas."

Obviously this conversation is stalled on the communication highway of life. At some point the two iNtuitives might figure out what the other is really trying to say. On the other hand, they might not.

In our workshops we are always finding how important it is to watch our words. For example, we have a purposefully open-ended exercise in which the participants are grouped by certain types. We ask each group to "use as much or as little of the environment as you wish and paint a picture." We provide them with no special equipment other than what is already sitting around the training room and the immediate vicinity.

You'd be astonished at how differently people can interpret this assignment. Much of the response is predictable:

◆ iNtuitives inevitably convert the assignment to a group experience, using a lot of colors, often centered around a rainbow theme, sometimes including accoutrements from the external environment: flowers, twigs, litter, and other found objects.

◆ Sensors inevitably approach us and complain that they

◆ A MATTER OF PRINCIPAL

All of us, at one time or another, have played to Sensors' literalism to skew if not eschew the facts. All types do it to their own advantage.

A fine illustration of this is in a story that goes back to Otto's junior high school days. Otto, a rambunctious seventh-grader, had once again opened his mouth one too many times. In exasperation the teacher sternly told Otto, "Young man, go and see the principal right now!"

With trepidation Otto left the room, aware that he was potentially in big trouble. But fate was on his side. As he walked down the hall, he noted that the principal's door was wide open, and the principal was in plain sight. Suddenly realizing he had obeyed the letter of the law, Otto returned to the classroom.

The teacher asked, "Did you see the principal?"

Otto, with total honesty, answered, "Yes."

"What did he say?" the teacher responded.

Said Otto: "Nothing."

And he was telling the truth.

cannot fulfill the assignment unless we provide them with paint.

As iNtuitives ourselves we're always tempted to believe that the Sensors are putting us on, picking apart our words for the sheer fun of it. As veteran Typewatchers we know differently. The directions instructed them to "paint," and although they want to comply, they cannot do so without having the specific ingredient called for. No matter that you can paint a picture with words, dance, or just about anything else. It rarely happens with Sensors. Even when they stretch themselves, trying to break away from the literal, they still remain very much grounded in the present, and the image is almost always something they can touch, see, hear, smell, or taste.

By the way, over the years we've refined the instructions given to the group. Now we ask them to "*Come up* with a picture. . . ." You'd be surprised at how much that has freed the Sensors to respond without trepidation.

Please understand: it's not that the iNtuitives are smarter or more capable than the Sensors. It's simply that the nature of the assignment, being so open-ended, favored the iNtuitive style. We could have designed an exercise that favored Sensors, asking for a very specific response to very precise directions, with a great deal of emphasis on details. ("Draw a picture of a two-story brick house using the red and green crayons provided. Make sure the house is no larger than the sheet of paper and contains at least five windows and two chimneys.") That would inevitably lead the iNtuitives to redefine the assignment in whatever ways necessary to undo the seemingly confining directions. They might find it so debilitating as to prevent their completing the assignment at all; or they might be moved to rebel and do whatever they wanted to do.

If you need further proof of iNtuitives' extreme difficulty dealing with specific details, consider what happens every

April 15, when the Internal Revenue Service asks all Americans to provide precise and timely information about a year's worth of finances. Most iNtuitives find it much more exciting to sit and try to redesign the tax form—or identify creative loopholes in the tax law—than to fill out forms and get them postmarked by midnight. It is safe to say that April 16 is a happy day for iNtuitives—at least those who didn't put things off by filing an extension.

As you are beginning to see, S-N communication difficulties aren't just verbal. Whatever the communication, whatever the communication mode, it is imperative to remember the high risk that key information can be lost in the translation. It's almost as if the two parties are speaking a different language. The futility of the situation can be likened to what can happen when you visit a foreign country and don't speak the native tongue. In trying to make ourselves understood, we often start by repeating things, but louder and more slowly, in the hopes that it will be more effective in getting the point across. But if the other person doesn't speak English, they may never understand what we're saying, no matter how slowly or loudly we speak.

It's the same thing with Sensors and iNtuitives. If we start from a very different perceptual awareness—a foreign "language"—it is possible that no amount of shouting or repetition will clear up the misunderstanding.

How do you overcome these obstacles? Our solution isn't quick and easy, but it's effective. It is a variation of an old training exercise called "active listening." In the exercise the listener cannot speak until he or she has repeated what the speaker has said to the speaker's satisfaction. "So," they begin, "what I heard you say was . . ." Or "You covered a great deal of material for me to repeat with any degree of accuracy, but let me try . . ."

Obviously this takes a certain amount of time, patience, and energy on both individuals' parts. However, when done

---

♦ MISERY LOVES COMPANY

Sometimes it's helpful simply to know we're not alone.

Several years ago we were working with a group of married couples. We asked a group of Sensors and iNtuitives to "describe time" on a sheet of paper.

The Sensors brought in a lengthy list of specific descriptors including hours, minutes, seconds, years, and the like.

The iNtuitives' much shorter list began with the following: "Time flies like an arrow. Fruit flies like a banana."

When the group saw this sentence, it broke up into hilarious laughter. One Sensing woman rose and, looking at her iNtuitive husband, said, "We've been married for thirty-three years, and I thought he said things like that just to drive me nuts. Tonight I learned that there are others like him. I don't know whether to laugh or cry."

---

conscientiously, it can work miracles by preventing communication gaps and garbled translations.

For our money, unless you are unscrupulously sleazy, you don't deliberately set out to mislead or miscommunicate. You start with good intentions that get lost through your preferences for handling what is said and what is heard. So unless your Typewatching skills keep checking the messages for surface-level accuracies and meanings, there's a high probability that you are heading down the road to frustration—probably in a powder-blue Ford Taurus.

♦

Thinkers and Feelers: Getting to the Heart of the Matter

No doubt you've heard it a thousand times: "Now, don't take this personally, but . . ." And the individual—a boss, a spouse, a so-called best friend—launches into something that can only be described as a devastating blow to your ego.

Did you believe the individual's preamble that it's "nothing personal"? Were you wondering, *Why am I even being told this?* Were you grateful for the honesty or hurt at the bluntness? Did you feel that the time and place of the comment were appropriate?

Your answers to these questions go to the heart of the communication differences between Thinkers and Feelers. And the differences are by no means trivial: the wording, timing, and delivery of nearly any message is a loaded gun that can easily misfire and harm any relationship. The kind of heightened communication skills that Typewatching brings can help keep messages on target and reduce the wounds—self-inflicted or otherwise—that often are fatal to friendships, marriages, and other relationships.

In the wide realm of communication problems, T-F differences can be the most difficult to overcome. Unlike Sensing-iNtuitive misunderstandings, which can often be clarified with relative ease, Thinking-Feeling communication clashes often carry with them emotional intensity and can quickly play to one or both parties' sense of self-esteem, or the lack thereof.

To understand further requires a quick look at each type's communication styles:

• For Thinkers, communication is any form of information that passes between individuals or groups, in which senders and receivers convey a message. It can be many things and take on many forms—verbal, nonverbal, written, artistic, physical—and can sometimes take on a life of its own. Most important, communication is what it is: information, and nothing more. In and of itself it is entirely impersonal.

• For Feelers, communication is an experience between two or more people in which the information conveyed is only the beginning. It involves trust, respect, admiration, empathy, and other emotive responses. If it is to be genuine, some or all of these ingredients must be present. When something happens to jeopardize or stifle these qualities, very little real communication can happen for Feelers. For them everything is personal.

As you can see, these differences are profound, to say the least. Even such seemingly innocuous conversation starters as "How ya' doin'?" can quickly become the building block for anything from a bruised ego to a knock-down-drag-out fight. For example, a Feeler, particularly an Extraverted one, might respond to the Thinker's greeting with "Well, I woke up this morning wondering whether my boyfriend and I really have a future together, and I'm not sure I want to take that Caribbean trip with him."

The Thinker is now in a quandary. The "How ya' doin'?" wasn't meant to elicit a dissertation about such delicate matters, merely to proffer a perfunctory greeting. The Thinker can respond in any number of ways. If the Thinker doesn't respond with empathy, the Feeler could be bruised, perhaps embarrassed, and even a little miffed at not receiving proper acknowledgment. If the Thinker tries to quickly put the matter to rest with something like "Well, things will work out in time," the Feeler might interpret that as the Thinker's depersonalizing the dilemma, and may walk away feeling frustrated and bitter. Of course, things could get really nasty should the Thinker respond with any comment tinged with sarcasm or rebuff—such as "Don't worry, there are a lot of fish in that Caribbean Sea."

Clearly the Thinker is walking a fine line. It would take a great deal of thoughtful insight to understand the optimal way to respond to that particular Feeler's needs on that particular day. As we've said, identifying with others' personal situations is not a Thinker's strong suit. And so it is not uncommon for the Thinker to say "the wrong thing," often at "the wrong time," leading to a clash.

Of course, the same principle works in the other direction. Let's turn the tables.

This time it's the Feeler who asks the Thinker, "How ya' doin'?" The Thinker responds with a similarly candid reply: "Not great. My boyfriend is threatening to break up just as we're getting ready to go on vacation." For the Thinker, that's intended to end the conversation. The question was answered, and there's no need to go farther. But the F is in a quandary. Genuinely interested, concerned, wanting to help, he or she is unclear how far to pursue the conversation. If the Feeler presses on, trying to elicit details and suggest possible solutions, there is a high probability that the Thinker may feel invaded, neither needing nor wanting to be rescued. If the Feeler avoids pressing on, not wanting to invade the T's personal life, the Feeler may become guilt-ridden about his or her inability to be helpful, and may even be angry with the Thinker for being so unresponsive.

As with so many other type differences what is exciting to one preference can drain or debilitate the opposite preference. For Thinkers, every communication is an opportunity for teaching or learning, and all communication is subject to continual improvement with the goal of achieving maximum benefit to both sender and receiver. It can therefore be quite common for a Thinker to interrupt a conversation in order to define or redefine some term, or to take an opposing stance simply for the sake of clarity. While this can be both enlightening and exciting for Thinkers, such behavior can frustrate and even anger Feelers, for whom the conversation had up to then been meaningful, understandable, and enjoyable.

For Feelers every communication is an opportunity to interact and connect with another human being. Their goal is not so much improvement of the communication as it is experiencing the moment: how it feels to be with the other person, the impact of the interaction on the relationship, and what if any motives might be involved. And then there's actual conversation: the flow and meaning of words, intonations, emotions, facial expressions, and a host of other interpersonal dynamics. All of these things combine to influence the Feeler's reactions during a conversation. He'll likely feel compelling urges to protect, defend, rescue, or even redirect the conversation so as to avoid what sounded like a potential conflict. While this may meet the Feeler's needs, it can become frustrating to a Thinker, who may simply be trying to impart some information.

Ironically, the Feeler's attempt to open up to the Thinker may actually cause the Thinker to become closed off, distracting or even blocking the Thinker's thought process. The T may respond by picking apart the F's words—"What do you *mean* I sound invested in the relationship?" That, in turn, can put the Feeler on the defensive, and genuine communication can go downhill.

It's no easier the other way. Feelers can be put off by what they perceive to be confrontational situations, even if that's not at all what was intended. For example, we know a man named Marvin who came home from work one day and announced to his girlfriend, Marsha, that he wanted "to confront the issue of our upcoming vacation."

Harmless enough, but not to Marsha, a Feeler, who heard the word *confront* as highly inflammatory. Her instant reaction was to head off what seemed to be an inevitable fight by offering him a drink. Marvin saw this as avoidance, which made him angry; after all, planning a vacation was supposed to be a fun experience. But Marsha was simply practicing a survival technique. After all, why should she willingly embark on something that from her perspective was guaranteed to be an exercise in yelling and screaming?

For Marvin, even if the situation should be reduced to yelling and screaming, it wouldn't necessarily be bad. That's simply part of the process—nothing personal. For all Ts, constructive feedback shouldn't be deemed as criticism. It is merely an effort to help someone improve a particular situation, offered in the spirit of the Golden Rule—"I would have appreciated someone telling *me* that."

Such constructive-criticism-turned-grudge-holding communication patterns are endemic to the Thinking-Feeling relationship. Therefore, Typewatching skills can be helpful in lowering some of the barriers that naturally occur and which hinder or inhibit effective communication.

The process, as always, begins with yourself: understanding how your own Thinking or Feeling preference affects your communication style. Are you too direct with your thoughts and opinions? Perhaps you should consider softening your tone to avoid unintentionally hurting others. Do you think

---

◆ HORSING AROUND WITH JUDGERS

We know a Feeling-Perceiver woman who wanted to celebrate her twenty-fifth anniversary with her husband by attending a couples' weekend workshop with us. She also knew that her Thinking-Judging husband would never attend such an event, let alone tie up a whole weekend with it. And, having known him for twenty-five years, she truly believed that once she got him there, he would have a great time.

So she told him that, as part of their anniversary weekend, they would go horseback riding. You can imagine the look on his face when he wandered into our conference center and learned he was facing a weekend of interpersonal encounter and marital communication.

His initial response was "I see the horses' asses, but where are the horses?"

As predicted, by the end of the two days he not only rated the workshop as a great experience, he shared with the group that this is why they've had such a marvelous twenty-five years of marriage: She learned how to communicate in a way that would get beyond his initial skepticism and allow them to share a world of marvelous experiences.

you're being direct when in fact you're beating around the bush? It might help to directly ask whether others understand what you are saying. Is the impact of your statements more personal or more impersonal than you intended? Consider the kind of impression you want to make. Do you see yourself as hypersensitive and easily wounded? Keep in mind that others' comments aren't necessarily directed at you. Do you enjoy arguing for the sake of arguing? Not everyone does; you might inadvertently be increasing the tension level of the conversation. Examining and monitoring such things can help you manage your own communication style and, at the same time, keep the airwaves relatively clutter free.

◆

Judgers and Perceivers: A Matter of Opinions

Whenever we think of Judgers and Perceivers trying to communicate, two vivid *Peanuts* cartoon images come to mind. One is of Charlie Brown, the Perceiver, finally garnering the force—and that's what it takes for a P—and shouting to Lucy: "You're not always right. You may sound right, you may think you're right, but you're not always right." And Lucy, the Judger, walking away with a smug, but-I-*am*-right look, totally unfazed by Charlie's uncharacteristic outburst.

The other equally vivid image has Snoopy, the happy-go-lucky Perceiving beagle, growling, snarling, and viciously chasing Lucy, who is running away in fright. Charlie Brown, observing the scene, shares with Linus: "Some folks don't like having their faults pointed out to them."

If there are two special symbols of J-P communication, those two vignettes capture them both. Most of the time Judgers sound right, whether they are or not. Js give answers, even when they haven't heard the question, while Ps search for new information and alternatives, while wondering of the Judgers, *How can they always think they have the right answers?*

The second issue is how much time the J expends criticizing everything, and freely pointing out faults. The topics may vary—a Feeling-Judger may be critical of social or moral issues; a Thinking-Judger may be critical of products or "the system"—but the process is inevitable: Js have to say what they think. And the problem, as Charlie Brown so aptly pointed out, is clear: not everyone likes having their faults pointed out to them.

Simply put, Js are life's advice-givers, while Ps are life's question-raisers. Without the benefit of Typewatching it's a free-for-all: Judgers and Perceivers are alternatively attracted to and repelled by their respective behaviors. Typewatching not only gives definition to the process, but offers some basic skills for coping with this phenomenon.

♦ FREE ADVICE

EJ Motto: When I want your opinion, I'll give it to you.

Because the J-P preference addresses the part of each of us that others see most readily, it is important to be aware of how their communication styles compare and contrast:

♦ **Judgers,** who need closure, don't mince words. They'll give you their judgment. They might repeat the same thought. If you ask them "Why?", they'll respond "Because," or say what they just said. It's not easy for Js to supply the data upon which their judgment is based. So they'll just repeat the judgment or decision.

♦ **Perceivers,** on the other hand, seem like they get paid by the word or the idea. Their communication style is just as open as their life-style, which tends to ramble from one thing to another. In making an argument they aren't beyond finding several ways to say the same thing, qualifying each point, often vaguely, often resulting in gigantic perceptual gaps. But then again, they may not. It all depends . . . maybe, but not always. Sometimes you can't be sure. Perceivers, especially Extraverted ones, can change thoughts midsentence and in-terrupt themselves, with no apparent need to complete— incidentally, did we mention that Ps, especially NPs, can appear very absentminded? On the other hand . . . Get it?

It doesn't matter what the configuration—a J communicating with a P, or two Js or two Ps trying to relate to one another. Whether jarringly different or strikingly similar, the J and P personality styles have the potential to confine if not confound communication:

+ Two Js tend to butt heads. In fact it is a J communica-tion style to say, "Yes, but . . ." (In fact, right now, Js reading this are saying to themselves, "Yes, but we do this for a good reason.") A Judger puts out an opinion, and the other J offers a counteropinion. And so the conversation becomes a series of sharply contrasting views. To the unknowing observer it can sound much more intense and severe than the experience of the actual conversationalists. A J-J conversation is likely to be limited in scope, relatively short in duration—unless some-thing or someone comes along with an alternative opinion.

+ A P-P conversation can be hard to follow (even for another P) because it can go anywhere, in all directions, at one time. Ps possess a conversational agility, often sharing a variety of ideas or other information, with a very low need to resolve any of it. One P may say something, the other P may ask an open-ended question about it or suggest an alternative thought. In either case the conversation may eventually come back to the original topic or head off in one or more totally new directions.

+ A J-P conversation is likely to be dominated by the J. It

may well end early if the P isn't ready, willing, and able to stand up to the J's argumentative style, or if the J can't handle the P's seemingly endless array of questions or alternatives. In the first case, the P might walk away grumbling, "Fine, have it your way." In the second case, the J might walk away with an abrupt, "That's just the way it is, and that's final."

There are few if any Ps who, in a conversation with a J, haven't experienced at least two phenomena typical of J-P communication. A conversation that a P intended to be merely a discussion or exchange of ideas can quickly turn into an argument, with the J unwittingly sounding defensive. ("You're not listening to what I'm saying. I said to you that all men have trouble making commitments in relationships. And that's true.") In addition Js, especially Extraverted Js, can sound angry when they're not. ("Why do I have to repeat myself? Just pay attention to me and you'll understand.") That can disarm, confound, and confuse a P, often resulting in an abrupt halt to the conversation.

The above generalizations notwithstanding, a J-P conversation needn't be an exercise in frustration. As the case of Rick and June demonstrates, Typewatching awareness can help each party meet the other's specific needs, leading to a win-win situation.

The setting is New Year's Eve. Rick (a strong Perceiver) and June (a strong Judger) are entertaining friends. As Rick describes it, "The atmosphere was a typical northern Christmas: snow outside, fire in the fireplace, and the warm buzz of good conversation. I'm in the kitchen mixing Spanish coffees for our guests, and June bursts in. With memorable urgency she began the conversation:

" 'I just remembered that next week at work, they're putting up the summer holiday schedule. We have to decide what weeks we want to take.'

" 'Do we really have to decide now?' I answered in typical P fashion, answering a question with a question. 'Can't we decide after our guests leave, or maybe tomorrow?'

" 'No,' said June. 'We have to decide now.'

" 'Why?' I asked, another question slipping out quite innocently.

" 'Because if we don't decide, I'll be thinking about it all evening and it will ruin the party for me.'

"At that point I realized several things," says Rick. "For one thing, the situation was not rational. That allowed me to recognize that June's personal needs of the moment overshadowed my need to put the discussion off. I also realized that the 'cost' of giving her what she needed was very low."

The rest of the conversation went something like this:

"Okay," said Rick, "I'll make you a deal. Let's pick some dates now, on the condition that as we get closer to the summer, we can change our minds."

"That sounds great," responded June.

Rick describes the outcome:

"The bottom line was that we came to a decision. I got the flexibility I needed, and she carried a tray of Spanish coffees into the living room and we had a hell of a good time for the rest of the evening. And she showed me how important that moment was later when our guests had left. Without Typewatching it could have gone very differently."

◆

Four Keys to Successful Communication

Here are several tips and techniques we've found especially helpful in breaking communication barriers:

◆ **Identify the differences.** When caught in a communication logjam, as always try to determine what's really going on in typological terms. For example, is an Extravert shouting and an Introvert not speaking at all? Has a Thinker given some criticism that a Feeler has overpersonalized? Is an iNtuitive being unclear? Does a Perceiver keep changing the subject?

Once you have pinpointed key differences, try any of the following:

—*If the difference is E-I:* Try to reverse roles, forcing the Introvert to talk and share information without internal editing, and the Extravert to listen without interruption.

—*If the difference is S-N:* Try to repeat to each other what the other has just said, without interpretation or further analysis. "What I hear you telling me is . . ."

—*If the difference is T-F:* Try to repeat each other's point of view. Then attempt to judge whether each party's perspective is too personal or not personal enough. Keep in mind that Thinkers respond more readily when asked, "What do you think?" and Feelers respond more readily when asked, "What do you feel?"

—*If the difference is J-P:* Try to determine what issues are negotiable, and which aren't. Then focus only on those things on which one party or the other is willing to move.

If none of these things can be done, you are in some deep communication difficulties and the situation of the moment may be too hot to handle. At this point you'd be better off putting your problem-solving on hold for a while—a few hours, a day or so—and trying again later.

• **Identify the similarities.** If, on the other hand, you determine that a communication problem stems from your being type alike—that is, two Extraverts, two Sensors, and so on—then there is a high probability that you are accusing the other of doing things that you are prone to do yourself. (Sometimes these are the very things we don't like about ourselves.) So, for example, Extraverts often accuse each other, "You never listen," when in fact what's true for one is true for both. Or two Judgers may rigidly accuse one another of being too closed to hear what the other is saying. Or two Sensors may accuse one another of being too hung up on meaningless details. What's happening here is that the problem is too close to home for them to see it.

The sooner the parties can appreciate what is happening, the more ready they will be to intercept the process—usually by tapping into their nonpreferences. For example, if one of the two Extraverts can manage to stop talking and start listening, that may begin to redirect the conversation and unfreeze respective positions.

+ **Own your own stuff.** In working things out—and in all communication, for that matter—the more either party can uses sentences that begin with the word *I*, the greater the opportunity for effective communication. So, instead of saying, "You're driving like a maniac," you will go farther faster by saying something like "I get frightened when you drive so fast" or "I don't like it when you tailgate." These are not guarantees for avoiding a collision—interpersonal or otherwise—but they are less accusatory and they place the onus on the person making the statement.

By the way, the same thing works when making positive statements. "Thanks, I really appreciate it when you drive more slowly" works better than "You're driving much better today." Even though both are complimentary, you'd be surprised how greatly people prefer hearing the former over the latter simply because it reflects a more personal investment. Trust us, it works.

+ **Sweat the small stuff.** This is almost embarrassing to mention, but we're constantly astounded by how frequently all of us overlook life's two simplest but most effective statements: "Thank you" and "I'm sorry." We hear repeatedly how refreshing a simple "I'm sorry" would be to mitigate a mistake or misunderstanding at work, at home, or anywhere else— instead of our seemingly more preferred defensiveness: "It wasn't me," "Gee, that's a shame," or "Things happen." We hear from parents, kids, employers, friends, and especially from mates about chronic insensitivity and ingratitude, all of which can be turned around with a few words. It's such a small investment that yields such big dividends.

EXERCISE

1

When Do You Know You're Loved?

Here is a good exercise for a couple in which one party is an **Extravert** and the other is an Introvert: Have both individuals write down as many responses as possible to the question "When do you know you're loved?"

After both have done this, read the list to the other and compare for similarities and differences.

Chances are, the Extraverted list will be based on social and verbal affirmations: "I know I'm loved when you tell me." "When you buy me presents." "When you go places with me and my friends." And so on.

The Introverted list will likely be more inwardly based, including such things as "I know I'm loved when you allow me space to be alone." "When you protect me from the demands of others." "When we can be in each other's presence and don't have to talk."

The differences often can provide insight into how different our communication styles are about something so seemingly universal. They may also speak volumes about the communication patterns and needs in your own relationship, and why one or both parties may inadvertently frustrate the other.

- ◆ BEING IN LOVE WITH Es

The secret to keeping an Extravert happy in a relationship is much like the secret to giving a successful speech. In the latter case the three key steps are 1) Tell 'em what you're going to tell 'em. 2) Tell 'em. 3) Tell 'em what you told 'em.

In the case of an intimate relationship with an E, the rule might be: 1) Tell 'em that you're going to tell 'em that you love 'em. 2) Tell 'em you love 'em. 3) Tell 'em that you just told 'em that you love 'em.

We can promise you that however distasteful or difficult this may be to do—particularly if you're an Introvert—the Extravert will be in heaven. The Extravert cannot hear it often enough.

EXERCISE

2

A Question of Questions

Here's a way for Js and Ps to work on improving their communication skills. The idea is for each party to focus on what doesn't come naturally.

It's very simple: Have the Judger write down three open-ended questions about him or herself and the other person. And have the Perceiver write down three definitive judgments about both individuals.

One of the things you'll find is that Judgers have trouble being open-ended. For example, rather than asking, "What are some of the things Peter does to get ready for a vacation?" a J is more likely to ask, "Does Peter ever bother to plan a vacation?" In the process the J begins the conversation with a rather loaded judgment in question form.

As for Ps, they often think they're being very judgmental even though their comments lack much direction. For example, they're likely to say something like "Joan has a pretty good idea of how we will spend our vacation," as opposed to "Joan always has a plan for our vacation, and it helps us to do everything we set out to do."

In the process of the exercise Joan and Peter can experience how difficult it is to communicate in their opposite preference. By doing so Joan can learn that she's often not as open-ended as she thinks, and Peter can learn that what he thinks is direct and straightforward can be construed as wishy-washy.

◆ SO, WHAT'S THE PROBLEM?

Judger: "The trouble with you Ps is that you answer a question with another question."
Perceiver: "Is that bad?"

EXERCISE
3

How's the Economy?

A very good J-P exercise is to jot down on a piece of paper a few thoughts answering the directive "Discuss the economy." Then have each party read his or her response to the other.

Judgers tend to create a list of opinions about the national state of affairs. In one glance of the list you'll know whether or not they are pleased with the country's present economic conditions.

The Perceiver, on the other hand, will respond with a series of questions defining the assignment: "Which economy—the world, the nation, the state, or city?" "The only real economy is the one in my checkbook." "How can I even talk about the economy without more direction?" "Do I even want to get into this?" Eventually, the list may eventually get to some conclusions, perhaps even a single "bottom line."

The value of this exercise is to show how very differently two people can approach the exact same assignment. That may lead to additional insights into how each of you approaches other things in opposite ways, such as cleaning the house, getting ready to go out, or raising the kids.

COMMUNICATION TYPE TALK

IF YOU ARE . . .

AND YOUR LOVER IS . . . .

	EXTRAVERT	INTROVERT
EXTRAVERT	• Repeat what you heard your partner say before you begin speaking.	• Demand quiet time and space from your partner.
	• Try not to both talk at the same time.	• Work at being direct and expressive now and then.
	• Try to hear what's being said without formulating your response. If necessary, count to five before you speak.	• Don't be afraid to shout to make yourself heard or understood.

	EXTRAVERT	INTROVERT
INTROVERT	• Allow for private time. Try to sit silently in your partner's presence.	• Fight avoidance by speaking out, no matter how awkward it may seem.
	• Now and then, put it in writing instead of saying it.	• Edit yourself out loud instead of inside.
	• Find alternative ways of expressing yourself.	• Enjoy the silence, appreciate the space, and love your partner's contemplative nature.

	SENSOR	INTUITIVE
SENSOR	• Work on restating the obvious in general terms.	• Remember that much of what you say—and don't say—will be taken literally.
	• Share your dreams with each other.	• Appreciate the specific and grounded help your partner gives to what you say.
	• Try to keep each other from always interpreting so literally what's being said.	• Remember that your partner prefers precision and facts before he or she can formulate a response.

	SENSOR	INTUITIVE
INTUITIVE	• Keep in mind that whatever you say, your partner will find different ways to interpret it.	• Be sure to check out each other's meanings about what is being said.
	• Check interpretations and meanings so you are satisfied with what's been said.	• Allow time for each of you to stop, look, listen, smell, feel, or taste. Don't be afraid to let your senses become overloaded.
	• Keep in mind that your partner may naturally give a general response to your specific statement.	• Translate what the other is saying into specifics: who, what, where, when, and why.

IF YOU ARE . . .

	THINKER	FEELER
THINKER	• Remember that each of you has emotions. Be sure to consider feelings in your communications.	• Don't be afraid to have a knock-down-drag-out fight now and then.
	• Be careful not to become too competitive in your conversations.	• Once in a while, try to express something negative without feeling guilty.
	• If others are present, be aware of how they will hear what you are saying.	• Avoid saying "I'm sorry" or "It's my fault" to your partner during an argument.
	THINKER	**FEELER**
FEELER	• Try to say "I'm sorry" once in a while, if only on general principle.	• Face the disagreeable with each other. Remember that it cannot be avoided.
	• Say "I love you"—whatever that means to you—with no purpose or goal in mind. Or, if you prefer, send a card.	• Try not to rescue or personalize what the other person says.
	• Keep in mind that when your partner surfaces an issue, he or she may want support, not analysis.	• Enjoy the affirmations and good feelings you give each other.
	JUDGER	**PERCEIVER**
JUDGER	• Give in now and then, even when you know you are right.	• Help your partner understand that he or she can't control everything— especially you.
	• Try to raise a question in place of giving an answer or offering advice.	• Help your partner see more than just answers and directions in what you are saying.
	• Remember that some things are beyond either of your control.	• Remember that what your partner is saying may not be final, even if he or she says it is.
	JUDGER	**PERCEIVER**
PERCEIVER	• Avoid putting your partner in a corner, conversationally. Allow room for him or her to move.	• Make sure that one of you makes a decision and follows through with it.
	• Help your partner sort out what you do not want, knowing that you can live with the rest.	• Help each other focus the conversation. Try to monitor when one of you strays off course.
	• Appreciate your partner's ability to generate alternatives. Don't be afraid to consider them.	• Try whenever possible to finish—hey, is that a new car?—your sentences.

AND YOUR LOVER IS . . .

6
SEX AND INTIMACY

*"Please try to say what
you're feeling as it's happening."*

Some people call it overrated, others can't say enough about
it. Whatever your opinion is of sexual intimacy, it's difficult
to overlook so critical a part of a relationship. Whether you
"do it" all the time, just once in a while, or hardly at all, the
way you perceive yourself and your lover in this arena can be
as important as anything else in making a love relationship
work.

When it comes to sexual intimacy, there are many layers
of things that can either make the act exciting or ruin it
totally. As just about anyone knows, defining and discussing
sexual matters is no simple task. When you get into the
subject of sex, you're not simply talking about a physical
activity. You're talking about something that involves traditions, values, taboos, mysteries, upbringing, religion, and a
host of social influences. What you may call flat-out immoral,
someone else may find not only normal but exciting. What
one person calls perverse, another deems erotic. What we
think boring may be what others consider just short of ecstasy.

All of this, and we haven't even introduced the impact of
personality preferences.

Coping with each preference's peculiarities in the arena of intimacy can be a challenge, to be sure. The challenge is to understand each other's needs and try to make accommodations accordingly. That's not always easy, given the heavy scripts and expectations levied by society on the "appropriate" roles of men and women in sexual relationships. But Typewatching offers a positive, nonjudgmental frame of reference that can ease the way.

As trained counselors we hear so many classic lines that reflect the issues we struggle with constantly. But you don't need a degree in psychotherapy to know the refrains: "I've never refused him." "He'll expect it and it's my wifely duty." "I've been obnoxious at the party, so I'm sure I'll be cut off tonight." "Well, I'm not going to get any tonight, so let's have another drink and I'll tell you what really happened." You get the picture. These lines and so many others like them indicate how we use and misuse the act of intercourse to

---

◆ EIGHT WAYS TO DO IT

Here is how the eight preferences typically behave during sexual encounters:

- **Extraverts** like to *talk*—before, during, and after.
- **Introverts** prefer to experience the moment in *quiet revelry.*
- **Sensors** are excited about *experiencing* the five senses—touching, tasting, seeing, hearing, smelling.
- **iNtuitives** are excited by *imagining* the thrills stimulated by the five senses.
- **Thinkers** want to *examine* the experience so it can be improved upon next time.
- **Feelers** just want to *appreciate* the moment without further analysis.
- **Judgers** prefer to *plan* it and execute their plan.
- **Perceivers** prefer to enjoy the *spontaneity* of the moment.

reflect anything from gender awareness to personal competence, from love to punishment.

Perhaps Typewatching won't eliminate all of the negative aspects of this subject, and it certainly won't erase years of ingrained behavior, but it can offer some constructive insights about how we approach one another on this vital aspect of an intimate relationship.

The influence of type on sexual intimacy works differently at different stages of a relationship. At any age, when boy meets girl, the adrenaline flows and for a certain period of time personality preferences can take a backseat to trying to get the fledgling relationship off the ground. Ironically, this intense period of mutual evaluation is probably a very bad time to be seriously sizing up a relationship. What appears to both parties to be "love at first sight" may really be a classic case of "bait and switch."

The reason: In our lovestruck euphoria we're far more responsive to the other person than aware of our own needs. Simply put, we're not being ourselves. For example, though it may be difficult for them to do, Extraverts work hard at listening carefully and Introverts expend great energy attempting to be social butterflies. There's a certain politeness that accompanies the time together: Judgers work at playing it cool while Perceivers enjoy taking charge of places to go and things to do. Clearly, both individuals seem to be aware that there is more to the relationship than what is happening on the surface. But the events of the moment seem exciting enough to make them want to forge ahead into the great unknown.

All of this is normal and a testimony to the power of sexual attraction. What is important to remember as the two see more and more of each other is that the relationship needs to move from excitation and adrenaline to the more natural state that encourages the genuine self to emerge.

The more the relationship moves toward intimacy, the more there will be bursts of self-doubt and self-confidence, trust and vulnerability, and a host of other emotions: "Can I handle a long-term commitment?" "Can I trust this person not to hurt me?" "Am I worthy of this person?" "Will this person leave me when someone better comes along?" "Is this really the person I've been looking for?" "How can I be sure?"

All of this inner noise is part and parcel of the struggle everyone goes through in the progression that leads to intimacy. There is no shortcut. There is no escaping the stress. If there is to be genuine union—symbolized for some types by sexual intercourse—that oneness is only attained in a slow, gradual, growing loss of self. It is not a matter of dependence, independence, or codependence. It is true interdependence in which each person is allowed to exercise his or her full potential, both individually and in the relationship, all the while aware that the other holds a significant amount of the ingredients necessary for completeness. In a successful intimate relationship the whole truly is greater than the sum of the parts. It's being mindful that no matter how good or competent or complete we are by ourselves, we are more of each by being part of meaningful intimacy.

The purpose of Typewatching, then, is to heighten the potential of intimacy by heightening self-awareness. It is important to assess your personal, physical, and emotional needs, and compare and contrast them with your partner's needs. As you understand more of your type, Typewatching can help you determine what you can do and what you can negotiate with your partner so that your physically intimate moments can meet the needs of each.

•

Sensors and iNtuitives: Imagination versus the Moment

Although each preference is important in the realization of sexually intimate oneness, let's begin with the S-N difference, which has to do with our basic perceptions. The various ways in which we perceive our own and others' intimate needs can significantly determine all that follows. If one party is excited about the immediate moment and the other is fantasizing about what could be, it's clear that the two individuals could pass like ships in the night, even though they experience a moment of physical closeness. If one person is comfortably trusting the situation and the other is still searching for the possible meanings of *trust*, they can, while being physically close, be worlds apart.

If you are a Sensor, it is imperative to remember that you are excited by the tactile world and your imagination *follows* the experience. Repeatedly, Sensors tell us that sexual turn-ons focus on the specific: a special place—the bedroom, in front of the fireplace, in the tub, or someplace that the S can describe exactly; or music, including a particular refrain of a particular song performed by a particular group—climaxing, as it were, at a particular moment. It is rarely a general description, but rather a detailed accounting of the lights, flowers, clothes (or lack thereof), perfumes, and other accoutrements. Such specificity rarely wavers.

If you are an iNtuitive, it is imperative to remember that imagination *precedes* the experience and often the actual can lag behind where your imagination had taken you. While Ns are certainly excited by the sensate world, they describe the moments in far more general ways. For example, they may report there was music playing, and when pushed they may eventually be able to name *Bolero*. Often their descriptions of what turns them on include generalizations that could describe most anything: "communications," "closeness," "ambience," "the right person," or simply "a good time." While this lack of specificity by no means diminishes the moment for the iNtuitive, it can appear to trivialize things in a Sensor's eyes. Obviously, if Sensors and iNtuitives don't realize this basic difference, it can lead to more turnoffs than turn-ons.

Sensors and iNtuitives offer a vital contribution to each

other in the act of intimacy. The Sensors, starting with a specific touch, smell, or sound, can be quickly stimulated to imagine much, much more, but the sequence of events is very important. The iNtuitives can get very excited by the sensual realities, but must be brought gently from their dreamy imagination in a way that builds on their fantasy rather than serves as a rude awakening.

You'd be surprised how these simple differences can lead to frustration and possibly conflict. A Sensor might complain, "I love the feel of his hair pressing against my breasts. I love to feel it on my fingertips. But I just can't ignore the offensive music playing in the background. I feel like my circuits are being jammed and I can't respond."

"Well, just ignore the music and let your imagination take over," replies the iNtuitive.

"It's just not that easy," answers the Sensor. "I can't do it."

"You could if it really was important to you," accuses the iNtuitive.

And suddenly sex has been transformed into sniping.

This can easily be avoided. Before things get out of control, the S and N would be wise to talk a bit more calmly about the irritations. Better yet, before they even get started, they could spend some time making lists of their respective sexual turn-ons and turnoffs. (Do the turnoffs first, just in case the turn-ons get you both so excited that you get distracted!) This will give you time and distance to more objectively share things that need to be said. You still may not agree, and there may be some bruised feelings, but if the issues are aired in a spirit of cooperation and mutual concern, they can lead to satisfying solutions.

Above all, if your discussions become too intense, stop the conversation, commit yourself to revisit the topic later, and give each other some time and space. It's not easy to do, but you'll benefit.

◆
Thinkers and Feelers: Head versus Heart

Since emotions are such a vital part of the intimate and sexual relationship, it follows that the different ways in which Thinkers and Feelers respond emotionally become very significant. In fact, the T-F dimension is the toughest area for couples to understand each other in when they talk about sex and intimacy. Because, as we stated earlier, there are some gender differences between Ts and Fs (men are overwhelmingly Thinkers, and women are overwhelmingly Feelers), we get ourselves caught up in social expectations about how men and women "should" behave in bed.

As we said in Chapter 2, emotions for the Thinker start with the head and, after some analysis, move eventually to the heart. The more a Thinker understands the emotional charge, the freer he or she is to experience it fully. In other words, feelings are there to be understood in order to be truly felt. It's a classic T line: "How can I tell you I love you if we don't understand what that means? We have to agree on a definition." Where a Thinker is concerned, "detached intimacy" is not a contradiction in terms. Rather, it is the key to knowing what intimacy is all about.

An ENTJ female friend of ours once said, "I have another ENTJ living outside myself on the ceiling. This other 'me' watches all of my moves, including my intimate ones. It is always with me, giving criticism and feedback in order that I might constantly improve whatever I'm doing." As a result, even during lovemaking, the "ceiling" ENTJ was watching, and would be ready afterward for a "meeting" and an instant analysis of her performance. For her, as for all iNtuitive-Thinkers, anything worth doing is worth improving upon— even life's most intimate moments. Each sexual experience must be measured and set against some set of objective criteria, so it can get better and better.

It is the Thinker's style to keep every aspect of life, and especially the sexual one, within a conceptual perspective: its meanings and significance to each individual's life. Gaining this perspective allows for total enjoyment and affords a challenge for each subsequent experience. It provides expressions of the particular emotions necessary for the moment. And through continued analysis it lets those emotions continue to be expressed ever more completely. If, on a particular day, the Thinker experiences joy, then "joy" should indeed be added to the list of emotions to be considered.

All of this can happen only if one stays detached and analytical. The more in control of oneself, the more full and meaningful the experience. And as learning improves, so does the physical act that is the foundation of that learning. At the very least, intimacy, including sex, is a mind-over-matter discipline. Who could argue with such a noble sense of self-improvement?

Feelers, for starters, could make a case against it. Any self-respecting F would look at the above paragraph—particularly the part about being "in control of oneself" during intimate moments—and be overcome with shock and amazement. After all, isn't being intimate all about losing oneself in another person—or at least in the experience of being with another person? How can this deeply emotional experience be regarded as a mere "discipline"?

Obviously, for the Feeler, intimacy is a matter of the heart. Such words as *unconditional* and *unending* drive the Feeler's grasp at intimacy. Not only is it an experience for which there is no "discipline," but the Feeler believes that to even attempt to understand it is to miss its essence. It is something to be felt, and you'll know it when you feel it. Don't try to dissect it, analyze, or improve it. For the Feeler intimacy, consummated in sexual intercourse, is the ultimate form of selflessness. Intimacy is loss of self in the giving of the moment, and finding each other in the oneness that makes the moment happen. Such moments cannot be objectified, and to add any conditions to such an event is to ruin it forever. (Even to refer to it as an "event"—as opposed to an experience—runs the risk of diminishing it.)

To define when one is being "intimate" sharply separates Thinkers and Feelers. For Fs intimacy can include trust, sharing, giving, forgiving, wanting, and helping. It means moving to new heights—and depths—and the discovery of oneself in this other person. It's the harmony of harmonies, a symphony of heart, body, spirit, and mind, played out into a crescendo of two becoming one. It defies analysis, it resists examination, it fades under scrutiny. And it is lost if it is not appreciated for what it is. Closeness, oneness, touching, and togetherness are the necessary and uninterruptible driving forces that allow intimacy to occur. If it is real, genuine, and unconditional, it will always have meaning—and that can't be improved upon, nor should it be. For the Feeler to step outside of this oneness—to analyze it, let alone try to improve it—is abhorrent. Such a move condemns an otherwise intimate couple back to separateness, which is not only jolting, but also becomes the setting for doubts, hurts, distrust, and possibly feelings of abandonment.

You can see the obvious dilemma. The Thinker cannot begin to ascribe all these qualities and emotions to any interpersonal event. Perhaps if he or she were given enough time to think about it and analyze it, some of those subjective traits could surface. But in no way could they all be given credence—let alone such intensity. At its worst Thinkers' inability to "keep up" with Feelers' emotional intensity may drive them away, as the Ts recognize that no amount of improvement and analysis will ever be enough.

And so the gap widens: The F begins to feel the relationship's failure creep in; the T begins to think about what's wrong, trying to discover what's missing and if it is hopeless.

Typewatching allows both Thinkers and Feelers to have their space. It is important for Ts to realize that they have contributed to an F's unconditional ecstasy, and to just let that be; the T isn't necessarily obliged to go along for the ride. The experience has given him enough to think about. And Fs must realize that they have contributed to a T's conceptualizing process, that nothing will be ruined by the T's analysis, and that the F isn't required to participate in that process. If both parties are able to move even slightly in understanding the other's needs and processes, the relationship will have a much greater chance for success, even in spite of their sharp differences.

If all of this weren't enough, there's also the gender difference to consider here. Remember that Thinking and Feeling is the only preference pair for which there is a gender bias: About two thirds of Ts are males, and about two thirds of Fs are females. There are strong pressures for those in the minority—Thinking females and Feeling males—to behave in ways that run against their preferences. And when it comes to sex and intimacy, that creates even more complex dynamics.

For example, consider the T woman. For her to engage in objective detachment and analysis during intimacy, though very natural to her Thinking preference, sets her up in our society to be the subject of scorn and resentment. One T woman we know put it this way: "There's no end to the struggle. When intercourse is over, it's over. And I want to think about it a bit and get on with things—either to go to sleep or do whatever is supposed to come next. My F boyfriend isn't ready to stop. He wants to snuggle, caress, and revel in the afterglow. It's hard for me to join in. But if I don't, he sees me as cold, heartless, and uncaring. It's not that at all. I'm just in a different place, usually in my head."

Such "man talk" by a woman can be all but emasculating to the male who doesn't understand what's going on. It raises all sorts of self-doubt in the T female unless she has strong feelings about a particular issue or a sense of what makes Thinking types tick.

For Thinkers, sexual tension can be created by discussing, arguing, engaging, competing, winning some, and losing some, because the engagement can be nearly as exciting as the act itself. You can imagine how stressful this process can be to a T woman. It inevitably raises questions of "What's wrong with my femininity that I get so excited by this competitive banter?" It would be helpful if she could recognize that there is nothing wrong with her or her femininity. It's not a matter of gender; it's a matter of type.

Ts, in their proclivity to rationalize, would do well to recognize that the attributes traditionally assigned as "male" or "female" are induced by society. Though time-honored, persuasive, and perhaps legitimate, they have little to do with a T woman's reality. If you want to lead while dancing, be on top during sex, or aggressively pursue a man in a bar, you may be out of step with what society says is proper for women, but it should by no means detract from your femininity. If, as a T woman, you can see all that as both pleasing and valid, and your mate agrees, then that's all that really matters. Be mindful, however, that you will be going against the mainstream.

◆ ALL IN A DAY'S WORK

Sometimes, a few simple words can go a long way to heading off problems.

Jack and Theresa were two Thinkers who had been married twelve years in what they described as a solid and satisfying relationship. There is no doubt that it was a positive relationship, but two things were unfolding that would have a dramatic impact on this couple. First, the two were taking each other pretty much for granted, and were not spending much time saying nice things to each other. As Jack put it: "We let the obvious speak for itself."

The second dynamic was in the form of Esther May, Jack's new office assistant. She was very expressive, a hard-core wearing-her-heart-on-her-sleeve Feeling type. As work demanded, Jack and Esther May spent quite a bit of time together, with Esther May regularly and enthusiastically sharing her positive impressions of Jack's business style.

Not surprisingly, Jack became excited and aroused. He would sit in our office and talk about her, denying the obvious, and looking to us to confirm that nothing was happening, that it was all his fantasy and nothing would come of it. Yet, as he would describe in his own objective and analytical way his time at home with Theresa and compare it to his office time with Esther May, the differences were painfully obvious: office time was affirming, homelife was not. Office time was flirtatious and exciting, homelife was routine and flat.

"I can't tell you how exciting it is to hear all she says to me," Jack would say. "Even if it's false or temporary, I've got to admit, I like it."

It was clear that unless something or someone intervened, Jack was headed for an affair.

We would ask Jack, "Is there any way Theresa could be as exciting to you as Esther May?"

"No," he would say. "I don't think so."

"Well," we countered, "we don't know that Theresa can't be exciting. She doesn't even have a chance, because you're keeping her on the outside. How about trying to equalize things a bit by giving Theresa a sporting chance? Why not try to win her back by courting her all over again? Take her to dinner, say nice things, seduce her. And give her a chance to respond to your advances."

There was no doubt Jack deeply loved Theresa. Further, he knew Esther May, however exciting, had no future with him. By helping both Jack and Theresa see how their objectivity had led them to take each other for granted, they were able to appreciate the need for being more expressive and responsive to each other.

Interestingly, as they talked about it in their own objective style, one readily followed the other's lead in sharing positive thoughts. With a little deliberateness and some direct requests for positive expressions, Jack and Theresa were able to fill some gaps that somehow unconsciously each had allowed to form.

In no time at all they centered their energies on some common hobbies and agreed to express verbally each day their affection and appreciation for one another in some meaningful way. They even turned it into a game, as each tried to outdo the other in showering attention and affection on their mate. Soon, being together became a part of the day to which each looked forward.

All of the above is exacerbated if the T woman is also a Sensing-Judger. A special dilemma confronts STJ women because they have a T preference that tells them to be objective, detached, and analytical, and their Sensing and Judging preferences lead them to a variety of traditional behaviors—"shoulds"—to which women are expected to respond.

A seventeen-year-old ESTJ woman brought this fact into sharp focus one evening while we had dinner with her and her family. During the conversation she blurted, "I don't even want to date anymore. It's lose-lose for me."

We were startled by the revelation, and asked her to explain.

"It's lose-lose because when my date picks me up for the evening and asks me what I want to do and where I want to go," she continued, "if I tell him, I intimidate him with my take-charge attitude. Taking charge, by the way, makes me feel good. If I play the passive woman, like a part of me says I should, and say, 'Oh, I don't care. Wherever you want to go is fine,' then I'm angry with myself all evening. I *do* care where we go, and I'd rather tell him that.

"On the other hand," she went on, "I tend to put him off if I dare challenge him about his choice. And that only gets us both frustrated. It's easier just to stay home and not date."

All of this at the tender age of seventeen.

Of course, what's true for a Thinking woman is also true for a Feeling male. Society places expectations on him that are contrary to his own inner workings and personality preferences. So he also can get caught up in a real bind between wanting to go with his natural Feeling preference—of nurture, empathy, and benevolence—which can put him at odds with society's expectations of masculinity: detached, tough-minded, and virulent. As was true with his T-female counterpart, the F male's dilemma is compounded if he is also a Sensing-Judger. The SJs proclivity toward "shoulds" leads to self-expectations of sharply defined masculine roles: breadwinner, head of the household, fearless leader. Obviously, this runs against his natural grain. It's not that SFJ males can't be breadwinners, heads of households, and fearless leaders. But spending too much time in these activities drains their energies and diverts their attention from their other natural preferences.

The F male sometimes deals with this dilemma by overreacting with behavior that includes unusually profane language or raunchy jokes. Or he may engage in a variety of sexual seductions—both physical and mental—to prove his manhood to himself and others.

However, in our sexist society the male once again has the edge over the female: if the T female tries to be "superfemale," she is usually called superficial and unreal. When she goes with her objective T side, she can be labeled a bitch. That's a lose-lose proposition. When the Feeling male behaves in a supermacho fashion, it's usually written off under the rationale that "boys will be boys." On the other hand, if the F male gives in to his nurturing side, he may be labeled a "Renaissance man." Either way, he comes out the winner.

Just as the F male's dilemma parallels that of the T woman's, so do the solutions. The first thing an F male must recognize is that "masculinity" is really more than social expectations or preference. It reflects a self-confidence about your gender and your capabilities in a host of actions, from the workplace to the household to the bedroom. What is important is how you and your mate—or prospective mate—behave in the privacy of your own relationship. If it works for both of you, society be damned.

As always, opposites can have a powerful attraction, and that's certainly true between Thinkers and Feelers. As we've said repeatedly, even the best-intentioned T or F can be undermined without a bit of balance from the opposite preference. For example, without the objectivity contributed by

Thinkers, Feelers can get wrapped up in the personalization of life. And Thinkers, lacking Feelers' touch, can become so detached that they can't relate to much of life.

◆

Extraverts and Introverts: As the Words Turn

It is probably both beautiful and beastly that when it comes to Extraverts and sex, what you see is what you get. For better or for worse, it's out there. You can pretty much break things down into the following categories:

* When sex is good, the Extravert tells all.
* When sex is bad, the Extravert tells all.
* When sex is in between, the Extravert tells all.

And so it goes. We're exaggerating, of course, but the point is that anyone who listens can become the Extravert's dumping ground. And they're not above telling veritable strangers in the office elevator about last night's star-spangled encounter.

Of course, all of this makes for one gigantic, anxiety-producing turnoff for Introverts. Not only do they not want their personal "dirty laundry" aired to the world, they don't want to hear others' conquests and disappointments. The anxiety is heightened by the prospect that anything they say or do is fodder for the Extravert's public pronouncements. ("If I tell her I love her, it will be all over the office by noon tomorrow.") For the Introvert there are certain things that are always private. And yet it seems as though the Extravert is always losing track of those boundaries. We've long believed that Introverts in intimate relationships with Extraverts walk around with permanently curled toes, constantly afraid of what intimate moment the Extravert is going to make public.

Extraverts can make or break an intimate moment with constant chatter, a sort of running commentary about the

◆ THE CASTRATION COMPLEX

When an Extraverted female marries an Introverted male, and they run into marital problems, there often surfaces a secondary problem we liken to a castration complex.

Our experience would suggest it is somewhat socially induced. After all, in our society we expect the male to take the lead and the female to take a more subservient, backseat role. When the roles are reversed, some outsiders to the relationship may have a hard time adapting.

An E female and an I male can actually be quite happy in their respective roles until the man's friends bombard him with such comments as "Can you go out bowling this weekend, or do you have to check with the boss? It's obvious she does all the talking for the two of you," or some other reference to the wife "wearing the pants in the family."

It's rarely a driving force of marital strife, but if the couple comes to see us for other problems, often this issue surfaces as well. ("While we're on the subject, another thing that yanks my chain is that you're always talking for me. . . .")

Others have witnessed this phenomenon. Ruth G. Sherman, a friend and colleague based in Hawaii who specializes in type-based marriage counseling, reported in the *Journal of Psychological Type* in 1981, "It is very possible that the very qualities in an Extraverted woman that the Introverted male lacked and which attracted him to her at the onset of their relationship, are the very qualities that create discord during the course of the relationship."

One explanation, says Sherman, is "the myth they may both be relating to: that the man is the one who is at ease with the world, who handles the environment, and the woman supports and follows his lead. When both become aware that this is not the natural order of things in their particular marriage, both may respond with disappointment."

events as they unfold. ("Well, we seem to be having a good time. We've been together for almost two hours now and we haven't run out of things to talk about. I'm really enjoying this and I think you are too. In fact, as we're sitting here finishing this bottle of wine, listening to this great music, I'm thinking about where this evening is going to go. We're having such a good time, it would seem a waste not to go for a nightcap. By the way, have I said how much I'm enjoying being with you?")

At any stage in a relationship Extraverts paint word pictures in an effort to excite. ("When I look at you I hear waltzes and I see us gracefully sweeping across the dance floor.") They make promises, brag, suggest, and describe—all of it done with words. Clean words. Dirty words. Seductive words. Subtle words. Extreme words. Whichever words work. They're not all talk: the words may be backed up with action—from an engaging smile to a tender touch to a sudden embrace. All of these things can continue, from the first date well into marriage. At the very least the sexual encounter with an Extravert will be louder in volume, enthusiasm, and action.

For Extraverts this is not just a one-way street. Not only do they fill the airwaves with talk, they demand responses: "Talk to me. Tell me you love me. Are you having a good time? Am I living up to your expectations?" Of course, not everyone—even other Extraverts—are ready, willing, and able to be that expressive, least of all on a demand basis. Failure to respond—or to respond negatively—can seriously bruise the Extravert and intimidate him or her in future encounters. It's a vicious cycle: the more the Extravert gets in response, the more the Extravert will demand.

Why would anyone be attracted to such a challenging, high-risk relationship? At their best Extraverts' enthusiasm and out-front style can bring life to an intimate relationship. It can be both refreshing and rewarding to have emotions, especially positive ones, expressed so freely. The power of positive speaking can reinforce the good things both parties bring to an intimate encounter.

Relationships for an Introvert happen in a much more private space. While they appreciate affirmations and verbal affections as much as Extraverts, for them such repeated exultations run the risk of becoming superficial and meaningless. For the Introvert to know without speaking has its own strength and beauty. The knowledge of being together yet separate speaks for itself, and words—particularly gratuitous or redundant words—run the risk of undermining the deeply personal nature of the moment and even cause distrust of the Extravert.

While you almost always know what an Extravert is thinking and feeling about a relationship, understanding and interpreting an Introvert can take some effort. For an Introvert, love and intimacy involve a quiet togetherness in which space and privacy are respected, and most important of all, there is the freedom to be oneself. "Go out there and make a fool of yourself or be a star," an Introvert might say. "But leave me and our relationship out of it. I have no need for the world to know what goes on in my personal life."

When it comes to verbalizing intimate expressions, Introverts tend to be as understated as Extraverts are overstated. They certainly can feel just as intensely as Extraverts, but they simply don't believe that everything that's going on inside needs to be shared—or that anyone would even be interested. Simply put, they have a high need to edit their thoughts and feelings before making them public. (Es, as we've said, edit as they speak.)

As a result you can be assured that when an Introvert does speak, there's probably much more going on than the words reveal. A seemingly simple expression of having a good time could reflect a feeling of borderline ecstasy. That, of course, requires a bit of decoding on the part of the Introverts' mates, a process that takes time and patience.

At crucial moments—during intense sexual encounters, for example—the Introvert's understatedness can be irritating and frustrating to the partner who doesn't understand what's really going on. Just imagine the scene: The two of you are in the heat of passion, with the temperature rising by the second. As things reach a crescendo, you, the Extravert, let loose with a loud litany of ecstasy, one rapturous compliment after another about your mate and the moment. (*"You are so wonderful! You make me feel like I've never felt before! I'm in heaven! Don't stop! I love you so much!"*) To which your Introverted partner, several minutes later, finally responds with a whisper: "Me too."

◆ VICARIOUS PLEASURES

Sometimes Introverts are able to break through their extreme privacy needs by the example of others.

Consider Mary Beth and Dean, both Introverted-Judgers, who came to us feeling insecure about their sexual urges. Sex for them was very private and, both being Js, neither was very open to improvisation or modification of their routine. Their sex was quite conservative, usually done in the dark with minimal nudity. They had considered it to be satisfactory until the apartment next door was rented to a highly Extraverted couple. Through the walls Mary Beth and Dean could hear the other couple shouting, exclaiming, chasing, and engaging in a variety of sexual activities.

Over time Mary Beth and Dean got to know this couple socially. Because of their through-the-wall voyeurism they got to know some of the couple's sexual code words. So when they overheard their neighbors say, "Do you want to go home and play catch?" Mary Beth and Dean knew exactly what that meant, and found themselves getting turned on by it.

This caused them a certain amount of anxiety, which got them to wondering, "Are we normal? Is it okay to have these rushes of sexual excitement when we hear this other couple, both in person and through the walls? Is there something wrong with us?"

A little help in understanding their Introversion and Judging, plus some assurance that "normalcy" and "sex" had a rather wide scope, was all these two needed to enjoy the external stimulus. By understanding that Introverts, though somewhat less expressive, can be excited and stimulated by the enthusiasm of others, Mary Beth and Dean were able to allow themselves to be tantalized by their neighbors' verbose activities. That enabled them to translate it joyfully for their own satisfaction.

The obvious danger of this communication difference is that Extraverts assume that Introverts aren't experiencing anything—or at least not the same things—and Introverts tend to discredit what the Extraverts say as superficial. What's vital is for each party to validate the legitimacy of each other's experience: Es aren't necessarily superficial; Is aren't necessarily without feelings.

Not that changing our behavior is a simple thing to do. It's natural that each of us can become insecure about ourselves and how we relate to others. And more often than not, when anything goes awry in the relationship, it surfaces most readily in the subject of sex. So if an Extravert becomes accustomed to saying certain things during sexual intimacy, even if they mean little or nothing to an Introverted partner, it may be hard for the E to keep quiet without wondering if he or she is still "performing" well. And Introverts who suddenly start being verbally effusive in bed may wonder whether such extraneous words cheapen the whole experience.

A good rule of thumb is that for sex to be meaningful to both Extraverts and Introverts, each must negotiate between their own needs and those of their partners. Sometimes it's as simple as declaring, "I need you to say 'I love you' more often," or "Please try to say what you're feeling as it's happening," or even "I want you to call out my name when you get excited." Or, from the Introvert: "I don't want you to tell anyone else about our experiences," or "Just be by my side and promise not to say anything for a few minutes," or "All I want you to do is hold me when it's all over."

Sometimes it's much more complex than this. Still, it's worth trying to find the right words, or lack thereof. Introverts can't expect Extraverts "to just know" something at the right moment without telling them. And Extraverts can't expect Introverts "to just say" something at the right moment unless they're asked. Obviously, the greater the differences, the more difficult all this will be. But through Typewatching, the more you know about each other, the faster you'll move through some of the barriers, and the greater potential for mutual satisfaction.

◆

Judgers and Perceivers: The Art of Scheduled Spontaneity

It's difficult for Perceivers to imagine that Judgers schedule sex, just as they schedule everything else. But it's true. They may not be quite as overt about it, they may not enter it in their Filofaxes, but it's "on the books," at least mentally, and it will be carried out if the J has anything to say about it. In fact, the more predictable the schedule, the more secure and confident the Judger feels and the better the sexual experience will be. The more familiar the Judger becomes with a partner, and the more routine the sexual moves become, the better the performance and the result, at least for the Judger. Not only do the times become quite predictable, but so, too, do the setting, the foreplay, and the ultimate act itself.

That doesn't mean that there isn't room in the schedule for flexibility, innovation, and maybe even a little surprise. But don't look for much. Too much change done too quickly with no warning can be intimidating to a Judger, the ultimate sexual turnoff.

That predictability can be an asset to someone trying to seduce a Judger. Consider the List, the J's ever-present com-

---

◆ **DON'T CALL US, WE'LL CALL YOU**

We know of two Judgers who have a standing rule with their friends and colleagues:
   "Don't interrupt us with phone calls of any nature between nine and ten P.M. on Saturday night. That is our time for sex."

pilation of scheduled things to do. If you tantalize a J with a little peekaboo of something to happen later—a new style, place, time, or position—the J not only will be ready for it, but may be wild with anticipation, having had it on the List for a while. Having it on the List gives time to review it, preview it, and ultimately do it.

It's just this simple: When it comes to sex with a Judger, you'll be most successful if you tell them what you're going to do, then do it, then tell them what you did. It's a marvelous J model that contains a scheduled event, execution of the event, and the opportunity to verify completion, so that the event may be crossed off the List.

There are always exceptions, of course. But be forewarned: Failure to allow for the J's need for structure and routine can be a cause of unending stress, particularly in intimacy, that can lead to frustration, failure, and perhaps even impotence.

If you're a Perceiver, and you've never experienced a Judger in an intimate relationship, you probably didn't believe what we've just described. For a P nothing could be a bigger turnoff than to schedule something so potentially spontaneous and free-flowing as sexual intimacy. How does one even know when "the mood" will hit (let alone *where*)? And therein lies a tremendous dilemma: "The mood hits because you schedule it," says the Judger; "I can't get excited on schedule," responds the Perceiver. "In fact," says the P, as some of the J's predictable foreplay begins, "anxiety and uneasiness set in." As the J puts on a particular song, the tension begins. When the J goes into the bathroom to "freshen up," the anxiety rises. By the time the J has, on schedule, lit the candles, dimmed the lights, and said, "How about a little cuddling?" the P's irritation level is off the charts. And from there, the two embark on an experience that will be one-sided, to say the least.

You can image what happens when a J is moving along, planning each seductive action, only to have it invaded or interrupted by the spontaneous behavior of a P. Or, worse yet, how about when a P gets the intimate urge, and makes an unplanned "hit" on a J, who isn't even thinking about sex, let alone ready to respond. You guessed it: Often the J's first response is to be bombastic and abrupt, a complete turnoff to the P, and putting the kibosh on whatever might have been emerging.

We call that "jangling the J," and though easy to do, it can have serious negative consequences. These include behaviors by the Judger that get interpreted as anger, though often they are simply an expression of frustration at having something unplanned suddenly added to the List. Often, hurt feelings can persist and subsequent sexual encounters can be both more difficult and intimidating. The P, meanwhile, can feel bruised by the experience—after all, he or she was just doing what comes naturally, something that's supposed to be enjoyable. But there's nothing enjoyable, thinks the P, when there are critical words and harsh sentiments that seem to last long after they're expressed.

Here's a better way to be spontaneous with a J. When the urge hits, try suggesting to the J that "it might be nice to snuggle later tonight," or something to that effect. It's most effective to "hit and run"; that is, suggest an idea—perhaps even an outrageous one—to a J, then leave the room immediately. ("Wouldn't it be great to neck in front of the TV like we did in high school?" Or even: "Have you ever thought about covering my body with chocolate syrup?") Or perhaps put on something seductive (or take something off) and dash through the room, allowing the J a glimpse and nothing more. However you drop the hint, get out of the way for several minutes or an hour or more immediately after doing so. That will allow the J to massage the idea, so to speak, turn the fantasy into a plan, and ultimately place it on the List of things to do. From there on the sky's the limit.

It's a win-win: the Perceiver has the opportunity to be spontaneous, and the Judger has the chance to fit this spontaneous act into some sort of schedule.

So far we've focused on when sex takes place—whether it's scheduled or spontaneous—but the same J-P issues come into play during sex itself. Judgers are more likely to be somewhat routine between the sheets, from their foreplay to their positions to who says and does what when. Perceivers, as in everything else, are much more likely to be excited by something new—a variation on a theme, different words, positions, and styles. Of course, either party is capable of both routine and innovation.

All that's needed is some basic understanding. Flexible, spontaneous Ps need to know that some routines can bring stability, security, and predictability, all of which can be freeing and enabling. And structured, routine Js need to know that moving beyond the routine can provide erotic excitement as well as ever-expanding ways to express love and affection in a relationship. It takes a lot of effort by both parties to keep a relationship exciting. A combination of old, reliable moves plus some nifty new ones is often a recipe for long-term physical harmony.

◆

Putting the Matter to Bed

What's important to keep in mind is that sex and intimacy are areas of extreme vulnerability for nearly everyone, whatever their gender or psychological type. That means trying to avoid making light of one another's approach to sexual moments and instead offering support and mutual understanding based on one's knowledge of type.

This doesn't mean that sex should be a serious subject that lacks teasing, laughter, and other light moments. But as with so many matters of an interpersonal nature, timing is critical. Any comment must be taken in the context of the moment and the state of the relationship. So what may seem warm, flirtatious, and seductive between two people at one particular moment can be interpreted as cold, insensitive, and inappropriate in a different time and place.

But there is so much more going on here than a few comments—or even a sexual act. The subject of physical intimacy is wrapped up in a never-ending stream of external issues in the life of a relationship: age, health, hormones, stress, pregnancy, child raising, and the potential for contracting any of a number of sexually transmitted diseases. And then there are the less direct connections: something so simple as missing the bus on the way home from work has the potential to mess up your evening's romantic thoughts or plans. Not to mention the seemingly unlimited issues that place distance between two people.

When it comes to sex, early scripts, role expectations, religious upbringing, and the like can have great impact on its significance as well as the enjoyment (or lack thereof) of the experience. Add personality type to all of this, and you can have fear, anticipation, duty, joy, expressiveness, silence, plus whatever else may be operating between two people. So, an Extraverted-Thinker can assume a touch means "Come and get me," or may respond with flirtatious words, while the Introverted-Feeling mate may wonder, "How did all this happen from just a touch? He or she must be an animal or a nymphomaniac."

It's hard to believe, but even in our sex-oriented, supposedly sophisticated nineties, there are those who are not sexually liberated. The double standards—that males can do things sexually that women should not do—are alive and well, and many people have been sexually abused, especially women. As a result, to take anything for granted about one another's sexual tastes, experiences, and freedoms can lead to all kinds of intimacy troubles. Particularly with sexual issues, things are not always what they seem, and couples must continue to check in with one another.

To illustrate, consider the case of Ellen and Tom, who on their early dates *seemed* quite free with each other, open and flexible. But after some time in the relationship, Ellen began to feel that Tom's flexible and experimental approach to sex was really a "lazy, you-do-all-the-work" attitude. Ellen came to think of Tom as very passive and disinterested in sex. Tom began to experience Ellen's openness about sex as demanding and filled with expectations. For them sex became labored, almost punishing. In our conversations with them one of the things they kept saying was "But you *used* to . . ." They kept holding on to those early, unconfirmed expectations and ideas.

As intimacy grows and interdependency develops, sexual expectations and behavior change and we need to be continually aware of this: where we are and what we need—and where our partners are and what they need. This way we avoid problems that stem from misunderstanding and mixed signals. But in any relationship that endures, problems are sure to arrive, even in the bedroom.

It's important to keep in mind that no one is "less" because of a sexual problem. Sex is not a performance, and the individuals are not performers. Though happiness and satisfaction are desirable, sometimes sexual intimacy is an expression of many other things, and so "ratings"—self-imposed or imposed by others—do not apply. Everyone brings a variety of needs that are expressed through intimacy. The more you know about your own needs and your mate's, the more it is okay to meet your own need and to help your partner meet his or her needs. If some needs are not met every time, it's not failure.

We really need to stop thinking about sex as win-lose, good-bad, and success-failure, and allow for differences in personality type, experimentation, learning, teaching, giving, and sharing by both parties. It's never a one-way street or a one-person issue. To say, "That's your problem," is totally inappropriate, unless you're ready to say, "I'll help you with it," or "I'm part of it."

◆
How Typewatching Can Help

In spite of the seemingly overwhelming odds against them, countless couples do manage to have satisfying sex lives. For a few of those couples things come naturally. For the overwhelming majority it takes a great deal of work.

We believe Typewatching can facilitate the process. Here are some tips on how understanding type can help:

+ **Extraverts: Know when to listen.** Be careful not to talk your way through the sack. The danger of being overly expressive is that it can become redundant, superficial, and meaningless to your partner. Try saying something once and letting it go at that. Allow time for your partner to respond or express his or her own feelings.

+ **Introverts: Say anything.** Don't assume that your silent ecstasy is being correctly communicated to your partner. Your silence could be interpreted as boredom or disinterest, among other things. Most important, recognize that while there may be a symphony going on inside you, unless you offer some direct expression, the music will be for your ears only.

+ **Sensors: Let your imagination go.** If it pleases your mate, it's all right to play different roles—farmer's daughter/traveling salesman, teacher/student, doctor/patient, casual acquaintance, or whatever—as a prelude to an exciting and explosive sexual experience. You don't always need to stay grounded in the moment. Some of these seemingly far-out ideas are neither crazy nor perverse. In fact, they can rejuvenate and enliven that part of some relationships that can become uninspired over time.

+ **iNtuitives: Stay with the moment.** Try to stop imagining a different, if not better, position, place, or person. Though you may find such fantasies exciting and erotic, your sense of presence with your partner may be somewhat dulled.

It may lead to your being unresponsive, or, worse yet, inappropriately responsive, saying the wrong thing at the wrong time.

♦ **Thinkers: Sex involves another person.** This may seem ridiculous to state, but sometimes Thinkers need to be reminded that the individual with whom they are sharing the moment has needs, feelings, and desires. And each of those may require sensitive attention. That means not turning every moment into a learning or self-improvement experience, for example. Your objective analysis of the experience can be read as mechanical and insincere. Instead of stepping back and watching a situation unfold, try to experience the moment without analyzing it.

♦ **Feelers: Sex involves another person.** Not everything is centered around you. Try to avoid personalizing every word and act. Sometimes sex is strictly a physical experience, and great gobs of love aren't always present. There's nothing wrong with that, and it doesn't mean the moment can't be pleasurable for both parties.

♦ **Judgers: Go with the moment.** Every now and then the unplanned happens. That's okay; it might turn out to be fun. Promise yourself right now that when spontaneity strikes, instead of reacting out loud, you'll count to ten. If you're still not ready to accept the situation, count to twenty, thirty, a hundred, or whatever.

♦ **Perceivers: A little routine can be nice.** Appreciate the dependability of knowing what will happen next. Within that context there's still room for flexibility and improvisation. Instead of fighting the plan or schedule try deciding spontaneously to accept it, and always remember there's plenty of room for modification.

You may have noticed that in the above eight tips, we've basically asked you to stretch a bit to get in touch with your nonpreferences. So, Extraverts may need to do some Introverting, Sensors may need to be more iNtuitive, and so on.

There are two reasons for this. One is that we bring our

preferences to the sexual act, just as we bring them to everything else. That brings us strength and confidence, but it also can make us complacent and lazy. By stretching a bit we can become more complete lovers.

Second, the sexual act also involves a certain amount of mystery, some of which also involves our nonpreferences. For Extraverts, for example, the mystery is in the contemplative, reflective side of the Introvert. For the Feeler the mystery is in the power of the analytical objectivity of the Thinker. Therefore, the more we can be in touch with this "mystery," the better able we'll be to satisfy our partners, whose differences were likely part of our initial attraction.

Believe it or not, sex isn't everything. Though some couples may find it hard to believe, other issues—namely, communication, finance, and conflict resolution—can be just as satisfying or destructive to a relationship. In fact, our experience has taught us that relationship troubles often begin with these other areas and manifest themselves between the sheets. So sexual problems aren't always a physical phenomenon. They may not even be the real problem. In the frustration of the moment that simple fact often becomes obscured.

Just as the lack of sexual meaning can reflect other problems, good sex is often the culmination of hard work, sensitive awareness of each other, and a keen desire to keep growing.

When it all comes together, it's like nothing else on earth.

◆ INTERCOURSE DISCOURSE

ESFP: Intercourse is the ultimate sensual expression of my love.
INTJ: Intercourse is the logical culmination of a stimulating encounter. And by the way, what do you mean by "love"?

EXERCISE

1

A Trust Walk

Here's a good way to help couples appreciate what's involved in letting go of themselves, depending on one another, and learning to trust their lover's intentions.

First, one person blindfolds the other. For the next ten minutes the blindfolded person will be totally in the care of the other. Neither is allowed to speak while the blindfold is on. The person who can see puts his or her partner through a variety of experiences: walking, touching, smelling, listening, eating, and exploring everything imaginable. After about ten minutes they reverse roles.

In the process, both can learn to experience the difficulty in trying to communicate when only one can see and neither can talk. They will also experience the awesome responsibility of their partner's being totally dependent on them for every move. Their safety, ability to move, and experiences are all dependent upon someone else.

Often the one who can see can become traumatized by the overwhelming responsibility, while the blindfolded one can discover how difficult it can be to depend so totally on another.

EXERCISE

2

Face-to-Face

In this exercise a couple faces one another, standing about six feet apart. When you are ready, approach your partner at whatever pace feels comfortable. Without talking, get as close to your partner as you'd like, then do whatever feels appropriate, all without speaking. Your partner is free to react however he or she would like. When the spirit moves you, back up to your original distance and stop the exercise.

Then, discuss the following questions:

* How did each of you feel?
* Would it have been easier if you could have spoken?
* Did you learn any new way to express your attraction to one another?
* What was the most awkward part of the exercise?
* How, if at all, was your partner encouraging or supportive to you?

The discussion that follows ought to highlight how little time most of us spend in experiencing the sensual, visual, tactile, and emotional parts of our mate. The closer we get to one another, the more we tend to turn out the lights, close our eyes, and talk feverishly. This exercise helps us learn how to experience our partners in new ways.

EXERCISE

_____ 3 _____

Head Trips

If you or your lover has difficulty giving up control to the other, you might consider trying this exercise.

Have your lover lie on the floor, facing the ceiling. Kneel down and gently lift his or her head in your hands. Then slowly move your lover's head in a variety of directions. After a few moments of doing this, gently lower the head to the floor. Then reverse roles and repeat.

When you are finished, observe and discuss the following:

* When you started to lift your partner's head, did your partner allow you to do it, or did he or she resist?
* Were you able to lead, freely moving your partner's head?
* How did each of you feel about controlling the other—and being controlled?

By doing this you can learn how difficult it can be to cede control of yourself to another person. Your neck, head, and spinal column, like each of our sexual organs, are sensitive to touch, and each of us is sensitive to the danger that can result from rough or careless treatment. Generally, the person holding your head feels a heavy sense of responsibility, and often can feel hurt if you won't relax and let him or her take over.

This exercise also can delve into the subject of power and leadership in the relationship—who's really in charge. For example, if one of you finds yourself unable to give up control of your head movements or unwilling to take control, it might speak volumes about how you approach each other in the relationship in general, and especially in sexual matters.

SEX AND INTIMACY TYPE TALK

IF YOU ARE . . .

AND YOUR LOVER IS . . .	EXTRAVERT	INTROVERT
EXTRAVERT	• Allow some time to listen to each other.	• Promise yourself to be more expressive about what's going on, what you think about it, and how it makes you feel.
	• Talk about the moment. Paint word pictures. But be careful not to compete with each other.	• Talk more than you personally feel is necessary. Say anything.
	• Make it loud and lovely, with a variety of expressions.	• Try to do more than just whisper. Force some loudness in expressing yourself.
	EXTRAVERT	**INTROVERT**
INTROVERT	• Allow time and space for your mate to reflect on the experience.	• Share some of what you are thinking.
	• Listen and affirm, rather than preparing a response while mate is talking.	• Remember you both need to push yourselves to disclose your experience.
	• Solicit and contract in advance for verbal feedback.	• Enjoy to the maximum the quiet, reflective closeness.
	SENSOR	**INTUITIVE**
SENSOR	• Forget all else and revel in the moment.	• Create pictures of your intentions, then act upon them.
	• Experience all the sights, sounds, smells, tastes, and touches available.	• Overload your space with sounds, smells, and other sensory experiences.
	• Don't worry about enjoying the moment too much.	• Be specific, tactile, and immediate.
	SENSOR	**INTUITIVE**
INTUITIVE	• Allow time to share previous experiences.	• Tease your fantasies, and have all needed props available.
	• Show and tell your partner what you want.	• Share your wildest fantasies, then act them out.
	• Do to your partner what you want done to you.	• Share your dreams and visions of the ultimate experience.

IF YOU ARE . . .

	THINKER	FEELER
THINKER	• The way to all good sex is through the mind. Think about it.	• Don't overpersonalize. Challenge your partner to discuss sexual ideas.
	• Share the concept of intimacy and discuss it.	• Plant thoughts of sex for later on.
	• Bait with an idea, hook with a mental image, and reel in with a challenge.	• Think and analyze so you can both learn from the experience.
	THINKER	**FEELER**
FEELER	• Don't be afraid to sound a little syrupy or sentimental. It won't kill you and your lover will appreciate it.	• Lose yourself for your partner. It makes you a happy, fulfilled martyr.
	• Afterward, be positive, affirming, and tenderhearted. Try not to be analytical.	• Help each other be positive and affirming, with many happy strokes.
	• Experience the moment without trying to improve it.	• Keep in mind that a little guilt plus a little absolution equals perfect togetherness.
	JUDGER	**PERCEIVER**
JUDGER	• It's on the List. Now is the time to do it.	• Recognize that a surprise, though exciting, can be more stressful than sexy.
	• Follow your tried-and-true routines. They bring security and freedom.	• Hit and run: Drop a few hints, get out of the way, and try to bring it up later.
	• Have your plans and share them. Decide who will be spontaneous each time.	• Remember, change and spontaneity for your partner happen slowly over time.
	JUDGER	**PERCEIVER**
PERCEIVER	• The more you know your limits, the more you will be free to experiment.	• Whenever, however, go with the flow. Enjoy—just let it happen.
	• Plan to stretch a bit. Now and then, "plan" to do something unplanned.	• Process the experience and seduce each other with erotic alternatives.
	• Announce your plans and intentions. Talk about what's negotiable and what isn't.	• Intimacy has no beginnings or endings. It happens when and where it happens.

AND YOUR LOVER IS . . .

7

FINANCE

*"Not to worry. It will all
come back to me eventually."*

Someone once said, "Money is not the most important thing in the world, but it sure is ahead of whatever is in second place." Woody Allen put it this way: "I'd rather be rich than poor, if only for financial reasons." However you view financial matters, you can't deny how dramatically they can affect any relationship, particularly an intimate one. Simply put, when money becomes a factor, relationships can be totally redefined, and usually not for the better.

Give a group of people—managers at work, a scout troop, an office pool—a seemingly innocuous exercise, then throw in a financial incentive, and you'll see behaviors change radically. All of a sudden complacent and even bored participants come alive. In general nearly everyone's behavior is transformed from docile and discontented to cunning and cutthroat. What was merely an exercise with a modicum of competition now becomes a do-or-die, winner-take-all battle. Folks who would never ordinarily think of cheating suddenly find themselves bending, or even breaking, rules and violating their own integrity.

All in the name of the almighty dollar.

The same things happen when money and relationships become intertwined. We know of couples who are getting along moderately well, coping with life in constructive and effective ways, whose lives are suddenly rent asunder with the introduction of some dramatic financial change—inheritance, job promotions, prize money, investment losses, or unemployment. Suddenly, these otherwise contented couples lose all sense of civility and yield to a host of ugly behaviors: distrust of just about everyone, jealousy of others' good fortune, and everything from selfishness to cynicism to suicidal tendencies.

Beyond the mystique of money itself there are many factors that influence how individuals cope with financial issues. Certainly it is our conviction that personality preferences play a very important role in how one addresses money matters. This is not to deny parental influence and that of the period in which one grew up (depression, war, affluence, and so on). Whether or not one "comes from" money, recently "came into" money, or never had any money, it can influence one's behavior almost as much as personality. Still, personality differences are the starting point for resolving nearly any conflict involving finances.

◆

Judgers and Perceivers: Saving for Later versus Enjoying It Now

Since so much of the concern of money involves goals and other measurable dynamics, the Judging-Perceiving difference may be the most important determinant of how two people relate to one another in matters of finance.

Consider what happens during our couples' retreats, when we ask groups of Judgers and groups of Perceivers to list their responses to the simple query "What to do with money?" The lists, made on large sheets of newsprint, are later posted for the entire group to view and discuss.

We can tell you with stunning precision how each group will approach the task and how the final list will read.

The Judgers' list is always organized and neat, and their responses are usually numbered or bulleted. Their list always reflects a conservative approach to money based on the premise that having money is the direct result of hard work and responsible living. Invariably the first thing on the Judgers' list about what to do with money is: SAVE IT. The rest of the list will include some version of the following:

* Invest it wisely
* Budget it
* Give it away appropriately
* Diversify investments
* Pay for kids' education
* Prioritize how it's spent
* Allocate it toward retirement
* Control its flow

The first thing on the Perceivers' list is almost always SPEND IT. The rest of the list frequently isn't a list at all but an apparent stream-of-consciousness outpouring that may be

---

* **RECORD PROFITS?**

Even though we all speak the same language, we often mean—and hear—different things. This is best illustrated by the story of a group of Judgers in one of our seminars. We had asked them to list on a large sheet of paper this response to "What to do with money." In their typical J fashion they got the job done with dispatch. Included on the list was "Buy CDs."

Problem was, in their haste to get the job done, they hadn't agreed on what "Buy CDs" really meant. It turned out that half the group thought it meant purchasing certificates of deposit. The other half assumed it had to do with buying music on compact discs.

written anywhere on the sheet, by anyone in the group, in any of a variety of colors and styles. (Just looking at the sheet drives the Js crazy, as they identify this as typical of how Ps maintain their finances. One might even be driven to look at the tangled array of words and numbers and comment, "That looks just like my mate's checkbook!") Among the things Ps suggest doing with money invariably will be:

- Do something fun with it
- Enjoy it while you have it
- Give some to someone who needs it
- Take a spontaneous trip
- Start a long-delayed project
- Fulfill an unfulfilled dream
- Buy presents for the kids
- Take my friends on a cruise

The answers have wavered little in the many times we have conducted this exercise. For example, in one group Js and Ps proved to be polar opposites. The Js, as expected, began their list with "Save it," and after prioritizing eight or ten items, ended with "Spend it." The Ps, working independently, began their list with "Spend it." At the bottom of their sheet of rather playful and random suggestions, they ended their list with "Save it." When the two lists were posted for all to see, this demonstration of exact opposites awed the group. They sat in stunned silence for a few minutes before breaking out in laughter—followed by a very insightful discussion about how so many couples had found themselves mated with individuals so different from themselves.

Clearly, this is a case of ships passing in the night. Js and Ps view money so dramatically differently, it's no wonder that this is the source of both attraction and stress. The Js see the Ps as people who may help them loosen their grip on their finances—and the grip their finances have on them. The Ps' spontaneous and flexible flair could offer Js a much-needed perspective on a part of their value system they may have lost in their overpowering need to have their finances under control at all times.

Perceivers may see Judgers as the answer to their financial prayers, bringing some order to their cash-flow chaos. The Js' finely tuned sense of organization and control is a welcome relief for those who simply can't seem to get a handle on their finances. It isn't that Ps don't have money or can't be effective with it, it's simply that they don't even want to think about it. And this affects all the basics, such as timely bill payments, monthly deposits into savings, checkbook balancing, and general recordkeeping. These things don't come naturally to Ps and usually take a backseat to almost anything else.

Logic might dictate that the organized, structured Judgers would be the ones best suited to managing money. After all, they pay bills on time, set budgets and stick to them, and generally have a good grasp of where their money comes from and where it is going. But don't be fooled: Both Js and Ps can be equally capable of managing—or mangling—their finances. Judgers, for all their organization, can be so locked into a financial course of action that they can miss opportunities or may be afraid to take some risks that over time could yield handsome rewards. And Perceivers, for all their apparent disorganization, can be adept at reacting to changing market conditions, possibly transforming a risky situation into tremendous financial success.

A case in point: We once worked with a brokerage firm in a major southern city in which all of the employees had an awareness of their personality types. We found that the Judgers were far more conservative with their customers' portfolios. But that wasn't good enough. The Thinking-Judgers, and especially the Sensing-Thinking-Judgers, were frustrating both customers and the company president because while earning a steady return, it was hardly enough to validate their salaries, let alone keep the customer satisfied.

In contrast the Perceivers, in particular the Extraverted-

Perceivers, seemed to take a more roller-coaster approach to their customers. They would paint such an exciting picture of a particular investment to both customers and company executives that everyone would become excited about its potential, overlooking a potentially high risk in the process. That approach was reflected in their track records: the Perceivers tended to win big or lose big, with very little in between. Obviously this was stressful to both customers and the company. Such brinkmanship is the bane of the Ps' financial life.

In our society, where people tend to be pretty conservative about what they do with their money, the Js' approach gives them an edge in the financial world, whereas Ps can be pushed aside and even scorned for their seeming reckless approach. That's not necessarily a good thing. Ideally, we need both types. Risk needs to be balanced by sound financial practice. Conservative thinking needs to be stretched beyond its boundaries so that growth takes place. It's true in finances, and it's true in the rest of life.

The financial dynamics that take place in the professional world are no less true for lovers. Judgers and Perceivers need each other to achieve balance around financial issues. It takes genuine listening to each other's point of view. And both sides have their strengths:

• **If you're a Judger,** generally speaking, you view money as something that provides security. It is a means by which you verify success and track your progress on a number of fronts. As with so many other aspects of life, you approach financial matters as a series of goals to be met. Once you know the limits of your financial situation, you are able to determine where there is some flexibility and where there is none. That knowledge frees you up to spend money as appropriate, up to and including a bit of self-indulgence.

• **If you're a Perceiver,** generally speaking, you view money as one of several tools available to help you live life to the fullest. You tend to make the most of it every day, without being confined by budgets. You find budgets useful, but only as guidelines. When you have money available, your tendency is to spend what you need to meet pressing concerns. If anything is left over, it's there for your pleasure, whether to be spent on indulgences or saved for a rainy day. If nothing is left over, or there's a shortfall, that's too bad. But not to worry: there will always be a new day and a new paycheck, bringing with it more possibilities and options.

♦ TO BUY OR NOT TO BUY?

Nowhere can Judging-Perceiving differences become more acute than when it comes to making a purchase. We run into this all the time in our own shopping. Janet, the P, wants to spend days, even months, collecting data, watching sales trends, and will put off a purchase forever if there's even a slight chance that the price could drop or the model could be improved upon. In fact, she can go into a store with a relatively clear idea of what she wants to buy, but when she sees all the different displays, it opens up so many options that she finds herself incapable of completing a transaction. In true P style she is more readily able to determine and rule out what she does *not* want than determine exactly what she *does* want. However, that still leaves an overwhelming selection from which to choose.

In contrast, there's Otto, the J. He almost always seems to know what he wants and recognizes that if ten different stores have the same item, their prices will be relatively the same and not worth driving from store to store to save a few bucks. Unfortunately, he has on occasion leapt too quickly, getting stuck with a purchase that didn't really fit his needs.

Fortunately, we've become pretty good at turning our differences into advantages. Janet does what she loves and does well: collecting all kinds of data and narrowing the decision to two or three top contenders. Then she calls Otto and says, "Here's what I learned. You decide. I can live with whichever one of these you pick."

◆

Extraverts and Introverts: Money Talks versus Talk Is Cheap

Imagine the stress of a couple we'll call Bert and Millie. Bert, an Extravert, can't help but offer a play-by-play commentary on their financial issues and transactions. He loves to brag about how much things cost—how he variously spent a fortune or saved a fortune—and the impact that has on his family's bank balances and investment portfolio. He even shares openly how much all of this stresses Millie, his Introverted mate, who ranks finances second only to sexual intimacy as something never to be discussed publicly. Laughingly, he says, "My even telling you this is probably going to get me in a heap of trouble. I can never understand why she seems so uptight about something so impersonal as money. Hey, if you got it, share and spend it. If you haven't, don't worry about it."

Meanwhile, Millie indeed cringes at Bert's behavior. In a series of sweeping comments, Bert is capable of divulging deeply personal matters about their finances, their private conversations, and their personal differences. This is embarrassing, to say the least, and probably unforgivable.

As you can see, Extraverts can be open books when it comes to finances. Often, the flamboyancy they bring to other parts of their lives is present here, which can lead to what others may consider inappropriate disclosures or braggadocios. Beyond that, they can stretch the truth somewhat, rounding up or down how much they made, spent, or saved. (Adding additional preferences—especially iNtuition and Perceiving—only intensifies the situation, heightening Es' creative potential and further lowering their credibility.) All of this can amaze or even embarrass others, especially Introverts.

For Introverts, financial matters—like most of life—are very personal and private concerns. Therefore, Introverts play their financial cards close to the vest, preferring to be very discreet about what they share with others. For them the amount of a pay raise, the price of a newly purchased car, the cost of their recent vacation, is nobody else's business. ("Let's just say that I got a good deal.") Even dealing with financial professionals can be stressful. Revealing basic salary information to a loan officer, for example, may be viewed as an invasion of privacy ("Do you *really* need to know these things?"), enough so, in some cases, to keep a strong Introvert from ever applying for a needed loan.

As usual, these differences can seem attractive at first. Introverts can be enthralled by the glorious tales laid out by Extraverts, impressed by their seeming generosity and the apparent ease with which they maneuver through the maze of money matters. Even if they are slightly turned off by the disclosures, and believe them to be a bit exaggerated, they may inwardly recognize that the disclosures hold at least a kernel of truth, making the Extravert credible at some level. Extraverts may view Introverts' withholding information as an appealing aloofness, a kind of mysterious quality and strength.

In either case there is a high likelihood that these attractions will wear thin rather quickly, becoming sources of stress, conflict, and, potentially, lasting bitterness.

That needn't happen. By increased awareness of each person's needs, a couple can allow space for their personality differences. For example, Extraverts can ask Introverts beforehand which, if any, aspects of their sensitive financial matters can be discussed with close friends. And Introverts can ask for time to think through privately their concerns about financial issues, then discuss them with greater insight with their Extraverted mates.

◆

Sensors and iNtuitives: Dollars versus Sense

There's a cute *Peanuts* strip that we think illustrates wonderfully the difference in how Sensors and iNtuitives face money issues. Lucy, a Sensor, is lamenting to Charlie Brown that "you get out of life exactly what you put into it—nothing more and nothing less." Snoopy, the iNtuitive canine, who happens to be listening, walks away, reflecting, "Somehow, I'd like a little more margin for error."

From checkbooks to investment portfolios, Sensors deal with money matters with sometimes excruciating exactness, very much in the present, and very specifically. In contrast, iNtuitives see money like the rest of life: as a general concept full of possibilities, all of which can accommodate a little "margin for error" in their execution.

Of course, both approaches are correct—and both, when done to an extreme, can open the door for all sorts of name-calling and other antagonistic behavior. Once again, something that initially seemed attractive can become a bone of contention without the insights that Typewatching affords.

For example, the iNtuitive may be drawn to the Sensor's natural affinity to the specific, exact, and immediate approach to money. For the Sensor, money is very tangible, something that you can (and should) measure with precision, a tool with which we do day-to-day business. When you have it, you have only the exact amount. It's in hand, and you can do as much as that amount allows. While you have it, live for today. And when you don't have it, go get some more before you make any additional plans. Live one day at a time. Money for Sensors is much like life for Lucy: you get out of it what you put into it—not a penny more and not a penny less.

This approach clearly can have advantages. Among other things it is less likely to get you financially in over your head. Sensors generally have a realistic view of their assets and liabilities at any given moment, a clear plus. Taken to an extreme, however, the Sensors' approach of constantly counting their pennies doesn't always make good sense. Sometimes Sensors miss investment opportunities because they are unable to see the long-term benefits.

On the flip side Sensors are often drawn to iNtuitives' rather exciting approach to money. For Ns, money is one more resource for adding fullness to life. It is a fluid dynamic, expanding and contracting on a regular basis, requiring a go-with-the-cash-flow attitude. For iNtuitives, the exact amount of money on hand at a given moment isn't as important as what possibilities that amount of money might afford, what opportunities it can leverage, and what doors it might open, recognizing that the only limits are self-imposed by one's lack of imagination. They can be drawn to investments with large potential returns, without sufficient regard for the risk. One reason may be that they are far less inclined to wade through the details and disclosures of an investment prospectus.

Like Extraverts, iNtuitives are masters at rounding off—either up or down—everything from purchase prices to checking-account balances. Some are known to round down in their checking-account registers any amount under $.50, and round up any amount over $.51. So, a check written for $19.45 would be entered as $19.00. "It all works out in the end," they likely say. A Sensor may greet the arrival of the monthly checking-account statement as an opportunity to balance it to the penny—no matter how long it may take. Meanwhile, an iNtuitive is far more likely to spend the time pondering the balance it shows, regardless of whether it is correct, redesigning the bank statement itself to improve upon its readability, or considering whether to open another somewhere else, thus alleviating the need to balance the statement with their check register. If the iNtuitive does spend the time it takes to actually balance the statement, it may be more for the intellectual exercise to prove it can be done than to conform to a monthly discipline. (We once knew an iNtuitive who looked at the bank statement and his checkbook, and if *anywhere* on the statement there was an item that also appeared in his check register, he considered the statement to be reconciled. Another iNtuitive would take his statement and canceled checks each month into the bank and say something to the effect of "You're in the money business, you do it.")

This is not to say that iNtuitives are incapable of financial success. Indeed, they are often in positions of significant financial positions in their jobs, from corporate comptrollers to branch managers of major banks. There's a case to be made that when it comes to money, iNtuitives' big-picture approach allows them a better perspective from which to view any financial situation, whether their own or someone else's. Our data show that financial planners and economic forecasters are among the professionals that tend to be more iNtuitive than Sensing.

Obviously, an approach to finances that rarely zeroes in on specifics can have its limits. While knowing the big picture and the ability to go with the flow can be assets, in the end the money realm is a very specific one, with high accountability. And in no time the initial excitement the Sensor has toward the iNtuitive's approach can turn to seeing the iNtuitive as being anything from cavalier to downright dishonest. What is initially seen as imaginative and bold can over time become very stressful to the Sensor because it seems to lack a solid foundation and builds upon such intangibles as instinct, gut reactions, and hunches.

Through the heightened awareness of Typewatching, Sensors and iNtuitives can work more easily at being clear in what they mean about financial matters. For example, a Sensor might ask, "Have you checked the specific details, or is this still in the idea stage?" That will help the S gain some insight on the N's latest hunch or idea. By recognizing that it may still be just a vague idea, the Sensor may help the iNtuitive sort through the issues involved to determine whether the idea has merit.

Typewatching can also help each party check the other's track record on finances. If the iNtuitive has done well by speculating, then the Sensor should probably be supportive, letting the N take the lead, but providing facts and details where needed. If the Sensor seems to be a financial success, then the iNtuitive needs to recognize that, then stand back, offering perspective where needed, but trusting the Sensor's instincts.

In each of these cases Typewatching can help both Sensors and iNtuitives appreciate one another and view their differences as a gift that covers both dimensions of any financial situation—the possibilities and the reality.

◆

Thinkers and Feelers: Power versus Glory

Power and control versus empowerment and service are key sources of stress between Ts and Fs in money matters. As with everything else, Thinkers approach money in a highly objective and impersonal way. Money is something to be used to gain or give power and measure success. Among the "things" that can be "bought" are people and relationships. It was no doubt a T who first promulgated the theory that everyone has his price. This doesn't take place merely in the world of corruption and greed. "Buying" relationships can take the form of such things as picking up the tab at lunch in order to impress someone or maybe have them "owe you one," or inundating a potential object of one's affection with a never-ending and calculated stream of gifts in order to win them over. Of course, the more money he or she has, the greater the ability of a Thinker to exercise power and control over others.

The apparent ease with which Thinkers approach financial matters is what Feelers can find attractive. For Feelers, money truly is the root of all evil: It induces guilt, fosters greed and exploitation, and engenders many of society's ills. They view Thinkers as being able to easily divorce their emotions from their pocketbooks. They are drawn to Thinkers with the hopes that the T might rescue them from their own financial frustrations and fears. Thinkers, believe Feelers, will be able to make life's tough choices—say, whether to go out to a nice dinner, save for the kids' education, or make an extra donation this year to the local animal shelter.

It's not that Feelers aren't capable of handling money. They can, and they do. For Feelers, money at its best is a servant to humanity. It can provide resources for those in need; foster growth and development, whether for individuals or entire nations; provide the means and incentives for people to move beyond their own limitations; or help improve a person's station in life, whether in his or her own life, that of a friend or loved one, or even the life of a veritable stranger. However, in every one of these cases money is always secondary to human need. So, whatever the purpose or cause, money must always help people, not exploit them.

Generally speaking, when Feelers get their hands on discretionary income, they are more likely than Thinkers to spend it—usually for some "good cause"—rather than save it for a rainy day. This is particularly true of iNtuitive-Feelers: as the consummate idealists, they look on money as the key to fulfilling their many dreams and ideals. So whatever the cause, any extra money—and even funds that could place the NF in a financial quandary—are best used when given to serve that cause. (For most Thinkers, *extra money* is an oxymoron.) Any concerns about the impact of their generosity on their own financial condition may be rationalized with a simple "Not to worry. It will all come back to me eventually." The wealthier the F, the more committed he or she may be to sharing that wealth with various causes.

Feelers and Thinkers share differing views on the meaning of work. It is difficult for a Thinker to imagine that anyone would work at a job for any reason other than to make money. And yet Feelers often have nonfinancial commitments to their jobs. They variously admire the organizational mission, enjoy being around the people who work there, respect the boss and the company culture. Partly as a result, across the job spectrum it is Feelers who are attracted to service-oriented jobs, usually the lower-paying ones: social workers, teachers, nurses, and clergy.

Thinkers, despite their relatively hardheaded approach to money, appreciate Feelers' idealism and good deeds. For them Fs are the embodiment of the solution to the myriad of causes and concerns that undergird late-twentieth-century society. And while Thinkers are less likely to become personally involved in such matters, they generally admire and respect the tugging on their heartstrings—and, usually, their purse strings—brought about by the endeavors of Feelers. In the process, Thinkers manage to rationalize their own philanthropy, once it is objectively determined that the charity in question is truly a "worthy cause." But only to a point: Thinkers, far more than Feelers, are in touch with the limits of time and money that they can afford to earmark for such causes. (If only we had a quarter for every T businessman who's stated to us how proud he is of the volunteer work in which his wife engages—as long as she's home in time to cook dinner.)

Differences between men and women on money loom large. Our society has traditionally had very definite expectations on how each sex should fit into the financial world: men, who are primarily Thinking types, are to fit in the role of the money manager; women, primarily Feelers, are to be the guardians of home and hearth, managing finances within a budgeted amount (often determined by the male).

Things have become far more complex in recent decades

as society has increasingly broken that mold. Both men and women who have gone against that traditional grain can find themselves struggling under the burden of additional stress. So, a Thinking female may intimidate the males around her in the objective way she deals with financial matters. And a Feeling male may face his own and others' criticisms for lack of a hard-line approach to money.

Consider the tale of Emily, a Thinker, and Paul, a Feeler, both twentysomething professionals of modest means who had been dating for about a year. Over the months they had grown to enjoy each other's company immensely, and never lacked for things to do and subjects to discuss. Among other things they loved to go out to dinner, and prided themselves on the number and variety of restaurants they had visited together. But trouble always seemed to be served up whenever it came time to pay the bill. First of all, the waiter or waitress almost always automatically gave the bill to Paul, which never failed to rile Emily, who prided herself on her independence and her equality in all relationships, financial and otherwise. Emily believed strongly that the traditional roles were outdated and very much wanted to demonstrate that she could hold up her end of the bargain. And so she always made a sweeping gesture of repositioning the restaurant check squarely between them, then, with equal flair, would proffer her half of the bill, pulling out cash or credit card as appropriate.

Paul understood and sympathized with her frustration, but Emily's actions never failed to undermine his masculinity. After all, he had been taught that men were supposed to pay the bills. And though he could appreciate the changing social scene—and genuinely welcomed Emily's financial contribution—he was intimidated and angered by her public display. "Why do you have to be so dramatic?" he would ask. "Can't you just hand me the money under the table or pay me back afterward?" Of course, both options were out of the question for Emily. Ever the realist, she would point out to Paul that because neither of them earned more than the other, it made sense that they should share the financial burdens of the relationship. Besides, she'd inevitably ask, "Why are you taking this so personally? It's only money."

Emily and Paul's dilemma goes well beyond the walls of restaurants, and can be found wherever men and women play nontraditional financial roles: T women executives who make tough budgetary decisions, F husbands who defer to their mates on investment choices, and so on. Whatever the situation, it is one ripe for frustration, conflict, and possibly the failure of the relationship.

This need not be the case. It would be far more constructive for those involved in such financial gender benders to put their money on the table, so to speak, owning up to their skills and interests, or the lack of them, in handling money. So, if one person loves the challenge of moving money around, and the other has less interest in these matters, it would make sense that these responsibilities be handed over to the former person, regardless of gender. If this decision is made together, it will be done in the spirit of collaboration, even if only one person is actually doing the work.

Of course, things will work somewhat differently if it turns out that both individuals—or neither—wants the responsibility. If both want it, feel equally capable, and can't otherwise seem to divvy up or alternate the chores, it might take a disinterested third party to help negotiate a way to take advantage of the best of each of their skills. If neither feels capable or wants to be burdened with these responsibilities, it might be worth considering finding an outside source of help—a bookkeeper, accountant, banker, broker, lawyer, financial planner, or some other appropriate professional.

•
Same Strokes for Different Folks

So far we've assumed that relationship money problems stem from type differences—that is, two people having more differences than similarities. But what happens when two people are largely the same type, or at least share key preferences and characteristics? There's little question that similarities can be just as problematic as differences.

Consider Noel and Sandy, both iNtuitive-Thinking-Perceivers, and both successful entrepreneurs. While they managed to amass a modest portfolio of real estate, stocks, and other investments, they accomplished this much in the same way as they do everything else: by gut instinct, with minimal expert help, figuring things out as they went along. Recognizing that they knew just enough about personal finance to be dangerous, and knowing that their investments had been made in a rather haphazard fashion, they agreed that they needed to seek help from a professional financial planner. Someone recommended a name to Noel, and three months later he got around to making the call. Finally they met with and retained the services of the financial planner, who analyzed their situation and made detailed and specific recommendations on investments they should buy and sell.

So far so good. Unfortunately it took these two busy Perceivers another three months simply to make the three phone calls and write the six letters required to carry out the planner's instructions. And in the process each blamed the other for not being on top of the situation. It wasn't that they intended to neglect business—in fact, it weighed heavily on their consciences that they were being negligent—but as Ps there was always some exciting event or other pressing business that required their attention. "In the end," said Noel, "we probably should have simply paid the planner a little extra to take care of it for us."

◆ THE CASE OF THE HAND-ME-DOWN GOWN

When it comes to financial matters, you never know what other aspects of a couple's value system will come into play. As we've said earlier, such things as tradition, religious upbringing, and personal tastes can play a role, sometimes in combination.

There's probably no better illustration of this than the story of Tracy. On her wedding day she and her husband faced their first major disagreement.

"I am an ENTP and he is an ISFJ, but of course we did not know that then," she says. "Money being tight, I purchased a wedding dress with a friend who was getting married a month earlier. We shared the cost. She wore the dress first and passed it on to me. My husband-to-be was unaware of our deal; I didn't even think it necessary to tell him about it.

"So, at our wedding reception, when another friend approached me about the possibility of buying the dress for her upcoming wedding, I thought *Great. My friend and I can recoup some of the original cost.* She made me an offer I couldn't refuse. Right then and there we made a deal, and I agreed to hand it over as soon as I changed into my travel clothes that afternoon.

"I changed and went to give her the dress," she went on. "And my new husband asked, 'Where are you going with that dress?' Upon hearing I had sold it, he stood and stared at me in total shock. 'What about our daughters? I assumed they would get married in that dress.' My reaction was that *if* we had daughters, twenty years from now the dress would be out of style. But the money would be useful today." Tracy went ahead with the sale.

In contrast there's the story of Ken and Christine, two Sensing-Judgers, who were trying to figure out what to do with the profits from the sale of their house. Because of Ken's work, which required him to travel a lot, they had decided not to buy another house right away, but to rent instead. By law they had two years to buy another house before the profit from their sale would be taxed by the government. As soon as they received their check, at the advice of a friend they immediately placed the money in one-year certificates of deposit, thereby locking their money up for at least twelve months.

Unlike Noel and Sandy, who missed opportunities because they procrastinated, Ken and Christine missed opportunities because they acted too quickly, coming to closure before it was necessary to do so. Not that they should have waited until the last possible moment to make their move. But taking the time to sort out their options might have resulted in a better bang for their bucks. Moreover, it might also have avoided the frustration—and the inevitable mutual finger-pointing—resulting from the realization that they could have done better with their money.

◆

Building a Financial "Team"

Building a financial relationship—whether with a friend, lover, or spouse—is much like creating any successful team: It requires appreciating each individual's contributions and compensating for their shortcomings.

How do you do this? Here are three steps to help maximize opportunities and minimize potential problems:

1. Understand who you are. As you look at the preferences of the individual involved, determine the strengths and weaknesses. What preferences are overrepresented, and what's missing? For example, if both people are iNtuitives, there's a high risk that details can be overlooked—incomplete paperwork, checkbooks unbalanced, bottom lines unexamined. Two Introverts may fail to communicate essentials—with each other as well as with outside professionals—regarding their own needs or changing conditions. So the first step is to inventory the preferences involved in the relationship.

2. Cover the bases. Having taken inventory, you'll be in a position to determine your potential weak spots and gain some insight into where you may get blindsided. For example, knowing that neither of you is an Extravert, you may want to devise a plan to ensure that financial matters are discussed with regularity and openness. You might want to have a regularly scheduled coffee klatch in which you and your partner discuss nothing but finances. You might want to schedule quarterly or semiannual meetings with financial professionals. On the other hand, if neither of you is an Introvert, it's important to ensure that financial discussions aren't just all talk—that listening takes place and is turned into action. That might be done by active note-taking during discussions, as well as ending a conversation with a commitment for one person or the other to follow through and report back.

3. Take stock of your success. Having taken your inventory and attempted to compensate for blind spots, the final

---

♦ PRESENTS ACCOUNTED FOR

In our couples' workshops we have an entire session on gift-giving. What surfaces again and again is that we tend to give gifts that reflect our personality preferences—that is, gifts that we want, rather than those that the recipient would appreciate.

For example, Thinkers tend to give books to their Feeling mates. Sensors tend to give something very practical to a dreamy, iNtuitive mate. Judgers can spoil a Perceiver's surprise by saying, "Here is a list of things I'd like for my birthday"; typically, none of those had even been considered by the P. Extraverts often throw parties for their Introverted mates, then wonder why the Introvert seems less than excited about the event.

To be able to separate oneself and put yourself in the other person's typological shoes is one of the great assets of Typewatching. It can help avoid the hurt that can take place when someone's effort at gift-giving seems unappreciated.

step is to agree on some way to measure your progress and recognize when things are going well—and when they aren't. Hopefully, this will avoid blame, keep each party interested and responsible, and allow for changing conditions and needs. Keep in mind that different types measure success differently. For example, some people more naturally think in the long term; others prefer to look only at the immediate situation. Both perspectives are necessary, and by staying mindful of each other's preferences you can ensure that the differences lead to complementary strengths and resources rather than contradictory excuses and blame.

In the end, keep in mind that money is meaningless; it's what you ascribe to it that gives it meaning. Problems begin when different personality types ascribe different things to it and try to interact harmoniously. As we've been saying all along, successful relationships involve knowing oneself, knowing one's needs and wishes, and negotiating in constructive ways to achieve fulfillment. This is most certainly true when it comes to dealing with money.

That doesn't mean money differences need bankrupt a relationship. As with all other conflicts, negotiation, perspective, and awareness of limits are essential ingredients to successful resolution.

--------------------------------- EXERCISE ---------------------------------

A Thought for Your Pennies

As with any difference between two people there is a series of steps that can be helpful in increasing each party's understanding of what's really going on. The steps use Typewatching to help define and clarify the issues in a constructive way.

The five steps are:

1. **Define the issues involved.** If someone has failed to balance the checkbook, what's really going on here? Are there other stressers that are symbolized in this action? Is the checkbook even the problem, or does it go deeper? It might and it might not. The key is to quickly get past blame and try to get to the heart of the issue.

2. **Try to put things into a typological framework.** Is it a case of an Introvert not communicating sufficiently? Is it a matter of an iNtuitive not paying attention to specific numbers and deadlines? Is it a Feeler's subtle way of rejecting this responsibility? Theoretically, any of the eight preferences are fully capable of mucking up this or any other situation. The more you are able to isolate specific typological behaviors, the more objectively you will be able to deal with them.

3. **Examine the likely cause of the differences.** Based on the above you might conclude that while the original conflict is about money, some underlying issues reflect one party's fear of the future, an unexpected and expensive dental bill, or something totally unrelated. It might turn out, for example, that the checkbook conflict is a symbol of another underlying relationship problem. Again, the more this can be put into typological terms, the better.

4. **Ask each party to identify with the other's point of view.** This is a crucial step that involves actually trying to step inside the other person's shoes for a moment. Try to experience what's going on from their perspective—what they see and hear and think. If you'd like, jot down a few thoughts onto paper; they can make the basis for a fruitful discussion. For example, one person might see that the other is resentful for having to always bear responsibility for ensuring that deposits are made, while the other person is the one who writes most of the checks.

5. **Negotiate compromises or contracts.** As a result of your heightened insight try to determine what each of you will do. For example, a Perceiver might agree to be more mindful of always entering check amounts in the check register. An Introvert might agree to always discuss his or her thoughts about the financial situation. An Extravert might

promise to be less blasé about the other person's financial concerns by listening carefully and responding thoughtfully. (We'll deal more fully with negotiations and contracts in Chapter 10.)

This is admittedly an objective approach to looking at a subject that is all too often far from being cut and dry. Money matters are filled with emotional baggage. One party inevitably makes more than the other, or may stand to inherit more from relatives. One party may bring more resources or wealth into a relationship, immediately creating an inequity. One may come from a background of never having had extra money—or always having had plenty of it. Child support, alimony, business debts, and other burdens also color the situation. In each case the dynamics created by these built-in differences—exacerbated sometimes by personality differences—often make objective decisions difficult at best. However, the more these conditions exist, the greater the need for both parties to be up front about them throughout the relationship.

Most important is for everyone to keep in mind that needing financial advice or assistance is not a sign of weakness in a relationship. Precious few of us are naturally born financial wizards. (And most people who think they are, inevitably learn otherwise—the hard way.) Open recognition of the problem is a key step to keeping the issue in perspective and will make resolution that much easier.

Certainly you won't make money problems go away by ignoring them or denying their existence. Seeking competent professional assistance could yield significant dividends—for both your pocketbook and your relationship.

———————

FINANCE TYPE TALK

IF YOU ARE . . .

AND YOUR LOVER IS . . .		EXTRAVERT	INTROVERT
	EXTRAVERT	• Decide what's private and what's public information, so you don't accidentally disclose sensitive matters.	• Demand that your needs and positions be heard on financial matters.
		• Try not to compete by bragging about your finances to friends and to each other.	• Make it clear to your partner about which matters are public and which are private.
		• Work hard at listening to each other's opposing points of view.	• Demand time for reflection— at least 24 hours—after discussing any financial discussions before taking action.
		EXTRAVERT	**INTROVERT**
	INTROVERT	• Respect that your partner's finances may be very private to him or her.	• Commit to regularly sharing your thoughts and feelings on financial issues.
		• Check in advance what can and cannot be shared.	• Remember that it is okay to seek help from financial professionals.
		• Beware of exaggerating, overpowering, fast-talking, or not listening to your partner.	• Work at keeping the communication lines open. Take nothing for granted.
		SENSOR	**INTUITIVE**
	SENSOR	• Though exactness is important, remember there is more to finance than facts and figures.	• Pay attention to the specifics and details, knowing you can trip yourself up if you don't.
		• Try not to bury one another in details.	• Draw on your partner's natural talents to deal with being practical and factual about finances.
		• Stay aware of precision and the present, but allow wiggle room for future fun.	• Help your partner see possibilities and future potential without demeaning his or her point of view.
		SENSOR	**INTUITIVE**
	INTUITIVE	• Work at balancing your need for exactness with some unknown possibilities.	• Given that neither of you is good with details, make sure someone is covering them.
		• Keep your partner aware of specific amounts, as well as your specific needs.	• Seek out someone who will implement your combined master financial plans.
		• Provide details to flesh out your partner's fantasies and big-picture ideas.	• Take some time to identify each of your roles and responsibilities in financial matters.

IF YOU ARE . . .

	THINKER	FEELER
THINKER	• Money can represent power to you both. Be careful not to let it become stifling or a source of abuse. • Remind each other there's more to life and your relationship than dollars and cents. • Recognize each other's financial strengths and use them accordingly.	• Be careful not to lay guilt on your partner over financial disagreements. • Respect your partner's objectivity. Don't be afraid to use it to absolve your personal guilt. • Avoid personalizing your differences. Hang tough during financial discussions and disagreements.
	THINKER	**FEELER**
FEELER	• Be aware that your sharp differences may not mean that one of you is "right" and the other "wrong." • Clarify your roles and be mindful of how each of you gives perspective to the other. • Help your partner recognize the limits of your finances, and sort out the causes without imposing blame or guilt.	• Resolve early on who is to be chiefly responsible and have the final word on financial matters. • Keep in mind that an outside financial consultant may be helpful in providing objectivity. • Avoidance and denial won't help. Success requires leadership with a minimum of personalization.
	JUDGER	**PERCEIVER**
JUDGER	• Be careful to avoid too much focus on money, work, and savings. • Schedule some unaccountable "fun money" for each of you. • Remind yourselves that money is not the goal, it is only a resource for achieving your goals.	• Remember that your partner will become stressed by a lack of structure, particularly with money matters. • Show your partner how windfalls and unplanned income can be opportunities for fun. • Help your partner see the need for both focusing and being spontaneous regarding finances.
	JUDGER	**PERCEIVER**
PERCEIVER	• Negotiate early on about your roles, responsibilities, and how you'll stay accountable to each other. • Try not to "one-up" your partner on financial matters. • Keep your goals in focus, but allow money for unplanned matters.	• Determine early on who will have major and who will have minor financial responsibilities. • Try to stay focused on your financial goals, knowing that you'll still manage to find ways to make it fun. • Support each other. Finances are not a strength for either of you. Don't hesitate to use outside help.

AND YOUR LOVER IS . . .

8

CONFLICT

*"Your silence drives me crazy.
It's so controlling!"*

Let's start with the basics: No one handles conflict well. Few of us move through life looking for a fight. Rare is the person who, when a conflict arises, can deal with it constructively. In the human situation there is nothing so explainable, at times so necessary, while simultaneously being so limiting and futile, as conflict.

The more intimate the relationship, the more vulnerable the parties are to devastating conflicts. It seems that the more intense the love, the more volatile and hateful conflicts can become. That may be because the more closely we relate to one another, the better we are at getting each other's goat. And we don't hesitate to pull whatever we need out of our respective bag of tricks when the situation warrants.

While each of the eight preferences responds differently to conflict, there is a big difference between this and the other three key areas of relationship problems—communication, sex, and finance. In those realms it's often a case of opposites attracting: Introverts attracted to Extraverts' conversational abilities, iNtuitives appreciating Sensors' check-balancing adeptness, Judgers finding Perceivers' sexual spontaneity exciting.

That isn't the case with conflict resolution. While some may be slower to deal with conflict, and others may handle it a bit more effectively, it's clear that most prefer that it never happen at all. And after it's over, practically no one is pleased with the way the situation unfolded. Conflict foments apprehension, insecurity, and anxiety for most of us—none of which is helpful in dealing with the situation at hand.

Not only do opposites not attract in conflict, they can make conflict worse. What had previously been an attractive part of someone's personality—the part toward which one is drawn—during conflict becomes a short fuse to an explosive situation. For example:

* The gregarious and shoot-from-the-hip Extraverted style can be seen as "You're a loud-mouthed fool who always embarrasses me."
* The contemplative, reflective listening skills of the Introvert get translated into "Your silence drives me crazy. It's so controlling!"
* The Sensor's precision and groundedness can become "Your constant nitpicking is so annoying."
* The anything's-possible, live-your-dreams inspiring style of the iNtuitive quickly can become "You're so impractical. You're such an airhead."
* The impassioned objectivity of the Thinker is turned into "You're a coldhearted, uncaring piece of ice."
* The Feeler's caring supportiveness can transform itself into "You're a doormat. You let everybody take advantage of you."
* The rock-solid-foundation forthrightness of the Judger can be viewed as "You're an angry and rigid person who always wants things your way."
* The Perceiver's spontaneity and free-spiritedness can translate into "You're an accident waiting to happen."

* * *

All of the above are the stuff from which conflicts are made, and made worse. We hear these lines, or some variations thereof, from so many people that they reflect the universality of how opposite personality types manage to turn previously attractive traits into the basis for fierce disagreement.

Consider the case of Ken and Jean, a married professional couple. During the time that Ken (ENTP) was gainfully employed, Jean (ESTJ) admired his philosophical musings and dreams. Ken, in turn, basked in her admiration. Then, as fate found him jobless and seeking new employment, Jean found herself irritated beyond measure by his endless philosophizing about what he could do next or what he was "going to" do. For all this talk Ken—at least from Jean's Sensing perspective—did nothing at all.

In the meantime all of Jean's highly honeyed home-management skills, which Ken had once found so appealing, in little time became viewed by him as qualities of a nagging, nitpicking wife who seemed to be constantly on his case about everything, never cutting him any slack. How could he be creative about his career decision, he wondered, with her endless badgering?

With Ken and Jean both sharing Extraversion and Thinking, much of their day together was being spent shouting, blaming each other for their respective faults. As we analyzed the situation, the mutual blaming was based on personality characteristics that up to then had been viewed as relationship strengths. In fact, both had enjoyed lively, hearty discussions and debates about a wide range of issues. They had also appreciated their opposite preferences: Jean liked Ken's ability to generate endless ideas (iNtuition and Perceiving) and Ken respected Jean's precision and keen sense of organization (Sensing and Judging).

While common Typewatching sense might have suggested that we focus on their typological differences—S versus N or J versus P—we thought it appropriate in this case to focus on their type similarities, which seemed to be keeping the situation frozen. With both of them Extraverting, very little real listening was going on. And in their natural tendency to remain objective they communicated very little caring and concern.

We suggested that they stop for a moment. In fact, we called a twenty-four-hour truce, during which time we asked Ken and Jean to spend as much time apart as possible, and when together not to discuss the problematic issues. During the truce period we instructed them to make separate lists of what each needed from the other in order to ease the daily stress level.

When the twenty-four hours were over, we all sat down and looked over the lists. We found that the lists had several things in common, including the mutual need for more overt expressions of love and support. From their own perspectives neither felt the other person truly understood what they were going through. In doing this the goal was to help them get past the shouting and blaming and move forward to carrying out some of the more supportive things on the lists: Jean not nagging every moment that Ken was not pounding the pavement for a job; Ken devising a concrete schedule and plan on his next career move.

From there each of them was able to see how their initial attractions had become a source of conflict in the other person's eyes. The heightened awareness brought about by Typewatching allowed them both to Extravert less, listen more to each other's genuine needs, and back off on the things that, under less stressful conditions, were really quite attractive.

Another example comes from Dave, an ISTJ, and Evelyn, an effervescent ENFP. From the start Evelyn viewed Dave as the "strong, silent type," who seemed to be in command of everything in his life. Eight years into their marriage Evelyn came to us complaining that Dave "communicates absolutely nothing about anything." She explained: "I would ask him,

'What's going on? What are you thinking? What happened today?' He would hardly look up, and barely answer in his own stoic style: 'Nothing.' "

At this point in their marriage Evelyn felt cut out of Dave's life, turned off by his behavior, and thoroughly angry at his apparent disinterest—in her and everything else. "It seems the angrier I get, and the louder I become, the quieter he gets, and the more cynical and controlling his silence becomes," she said. "He no longer notices anything I do. I could swing naked on the chandelier and he wouldn't even know I was in the room. Some days I fantasize leaving him, but I fear that it would take him three days just to notice I was gone."

Evelyn's plight, albeit serious, is all too common: a couple seemingly unable to communicate on any issue, with one or both parties very angry about the conflict in styles and needs. While Typewatching has its limits—it can only unfreeze people who are willing to be thawed—we did manage to help Dave and Evelyn move their respective positions a bit. Recognizing her hunger for communication by the time Dave came home from work each day, and his need for solitude after a day of office bustle, Evelyn agreed not to pounce on him verbally as soon as he walked through the door. After some negotiation it was further agreed that Dave could spend the first half hour or so at home indulging himself in his study—going through the mail, reviewing the day's events, and organizing things for the next day. Dave agreed that, after spending some time alone, he would spend a minimum of thirty minutes sharing his day with Evelyn, and discussing whatever else either of them wanted to talk about. In addition, Dave agreed that when asked a direct question by Evelyn, he would try to answer as fully as possible, even if the answer seemed simple and obvious. Over time, as this began to work for them, it inspired Dave and Evelyn to expand the various ways they could spend satisfying time together.

Ultimately, the couple was never able to recapture the close sharing and intimacy of young romance, but through Typewatching they were able to come "unstuck" from their respective destructive positions and managed to rekindle some of the respect and mutual admiration that had brought them together in the first place: her bubbling enthusiasm, and his silent strength.

•

Thinkers and Feelers: Getting to the Heart of the Issue

When it comes to understanding the impact of personality differences on conflict, the best starting point is the Thinking-Feeling preference. One reason is the gender factor unique to his preference: as we've said before, two thirds of Thinkers are male and two thirds of Feelers are female. From our very earliest childhood scripting, the T-F gender factor plays a major role in how we view conflict. For example, girls aren't "supposed" to hit or be hit during a fight. Boys, meanwhile, aren't "supposed" to cry or show any weakness. When males fight, it's simply a case of "boys will be boys." When females exhibit the same behavior, they are called anything from "bitchy" to "catty." Males are taught to compete—it is a tough, masculine thing to do—which inevitably sets up a win-lose model. On the other hand, females are taught to be conciliators—considered to be soft and feminine—a more

---

• **A NO-WIN SITUATION?**

Feeler: Winning isn't everything.
Thinker: Winning isn't everything—it's the only thing.

collaborative model leading to compromise, win-win situations, or even lose-lose scenarios where both parties go down together.

As a result of this scripting, nearly any male-female conflict begins on an unlevel playing field, with each party expected to exhibit certain behaviors and avoid others. Thinkers approach conflict with an immediate need to win. In the classic T model, conflict is a chance to prove oneself and improve one's position, an opportunity to secure one's position as king of the castle. In the end it is very T to stay objective, impersonal, and above all, not embroiled in the experience itself. "Now, now. One mustn't lose one's head" is a typical T refrain. In fact, thinks the T, if everyone were to stay rational, this conflict, though momentarily stressful and perhaps even painful, can become quite productive and helpful in the final analysis. As a result Ts often see conflict as a situation in which opposing points of view may create positive results. Conflict, then, is not only healthy in small doses, but also a good thing to have from time to time—a cleansing experience that can sharpen a relationship.

That's a little different from the way Feelers view conflict. Rarely, if ever, does an F find anything constructive about a disagreement between people. Feelers see it as destructive, hurtful, often deeply scarring, and something to be avoided at all costs. Until one has encountered a genuine F in some kind of conflict situation it is difficult to comprehend how severely stressed and evasive the F can become. Anything from a raised voice to specific words can be taken personally, even perceived as inflammatory. So, while a T may be merely unconsciously defining terms, not even expressing anger, the F may feel threatened, personalizing every word, feeling bruised, and looking desperately for any way to escape what looks like an impending bombastic exchange.

To appreciate the sharp differences you must hear the story of Frances, an F, going out to dinner with Tim, her T boyfriend. The event was their fifth "anniversary," marking their first date. The evening as planned consisted of dinner at their favorite French restaurant, followed by dancing the night away. In short, the quintessential romantic date.

They arrived at the restaurant at eight o'clock, precisely the hour for which Tim had reserved their favorite table. But the maître d' informed Frances and Tim that their table wasn't ready, and that it would be another fifteen minutes or so before they could be seated. He suggested to the couple that they go into the lounge and have a before-dinner drink.

But Tim would not be that easily appeased. "We had an eight o'clock reservation. We're here on time, where's our table?"

The maître d' responded coolly, "There's nothing I can do, *monsieur*. There are simply no tables available, including the one you requested."

"Well, then, the drinks are on you," responded Tim angrily, "since it was your mistake."

As Tim's voice and anger rose, Frances could feel the rush of embarrassment and anxiety. She wasn't at all comfortable with Tim's public display of anger. And his inflammatory words, and his bold demand for free drinks, made her wish she were somewhere else.

"*Au contraire*," the maître d' responded defensively, "I cannot control how long it takes for people to eat. And I certainly cannot buy drinks for everyone who doesn't get their table on time."

"Well, then, you shouldn't be in business," Tim shot back, almost shouting.

Frances, in an act of desperation, took Tim by the arm and led him to the bar, saying to the maître d', "I'm sorry. It's really no big deal." As they walked away, Tim gave her a stern look and icily said, "Why are *you* sorry? You have nothing to do with it. It's not your fault. It's not even your problem."

They finally got their table and their meal, but it was far from the romantic evening they had envisioned. Tim acted as if nothing had ever happened. From his perspective the restaurant had done him wrong and he had tried to negotiate the best possible deal under the circumstances. But Frances never seemed to recover. She was shaken by the episode and felt embarrassed and guilty about Tim's behavior. On the way out the door, and without Tim seeing, she deftly slipped the maître d' a twenty-dollar bill with an additional apology.

They never got to go dancing. Feigning a headache, she asked to go home early. Tim, aware that she was still upset about the earlier incident, tried to put things in perspective for her. "You've made too much out of this. You always take these things personally. You just can't seem to handle it when people argue."

Frances's reaction was a typical F response to conflict. Feelers are masters at denying conflict. But that by no means makes it disappear, as they wish it would. In fact, despite their desire to avoid unpleasantness between people, the opposite actually occurs: the things they'd rather not deal with (or wish would disappear quickly) tend to linger for great periods of time, surfacing where least wanted or expected, sometimes totally out of proportion to the current situation.

"I can forgive but I can't forget" was probably spoken by a Feeler. Such a statement has an oxymoronic nature to it because the latter contradicts the former. By definition to forgive is to forget, a process that Feelers find particularly difficult. When it comes to being slighted or hurt by others, little compares to a Feeler's capacity to remember for a long time. Again, this is the very opposite of what they want to happen. The failure to confront, dump, test, explore, and talk through with others—all of which Feelers find difficult to do—is the very thing that must happen to put the situation behind them. Clearly, Introverted-Feelers have an even more difficult time.

Feelers could avoid a lot of this difficulty by keeping two simple things in mind: 1) however distasteful conflict may be, it is a reality we must deal with, and life will go on; and 2) though tense and stressful to a relationship, if the situation is dealt with thoroughly even the Feeler will be better off for the experience, and generally glad for the positive resolution. However difficult this may be to do, it certainly is worth the effort.

It's nearly impossible for Thinkers to even come close to the F's perspective on this. Though perhaps equally distasteful for them, conflict will produce learning, and there's a high probability that growth will take place. Therefore, it is imperative that we confront it, talk it through, and push for resolution. And most important of all, if you say it's resolved, say you forgive, or clink a glass in settlement, then it is verboten to the Thinker to bring it up again. It is over, and harboring it any longer is in poor taste, ethically questionable, and will produce no good for anyone.

As we've said, gender plays a key role here. And nowhere is that role more pronounced than when men and women are out of step with society's expectations—that is, with Thinking females and Feeling males.

T women swim upstream against a rather swift current. Statistically they are outnumbered. Interpersonally they often behave—naturally, albeit quite unconsciously—contrary to societal norms. Internally there is often a psychological conflict of interest—"Do I go with my natural instincts, or do I do what's expected of me as a female?" During the course of a busy day, dealing with spouses, friends, colleagues, kids, and the rest of the world, making a continuous stream of such instantaneous choices is an unfair extra burden. Nonetheless it's a real one that must be dealt with by T women.

The T woman can't win. If the Thinking woman gives in to her objectivity, she can often be quite intimidating to those around her. On the other hand, if she makes some

♦ MIXING IT UP

The T-F issue reaches a new level of complexity when you consider the various combinations of gender and preference. Their approaches to conflict might sound something like this:

T male versus T male: Winner takes all, and may the best man win.

T male versus F male: Winner takes all, and I (T) am the best.

or

If I (F) don't win now, I'll get you sometime.

F males versus F male: I disagree, but I sympathize with your point of view.

T female versus T female: We have a real difference, although I know we can resolve it mutually.

T female versus F female: We have a real difference, and I (T) think we should confront it now.

or

There is a real difference, and I (F) would like to understand your point of view.

F female versus F female: I don't see why we can't disagree and still be friends.

effort to compensate for her impersonal approach, by softening her style, she may be viewed as false or superficial. In either case it's not a very pleasant array of stereotypes to bring to a conflict. What's worse, conflict is rarely planned or strategized, and it can escalate very quickly. In the heat of the moment it's natural for all of us to fall back on our trusted preferences. In this case that means that the greater the need to react in the moment, the more likely it is the T women will react in typical T fashion: objectively, analytically, impersonally, and perhaps intimidatingly to others.

All of this can become very convoluted. Without awareness of type things can get misunderstood immediately. "I don't understand her," people say of the T woman. "She looks like a woman but fights like a man." And once labeled, the opportunity for resolution of the conflict is further reduced.

The good news is that we believe that most T women, by virtue of their upbringing and scripting, still tend to have a reservoir of nurturing and interpersonal awareness—as much or even more than a Feeling male. As a result the T woman, if she can maintain her equilibrium during the stress of conflict, can call upon the best of both worlds: objectivity and subjectivity, competition and collaboration, impersonal and personal. All are qualities that can be of benefit in resolving a conflict.

Unfortunately the opposite isn't necessarily true for the Feeling male. Life's scripting tends to confront F males with a very different set of issues. It's not that the F male isn't capable of collaborating or negotiating. It's just that "maleness," for lack of a better term, gets in the way. This is a classic case of the "Me Tarzan" syndrome, which says that boys must be boys and men must be men, with the "gentler sex" filling their respective role. And never the twain shall meet.

Couple this Tarzan syndrome with the Feeling type's fear

and denial of conflict, and Feeling males find themselves on the road to behavior unpredictable even to themselves. Super-machoness takes over: "Just be cool. Don't be afraid. Don't let on to what you're really feeling. Act big and talk tough. And above all, never be afraid to do battle, because real men aren't afraid of anything."

This is strange indeed because as a Feeling type, the F male disdains conflict and certainly would prefer to avoid it if at all possible. Further, were he able to stay in touch with his Feeling side, the F male would likely be quite effective during a conflict: enough "maleness" to convey strength, enough Feeling to value concern and sympathy over winning and losing.

♦ LETTING HIM WIN

Often gender overrides personality preferences when conflict arises. In such cases things become a male-female issue more than T-F. The two genders' approaches are amazingly similar:

Male: I've got to win, to prove I'm a man.
Female: I've got to let him win, so his ego survives.

We once saw a cartoon that summed it up this way: "Love is letting him win, even when you know you can."

As a result any form of conflict can bring a response from the F male quite out of proportion to the situation. Not willing to be seen as "soft" or a wimp, his almost instant reaction to a relatively simple stressor can be quite volatile. While this will be most evident with Extraverted and Judging Feelers, it can also take place with Introverted Feeling males.

There are some things to keep in mind when dealing with T-F conflicts. First, as the issue erupts, it can be helpful for one of you to declare a Dumping Session—a brief period where the issues are "dumped" on the table by each of you, with no further discussion allowed.

For example: "I'm really mad that I end up doing all the housework just because I'm the woman. I want you to do your share without my having to tell you what needs to be done."

The mate adds: "I'm frustrated that I always have to take care of all matters with the car. You never even fill it with gas, but leave it on 'empty' for me." You both continue alternating your "dump" for the prescribed amount of time.

At this point each of you would no doubt like to respond to the other's arguments. But for now it's inappropriate. After the Dumping Session is over, you must leave the subject alone for at least a half hour. Then, when you spend some time discussing it, you'll probably both see the issue for its merits, with less personal and emotional charge.

◆ WHAT GOES AROUND COMES AROUND

Janet, a Feeler, raised her three children in a way that reflected her need to ensure that no conflict would end without harmony. When a dispute was settled, even tentatively, she would make the entire family stand in a closed circle, arms around each other. "We're family," she'd say. "We are each other's support. We need to remember that and be there for each other. Now, I want everyone to give each other a hug."

The kids didn't completely buy into the process. They found it a bit hokey. But they must have found it meaningful: **now** more than two decades later they've instituted the practice with their own families.

That brings us to the second key to managing T-F conflicts: Each of you must distinguish between personal attacks and genuine issues that need resolution.

How do you do that? Take a look at what's really going on. Is the housework really the issue, or are you angry about general sharing of responsibilities—in social situations, in bed, wherever? Granted, these things aren't always crystal clear, but the more you can step back and try to look at the real issues, the better the potential for a positive solution.

Finally, it's important to remember that all of us—Thinkers and Feelers alike—have emotional hot buttons that can get pressed by people who are close to us and who know our vulnerabilities. Typewatching won't help us avoid such moments, but with luck it will help us move through them with as few scars as possible.

There's much more to this puzzle than the Thinking-Feeling dimension. As each preference is added, the complexity grows.

◆

Extraverts versus Introverts: A Space Odyssey

We have an exercise we use in our couples' workshops in which Extraverts and Introverts are asked to generate on a list "things I want others to know about me during a conflict." Almost always the Extraverts' lists begin with "I'm going to talk louder and faster." And Introverts' lists usually begin

---

◆ STOP THE WORDS, I WANT TO GET OFF

Extravert: With just a few more words we can clear up this entire mess.
Introvert: If I hear one more word, I'm going to go crazy.

with something like "The madder I get, the quieter I get." Extraverts further report that "I tend to exaggerate to make a point. I get overly enthusiastic and want to monopolize the conversation." Introverts, meanwhile, say "I store what's said for future reference. Someday, when I get mad enough, I'll let it all out."

That pretty much illustrates the tremendous communication gap between Es and Is where conflict is concerned. It also points up how difficult it can be to resolve problems when the levels and styles of communication are so disparate.

Whenever we display the Es' and Is' lists, there is always an initial sense of hopelessness about the potential for ever working things out. It is clear to us that if conflict between Es and Is will ever be resolved, it will demand deep understanding and dramatic behavioral modification on the part of both. One of the hardest things for an Extravert to do is listen without preparing a response, and yet that's what must happen. One of the hardest things for an Introvert to do is be expressive without internally editing, and yet that's what the situation demands.

This internal editing process is doubly troublesome during a conflict. Not only does it irritate the Extravert, who perceives the Introvert to be withholding and maybe even deceiving, the silence also affords the Extravert license to jump in with criticism. This, in turn, is doubly troublesome for the Introvert. For one thing, it further compounds the internal mindjam: Just when they were beginning to figure out an appropriate response, there's new data to consider. For another, the Extravert's rambling dominates the airwaves, making it even more difficult to get a word in edgewise.

If you are an Introvert, as conflict arises your first inclination is to take the issue inside, where it can be thought about, inspected, interpreted, readied for action. Because of your introversion it is natural to trust this process far more than anything you can accomplish out loud. Remember: to the

Introvert the external world is foreign turf, which drains your energy and exposes your shortcomings. Of course, in something as uncomfortable as conflict, the sense of vulnerability is heightened, making your inner world of thoughts and ideas that much safer and more secure. As a result, conflict is something that one needs to think about for a while—perhaps overnight, or even longer—before responding. The important thing is that you need to be allowed space to prepare an appropriate response that will reflect your actual thoughts and feelings about the issue at hand.

In a society in which Extraverts outnumber Introverts three to one, and where Extraversion is rewarded throughout our lives, Introverts must be aware that any time they engage in a verbal altercation with an Extravert, the Extravert is operating with "home-field advantage." Even if an Introvert has mastered good verbal skills, the Extravert will still have the upper hand simply because the exchange is taking place in the external world that is home to the Extravert. If Introverts heed only one piece of advice, it would be to occasionally say to an Extravert, "If you want to continue this discussion, type your thoughts into a computer or jot them down so I can read them in my private time and prepare a reaction."

Not only is that good advice, it also helps prevent Introverts from exhausting themselves by overextending themselves verbally, or by being the recipient of some Extravert's dumping. Clearly, Introverts, when they are fatigued by such interactions, run the risk of letting loose with their own verbal outpourings. These may include any number of issues, some totally unrelated to the matter in dispute. And there is a high probability that the outburst will be charged with a level of emotion seemingly disproportionate to the overall situation.

This has an interesting secondary effect: Feeling that they have overreacted in an extraverted manner, they can end up feeling foolish, embarrassed, and convinced that they should have never opened their mouths in the first place. This can make it even more difficult to deal constructively the next time conflict surfaces.

So much for the problems faced by Introverts when dealing with Extraverts. Two Introverts embroiled in conflict only compound their mutual nonexpressiveness. This is perhaps best illustrated in the story of Debra and Barry, both Introverted-Judgers. Their marriage was marked by quick but incomplete resolutions of conflict. Over a period of seventeen years unresolved issues often grew to a point of explosion, then were avoided in most stifling ways. Finally the two Introverts sought marriage counseling, which was for them the appropriate (J) way to deal with this very private matter (I). Interestingly, in the counselor's office, seventeen years of conflict was dumped—with anger, frustration, and all the other emotions that reflected their long-pent-up feelings.

However, upon leaving the counselor's office, the two returned to the familiar behavioral pattern of avoidance and mutual accommodation that had gotten them where they were. It seemed the only way they could communicate about the conflicts was in the presence of an objective outsider. And even that soon grew wearisome. Unfortunately, for this couple, divorce was the only alternative. But in their note to us they sent the following advice:

> Learn at the beginning how Introversion and Judging impact on how one relates. Then practice communicating, promising above all not to bow to silence.

Clearly, continued genuine communication is central to effective conflict resolution. It is certainly all right, maybe even necessary, to build in "rest stops"—quiet zones on the road to resolution—but let that not be a detour from reaching your final destination, which is openness and honesty in facing the issues.

Just as the lack of communication can spell early death to the conflict-resolution process, excessive, unending Extraversion can be equally deadly. Extraverts want to move the substance of a conflict to the external domain, just as Introverts prefer to work the issue inside themselves before sharing with others. For Extraverts the external sphere is where their ultimate confidence lies, and therefore offers the greater opportunities for resolving a conflict. The external arena becomes a proving ground where both perceptions and judgments are tried out and, if deemed worthy, built upon.

Because of this, and because of Extraverts' natural proclivity to exaggerate, many, many things will be blurted out, not all of which are either important or intended to be heard by others. This shooting-from-the-lip phenomenon carries with it tones of enthusiasm, anger, and deep involvement, often done in a progressively louder and faster fashion. And it can convey to others the idea that the Extravert is highly knowledgeable ("He surely sounds like he knows his stuff"), full of conviction ("She obviously believes what she's saying"), or highly volatile ("He sounds like he's nearing the breaking point"). Ironically, none of these may be true. The Extravert merely may be getting things out into the open where they can be examined, refined, and ultimately acted upon—or abandoned.

What frequently happens in the process is that such outpourings are followed by an interruption or response by whoever is within listening radius. Whatever the response, it inevitably engenders another outpouring, often even louder and more defensive. This is particularly true of Extraverted-Judgers, who can end up defending a variety of things in which they don't really believe. Obviously, this can frustrate both the Extravert and the listener, both of whom can become confused about how things got so quickly off track. It might go something like this:

Extravert: "No, I don't want to go there for dinner. We always go there."

Significant Other: "Always? We haven't been there in ages."

E: "Baloney! Don't tell me. I know we were there just a week or two ago."

S.O.: "A week or two ago? Be more specific."

E: "I don't need to. I remember it clearly. Why do you always have to pin me down?"

S.O.: "I'm not pinning you down. You're the one who's making inaccurate statements."

From there the conversation may proceed to an in-depth analysis of whose statements are more accurate. And over the course of all this dumping, exaggeration, and defensiveness, the couple may or may not actually get to a restaurant before closing time. While both parties can and should accept blame for this state of affairs, one key contributing factor is the Significant Other's interrupting the Extravert's verbalized stream of consciousness.

The "stream" metaphor may be appropriate. Think of an Extravert's outpouring much like a river that must flow downstream. The more it is diverted or blocked—by rocks, fallen trees, and the like—the greater its force and the greater its tendency for unleashing such powerful forces as waterfalls, whirlpools, and cascades; it may even meander in new directions, creating streams and tributaries.

As an Introvert you have several options in dealing with this undeniable phenomenon of nature. You can jump in and go wherever the flow takes you, risking whatever unforeseen dangers you encounter along the way; you can stand on the shore and watch the wonder of it all, waiting—perhaps in vain—for calmer waters; or you can wade in to whatever depth you feel comfortable, hoping you'll be able to maintain your balance and control. If you're up to the challenge, you can even jump in and fight the natural forces by trying to swim upstream, despite the high probability that you won't get far before tiring.

In the end, chances are you'll be most satisfied by achieving some kind of balance: an opportunity that allows you to spend some time in the stream, and enough time onshore to feel grounded. That gives ample time for both the Introvert and the "river" to interact, yet do what comes naturally.

Translated back onto dry land, that means there must be opportunity for both Extravert and Introvert to hear each other's point of view. That must take place in spite of the Extravert's difficulty with just listening and the Introvert's difficulty with verbalizing without running things through their internal filters. The key to success in our minds is that there must be sharply defined periods for extraverting—on everyone's part—then some reflective time—again, for everyone—with the goal of sorting out those things that are necessary for resolution from things that are better ignored.

Not allowing such E-and-I space can lead to another classic scenario. It begins as an Extravert perceives the Introvert's quietness as anger or distress. Attempting to ferret out the issue, the E asks, "What's the matter?" or "Is something wrong?" To which there is a curt reply: "No. Nothing's wrong."

Clearly such a response to an Extravert is an invitation—almost a mandate—to pursue the issue. The E's challenge is to pull it out of the I at all costs. The E begins with teasers, which range from "You're putting me on—what's up?" to "All right. I know something's bugging you, but I'll be damned if I even care to know what it is."

Now the ball is squarely in the Introvert's court. Does the Introvert take the bait and tell all, or respond with an equally oblique retort that can range from "Well, it's none of your business anyway," all the way to "If you had any sensitivity, you'd know what it is without my telling you."

The Extravert's intent may well be to simply get things

out in the open where they can be discussed and hopefully resolved. And the Introvert's intent may well be not to bother anyone else with this particular issue. Regardless, such conversational baiting can get both parties hooked into a winner-take-all situation, in which the mere act of initiating the communication becomes the focus and the parties involved are already invested in the diversionary issues.

♦ NOTHING BUT THE TRUTH

During conflict both Extraverts and Introverts have a tendency to distort things, and each can accuse the other of lying.

In the heat of an argument Extraverts tend to exaggerate to underscore a point. Introverts hear the hyperbole and view it as a bold-faced lie.

Introverts, meanwhile, in not disclosing certain things, can be branded as being deliberately deceptive, perhaps even trying to hide the truth.

Neither is lying, of course, but with such divergent styles it's hard to convince the other party that this is the case.

Interestingly enough, both the Introvert and the Extravert were being pretty true to themselves. The E picked up some vibrations and verbalized a reaction. The I, not ready to respond, may have felt invaded by the E and responded accordingly by retreating inside. And the rest is history—if not hysteria.

Here again is where an awareness of each other's differences can convert a potentially ugly situation into one that is at least manageable. If the Extravert can be aware that he or she has responded true to type and has invaded the Introvert's space, then it could be helpful for the E to acknowledge this: "I'm sorry. I may have invaded your space. To me it seemed you were upset and I wanted to help. Let me back off and perhaps we can talk about it later."

The Introvert could also have initiated a response: "I'm sorry, but I wasn't ready to say anything. I appreciate your desire to help. But the matter really has little to do with us. I'll try to discuss it with you later."

Those relatively few words can give both of you all the space and freedom you need—for the Extravert, letting go of the rescue and getting on with life until the Introvert is ready to discuss the matter; for the Introvert, an opportunity to internalize the issue, think about it, and get it ready to present to the Extravert or solve internally.

◆

Sensors and iNtuitives: The Forest versus the Trees

Since so much conflict starts with some kind of perceptual misunderstanding, and since Sensing and iNtuition have to do with how we perceive the world, it's easy to see how two or more people can get off to a bad start when their perceptions of the same thing are very different. As we've said before, if one person sees a forest and the other sees the trees, both are convinced they are right about what they see, even though they may describe the scene in very different terms.

Both Sensors and iNtuitives get each other's goat through the Sensor's need for details and the iNtuitive's disdain for same. The N makes a broad, sweeping statement, refuted by the Sensor, who supplies the countering facts and details. And in no time the two are off and arguing. Or, a Sensor asks a very specific question and gets a seemingly unrelated, unfocused answer.

All of this happens very quickly. We often conduct an experiment in our training sessions to demonstrate S-N differences. For example, Otto puts a chair on his head and walks around the room, throwing pennies at the assembled group. We then ask groups of Sensors and iNtuitives to describe what has just happened, writing their answers on large sheets of newsprint.

You'd be amazed at how the two groups respond. In one session the only thing the iNtuitives reported was, "Otto has lost his cents," a classically iNtuitive play on words. In that same group the Sensors began their list by saying, "Otto entered the room with a chair on his head, held by his left hand. He walked counterclockwise around the room and threw thirteen pennies at the group. Three of the pennies were picked up by women. . . ." At which point one of the iNtuitives interrupted with, "Where did you get all that?" To which a Sensor answered, sharply and self-righteously, "That's what happened. Why didn't you see it?"

And in two sentences more they could have been rolling up their sleeves, in a full-fledged argument.

Ns can't understand that someone would report the obvious—exactly what happened—and then defend it as "the truth." Obviously, everybody saw that, so it seems clear to focus upon the heart of the matter: the meanings and possibilities of what took place. To the Sensor the specifics—the actual details—are the heart of the matter. If both parties are sufficiently invested in their version of reality, it inevitably leads to conflict.

The problem is heightened because, in the iNtuitives' disdain for the details (which seem too obvious), there is often an accompanying arrogance that not only aggravates Sensors, but also can leave them feeling put down. Ns argue haughtily that they have their own reality, and that's all that really matters. It is a waste of time to deal with the mundane, and certainly anyone who thinks otherwise is lacking in intellectual acumen.

We love the story of our two friends Maggie and Mitch.

Maggie, the Sensor, had rearranged the family room in anticipation of a party they were having that evening. Over the course of a few hours she had single-handedly labored to move the couch and other large pieces of furniture out of the main flow of traffic, and set up tables for the buffet and bar they had planned.

When Mitch came home from work, he wandered through the newly arranged family room on his way to the kitchen and walked right into one of the tables Maggie had set up, knocking it over and spilling the platter of petit fours sitting on it.

"What the hell's this table doing in the middle of the room?" asked an irritated and obviously bruised Mitch.

"Don't be so stupid. If you had bothered to look, you would have seen the table and walked around it," responded an equally miffed Maggie. "How could you miss something so obvious?"

"I needed to get this bag of ice into the freezer as soon as possible. Besides, there's not usually a table here. How could I have known there'd be one now?"

"As usual, you're not paying attention," snapped Maggie. "For once, why don't you try keeping your eyes open and your mouth shut?"

By now we're well on our way to a serious fight. Which is exactly how we found them when we showed up to help them add the last-minute touches for the party. The two had hardly spoken since Maggie's last swipe, and as we entered the room, the tension was so thick you could pierce it with an ice pick.

From Mitch's perspective he was being unduly criticized for having been in the wrong place at the wrong time. It wasn't, as Maggie charged, that he hadn't been paying attention. For him the focus hadn't been on the here and now, but on his immediate goal (getting the ice in the freezer) and the task after that (setting up the bar). Not only had Maggie not appreciated his efforts to do his part for the party, she had added insult to injury—literally—by berating him for his mishap.

Maggie didn't see it that way. She was tired of Mitch constantly overlooking significant details. As far as Mitch was concerned, she could dye her hair blue, buy all new clothes, and hang all the pictures upside down. In this particular case she had worked hard to get the room in shape, and Mitch—typically—had not only been inattentive, but his scatteredness had helped to undo some of her efforts.

Typewatching won't prevent the Maggies and Mitches from bumping into things—and each other. However, it can help reduce stress by keeping in mind Sensors' and iNtuitives' divergent perspectives. That means, before we take the leap of defending our perspectives—and, in the process, putting the other person on the defensive—it might be helpful if we can understand the other person's point of view and how ours may be perceived.

In the case of Maggie and Mitch, who had been together long enough to know each other's foibles, it might have helped if Maggie had either met him at the door, saying, "Be careful. I've rearranged everything," or put a note on the garage door informing him of the situation. And Mitch, knowing Maggie's propensity to go all out for a party, might have anticipated that the house might look different than it had when he'd left for work that morning.

In other words, a minute or so of anticipation and preparation, based on an awareness of personality differences, could have prevented an evening's worth of stress and strife.

Experience has taught us that when Sensors and iNtuitives work together, their combined perceptions of anything are always more complete and accurate than either of their most perceptive separate views. The tough part is for both individuals to be sufficiently aware and mature enough to look past the frustrations caused by their differences in order to reap the benefits of their combined perceptions.

As always, recognizing and appreciating the differences is the first step.

◆

Judgers and Perceivers: A Conflict Waiting to Happen

"When I want your opinion, I'll give it to you."

What could be more fight invoking than this highly opinionated and rigid statement? And yet that's not an uncommon starting point for some Judgers, who are quick to

---

◆ HITTING AND RUNNING

As we've said before, one of the credos of Judgers is "I don't like surprises." And yet it is necessary (for some types, even fun) from time to time to confront Js with unexpected ideas or plans. Here's a simple but very effective technique we recommend on how to do this with minimal stress and conflict for the parties involved. We call it the "hit-and-run approach."

It works like this: When giving a J a new idea, drop the information in his or her lap, get out of the way, and come back and discuss it later. That will give the J time to moan—if only internally—before he or she puts the item on a list so that it can be dealt with on its merits.

---

state their minds, consequences be damned. A typical Perceiver retort might be "Who died and named you God?" or something equally resentful and feisty. And things go downhill from there.

As we've stated earlier, the J-P difference is usually the most obvious of our four preferences, the one most easily and quickly detected by others. Introverts can masquerade as

Extraverts, Feelers can take the hard-nosed line of Thinkers, and so on. But when Judgers open their mouths, directives and commands inevitably follow. And when Perceivers speak, it is more often than not in the form of a tenuous question or open-ended information.

Is it any wonder Judgers and Perceivers often find themselves at each others' throats?

Consider a simple conversation gone awry:

> **Judger:** Do you want a bowl of peaches before you go to bed?
> (*This is not a question for discussion. For the Judger it requires a yes-or-no answer.*)
> **Perceiver:** We haven't had peaches in a long time.
> (*This is the P's way of answering affirmatively, although it isn't the answer the J had in mind. So the Judger, somewhat irritated, must ask again.*)
> **Judger:** I asked if you wanted peaches. It's a simple question: yes or no?
> (*Hearing the irritation, the Perceiver gets defensive.*)
> **Perceiver:** What are you so upset about?
> (*By this time, the Judger deems the situation beyond redemption.*)
> **Judger:** Forget it. If you're hungry, get your own snack.
> (*Now the P is angry too.*)
> **Perceiver:** Why are you being such a jerk? You always sound so angry!

And now the name-calling has begun. The J is bruised, having been rebuffed when she was only trying to be helpful. The P, meanwhile, is equally upset because he doesn't understand how they got into an argument. And the more he seeks to understand the situation, the more irritated and embroiled both become.

When you more closely examine the two preferences, you can see how each of them is a conflict waiting to happen. For example, much of the P's speech is nondirectional—that is, open ended and seeking alternatives—which requires more analysis and translation than most Judgers are willing to invest. For Judgers that makes them one step away from being spacey and unfocused. Judgers, meanwhile, tend to speak with much more direction—that is, seeking closure and results—which is only a short step removed from being closed and rigid.

♦ APPEASING Ps

If you are a Perceiver, it is your nature to generate alternatives. That is your contribution to the world—your creativity and your dynamism, and probably part of your attractiveness in a relationship. But this process can be very frustrating for others.

There's a very simple way for you to help Ps sort things out during a conflict. Push the P for closure, saying "Let's do this" or "Let's do that." That will often help the P decide what he or she *doesn't* want to do. That will facilitate the P's natural decision-making process, which is to rule out what they don't want, thereby keeping their options open.

Even when the two types try to put themselves in the other person's shoes, it can be done in a rather clumsy fashion. The J, trying earnestly to be more flexible and open to new information, often approaches it in a very closed-minded way. ("Where'd you get that sweater?" when the J really wants to say, "I like your sweater. Tell me about it. Is it new? Is it handmade? Who knit it?" Meanwhile, the sweater wearer might have interpreted the J's initial query as a criticism. "What's wrong with it? Don't you like it?" Or: "Why can't I buy what I want?")

The P, on the other hand, in an effort to respond to a question of "Should I wear this outfit?", answers either in questions or open-ended comments that seem to go nowhere. ("You have other outfits that I like better." Or: "What other sweaters do you have that go with that outfit?") The P may consider those as definitive responses, but it will take some interpretation to give the response actual meaning. That may frustrate the Js, who prefer a direct answer to a direct question.

In the Js' desire for closure they often sound harsh, angry, or defensive. If it's an issue that involves the J's personal values or commitment, the intensity increases. Stir in a little stress, and you now have an individual who is rigid and needs to control everybody and everything within reach (or, for an *Extraverted*-Judger, within earshot).

◆ THE CHILD IN SOME OF US

During the 1970s there was a popular method of psychotherapy called Transactional Analysis, or TA, developed by Eric L. Berne and popularized in Thomas A. Harris's book *I'm OK—You're OK*. In TA everyone has a parent, child, and adult within them, and it is the confusion among these, Berne said, that leads to interpersonal stressors.

In type terms, if your last letter is J, behaviorally you have an overabundance of "critical parent." And if your last letter is P, you have an overabundance of "natural child." While both traits have their strengths and weaknesses, they make for some very difficult communication problems.

In any conversation a "critical parent" can begin "talking down" to others, leveling all sorts of criticism. Meanwhile, "natural children" approach conversations with a lot more playfulness and spontaneity, which can be perceived by others to be immature and irresponsible.

The flip side for Perceivers is that in their desire to remain open ended, it is natural for them to raise questions and probe. Often the questions don't even need answering; they're only frames of reference to stimulate ideas and alternative ways of thinking. If it's an Extraverted-Perceiver, the person can seem to flit about, jumping from subject to subject and person to person. Stir in a little stress and the Perceiver is likely to become hopelessly scattered and seemingly unable to function.

Because both Js' and Ps' behavior can be so obvious, it can be a source of instant frustration: the Judger sees the P's scatteredness and tries to shape him or her up; the Perceiver experiences the J's rigidity and implores him or her to "hang loose" or "stay cool," which further infuriates the J. So both parties' best intentions go awry.

That needn't happen. Things might go more smoothly if the Judger pitched in and helped the Perceiver make a decision about whatever seems to be frustrating him or her, rather than being critical about the P's indecision. And the Perceiver might do well simply to stay out of the Judger's way until the J has cooled down a bit and can see the need to schedule some relaxation. For the P, doing nothing might be the best course of action in this situation.

Even something as simple as going for a walk can lead to conflict between a Judger and Perceiver. Witness Joan the Judger and Peter the Perceiver. Here was a couple who decided they needed some fun together. With both of them working full-time, the hour from six to seven o'clock was deemed to be the best time for them to try a little togetherness in the form of a nightly walk. It would cost no money, there would be no interruptions, and the time was available to both.

Peter wanted to walk in an area that was aesthetically pleasing to him. They did not have time to drive to a park he particularly liked, so they settled for a tree-filled area not too far from their house. Joan wanted the walk to have a purpose:

to get exercise. She wanted to walk briskly so they could get their heart rates up. But Peter wanted to saunter through the neighborhood and enjoy the scenery. Joan soon became annoyed with Peter because he would not cooperate and was holding her back. However, she did not tell him this because she didn't want to upset him. Meanwhile, Peter was annoyed with Joan because she was rushing him. He didn't want to say anything to her because he didn't want to start a fight.

The more Joan pushed Peter to walk faster, the more tense he became. The more Joan tried to slow down to meet Peter's needs, the more tense *she* became. This hour of what was supposed to be "fun" turned out to increase their anxiety and anger. In the end they couldn't wait to get back home to their own activities—safe in the knowledge that the other didn't even know how to take a walk.

The Joan-and-Peter stories are endless. Yet Js and Ps will continue to be attracted to one another, and without some basic Typewatching skills will end up spending much of their time in conflict, turning even "fun" walks into exercises in frustration.

◆

Tips for Dealing with Conflict

Though type awareness won't resolve all conflicts, it certainly can help in easing those inevitable moments of disagreement as well as provide some insights into the more chronic disputes that can plague intimate relationships.

Here are some time-tested tips to keep in mind during conflict:

◆ **Stop, look, listen.** As things escalate, take the time to make sure that the subject causing the tension is what's really the problem. Rather than simply talking (or shouting) your way through it, try to step back and get a handle on what's happening. For example, before you blurt out an accusation, think about whether that's really what you want to say. It may be that there are other issues on both sides which compound the dilemma.

+ **Turn it into type.** The more you can put the dispute into typological terms, the greater the chance for a satisfying resolution. For example, is the Judger in you jangled by the unexpected—bikes in the driveway, dinner being late, unbearable commuting? Or is the Perceiver in you totally scattered and frustrated because you haven't been able to accomplish a single thing on your day's list? When you can segment one or more personality preferences that may be coming into play, you have an opportunity to deal more constructively with the issues at hand.

+ **Chill out.** Think about declaring a cooling-off period— a few minutes or an hour (depending on the situation)— during which you get away from one another, preferably spending some time in reflective silence. This simple act can be a marvelous catalyst for achieving an effective and mutually satisfying resolution.

+ **Check luggage tags.** How much of what's stressing each of you is current, and how much is "old baggage"? Friends and lovers have a way of carrying stuff into new conflicts, and dumping old business into new scenarios at inappropriate and often vulnerable moments. For example: "And another thing, while I have your attention, I'm still mad about the way you treated me on my birthday." Or: "I hate when you do that. It's just what my father does to get even." If you can identify such baggage, call it what it is and stop the process immediately, or the situation will only wander and worsen. The original dispute will become obscure, unresolved, and fodder for the next fray.

+ **Make a list and check it twice.** Try to develop a list of each of your sensitive points and ways in which the other person "pushes your button" during conflict: loudness, silence, nitpicking, arrogance, pouting, guilt-tripping, and so on. If these are shared openly between you, they can be more readily identified during the conflict. In doing so, you might come to terms about which behavior is acceptable ("I'll allow you to pout if you'll let me yell when I need to") and which is deemed inappropriate ("I'll agree not to nitpick about your grammar if you'll promise not to bring up my mother").

• **Is this a love-hate scenario?** Try to determine whether the things that are bothering you about the other person are also some of the same things you find attractive about that person. For example, you may love her keen sense of organization and structure, but for the moment feel totally controlled by it. Or you may appreciate his nurturing and affirming style, but be offended by his seeming inability to be objective about the situation at hand. If you come to the realization that you are currently hating the things you otherwise love, it is imperative that you stop the conflict immediately and go to neutral ground. Do not deal with the subject further until you can deal with it in a different state of mind. We are convinced that to engage in a serious conflict, exacerbated by such love-hate issues, leaves deep scars. In no time what had been excitement and attraction gives way to resentment and deep wounds from which there may be no genuine recovery.

• **Know when to say "when."** As we said at the beginning of this chapter, no one handles conflict well. There is no crime or shame in asking for help—from friends, relatives, or professionals—usually the sooner the better.

• **Don't sleep on it.** It's been said many times, but it's worth repeating: no matter how severe the conflict, try not to go to bed angry. Ideally, find some way to clear the matter up, or to put it on hold without a grudge—admittedly, very difficult—until some designated resumption time. Going to bed together (or worse yet, separately) when you're angry and hurt without a chance for making up can be far more destructive than constructive for most relationships.

When it comes to conflict, it's important to keep in mind that we don't live alone on the planet. This is obvious, of course, but we all have the potential to act as if we're the only one that matters. So even though you might not need an "I love you," someone close to you may. As part of our relating to others, we need to find ways to meet their needs as well as our own.

Think of the act of driving at dawn or dusk without your headlights. You may think there's no reason to turn them

---

♦ THE LIMITS OF TYPEWATCHING

It is important to remember that Typewatching is most effective in those day-to-day conflicts that can bombard relationships. When a relationship has gone so far that both sides' views become polarized and neither is interested in moving toward the other, that is a different situation that requires a more intensive form of help: marriage counseling, psychotherapy, or whatever.

Typewatching's most effective contribution in dealing with conflict comes with the everyday "rubs" that can plague any relationship. Typewatching can make those situations palatable, manageable, sometimes even laughable, before they become destructive.

---

on—after all, you can see perfectly well without them—but others may not be able to see you and you are therefore a danger to them and yourself. No one is ever on the road by themselves, and so for the safety of all concerned, you may need to turn your headlights on, even if you think it's unnecessary.

It's the same way in relating to someone else. Your needs

always have to be measured against the needs of others in the relationship. And some sort of compromise is usually necessary if you are to live responsibly, sensibly, and respectfully.

Conflict is an inevitable part of a growing relationship. The closer the parties, the more the potential for damaging, hurtful, and destructive conflict. The greater the awareness of differences as well as their strengths and liabilities in a relationship, the more conflict can become one more step in the maturing and developing stages between two people.

Sharing and Comparing Profiles

When conflicts become frequent or persistent, it may be helpful for both parties to step back to get a clearer picture of the issues and personalities involved. One effective way to do that is to use the profiles in the back of this book.

For example, you and your partner might read your own profiles and highlight the parts with which you agree and disagree. Then, swap profiles with your partner and read each other's comments. That will provide the basis for further discussion. How much do you agree or disagree with your partner's perceptions? In what ways are the two of you similar and in which ways different? Are there any surprises? How much of the current conflict has to do with your personality differences?

The more you can view your conflict in the light of these questions, the more you will be able to deal objectively with the situation at hand.

More daring couples might reverse the process and begin by reading each other's profiles and highlighting where they agree and disagree about how well the profile describes their partner. They might then swap profiles. It would be enlightening, to say the least, to learn how your partner perceives you.

Most daring of all is to go back to Chapter 3 and answer the questions as if you were your partner. That, no doubt, will stimulate a fascinating evening of discussion.

By the way, more in-depth versions of the profiles can be found in our book *Type Talk: The Sixteen Personality Types That Determine How We Live, Love, and Work.* Workplace and management-style profiles are illustrated in our book *Type Talk at Work.*

———————————

◆ FIGHTING TYPES

We don't plan our conflicts and fights—or not as a rule. When they erupt, it is usually a surprise and we most naturally fall back on our strongest preferences:

- **Extraverts** talk louder, faster, and know that if they can "just say one more thing" the whole issue will be cleared up. They want to talk about problems *now;* if they can't, they may get frustrated, even panicky.
- **Introverts,** who are most often at a disadvantage in this setting, are at their best when they have time to think through, rehearse, and have some advance notion of the issues at hand. But fights aren't usually prearranged or rehearsed—unless they are about recurring themes.
- **Sensors** like to argue the facts, the more specific the better. They are prone to sidetrack a bigger issue by focusing in on smaller, less relevant issues.
- **iNtuitives** like to make broad generalizations, often blowing a specific incident into a sweeping pattern. They see the Sensors' emphasis on facts as nitpicking.
- **Thinkers** tend to get too analytical of a dispute, often missing the emotional side of things. Their logical side of the argument may have little to do with the hurt feelings involved.
- **Feelers** tend to personalize everything, even things that weren't intended to be personal. They view disagreements as something to be avoided, and tend to "give in" before an issue is resolved, if only to reestablish harmony.
- **Judgers** "know" they're right. Because they tend to see things in black and white—they demand that others do too—issues for them are very simplistic in nature—it's either this or that, right or wrong, good or bad, et cetera.
- **Perceivers,** who tend to see many options to everything, like to play both (or all) sides of an issue. Unlike the case with Judgers, few things are black and white to Perceivers. They have trouble settling a dispute because there is always more data to examine and another possible solution.

CONFLICT TYPE TALK

IF YOU ARE . . .

	EXTRAVERT	INTROVERT
EXTRAVERT	• Stop competing. Have one party play listener while the other talks. • Remember that the last word may not be the final word. • Try to argue the other's viewpoint. Repeat what you hear the other person saying.	• Demand he or she be silent for a while and listen. • Try to blurt out the first thoughts that come to mind without editing them in advance. • Commit yourself to share your thoughts, even if you need to write them down first.
	EXTRAVERT	INTROVERT
INTROVERT	• Avoid overkill and redundancy. • Say your piece, then back off and allow your partner time to respond. • Jot some thoughts down on paper, perhaps just a list, and show it to your partner.	• Force yourself to speak on issues. Above all, do not avoid conflict by being silent. • Commit yourself to working out the issue together, rather than internally by yourself. • Assume that your partner is experiencing at least as much stress as you are over the conflict.
	SENSOR	INTUITIVE
SENSOR	• Beware of overloading each other with facts and specifics. • When you disagree on details, stop the action, and check each other's accuracy before continuing. • Try to explore the impact and implications of what you are saying.	• Respect that specific facts may be necessary to resolve the conflict. • Help your partner see meanings and implications of the details he or she presents. • Avoid trying to win an argument by focusing only on the big picture.
	SENSOR	INTUITIVE
INTUITIVE	• Keep your partner grounded and specific. • Try to grasp the implications and meanings of what is being said. • Avoid introducing so many details that you lose sight of the bigger picture.	• Recognize that you both tend to avoid facts, or "bend" them to prove your case. • If you disagree on a perception, stop and check it for accuracy before the conflict escalates on misinformation. • Work hard with each other to stay grounded, precise, and in the present.

AND YOUR LOVER IS . . .

IF YOU ARE . . .

AND YOUR LOVER IS . . .		THINKER	FEELER
	THINKER	• Know when to stop analyzing and competing.	• Try to remember that not all criticism is directed at you.
		• Recognize you both have emotions and that hurt feelings may result from your disagreement.	• Stand your ground. State your position and try to stay objective.
		• It is okay to lose the argument. Life will go on.	• Avoid saying "I'm sorry" or "You're right" as much as possible. It's okay to argue. Life will go on.
		THINKER	**FEELER**
	FEELER	• Keep in mind that whatever you are saying will be taken personally, even if you don't mean it that way.	• Face the conflict. Stand tough and don't avoid it.
		• It is okay to say "I'm sorry" when you mean it.	• Try not to press for early resolution of the issue in the name of harmony.
		• Try to show your human side during the conflict.	• Remember that conflict can be a positive experience and that both of you can learn from it.
		JUDGER	**PERCEIVER**
	JUDGER	• Conflicts can't be scheduled—but resolving them can be.	• Recognize that your partner may sound more angry than he or she actually is.
		• Bring up the issues, then schedule a time to deal with them later.	• Help your partner seek alternatives. Keep him or her from trying to come to a quick win-lose resolution.
		• If an issue isn't yet resolved, don't say that it is just to bring closure to the situation.	• Hit and run: Drop the topic of the conflict and leave, then come back and deal with it later.
		JUDGER	**PERCEIVER**
	PERCEIVER	• Allow some latitude for your partner to explore different aspects of the subject.	• Help each other stay focused on only one issue at a time.
		• Push for closure for a positive resolution, not to win an argument.	• State as clearly as possible your opinions and needs. No waffling!
		• Help your partner stay focused and deal with one issue at a time.	• Try to negotiate win-win solutions. Or, decide which of you can "win" and "lose" each issue.

III

PUTTING
TYPE TALK
TO WORK

9

NEGOTIATING THROUGH THE CRISES

"Don't hold me to what I'm saying quite yet."

The success of any intimate relationship is largely based upon the ability of both people to negotiate their needs in such a way as to achieve mutual and guilt-free satisfaction. It is simply not constructive to say yes when you mean no. It can be debilitating to say no and then be shrouded with guilt. Like everything else it's a matter of give and take. The more up-front and direct each party is with that process, the better the relationship will be.

What we're talking about here is negotiating your way through whatever problems arise. That's easier said than done, of course. Some people are naturally good at it, and others would rather do just about anything else. But for everyone it's a necessary process.

It's corny, but true: If you can view the negotiating process as a vehicle to your growth as a couple, every day and in every way you'll get better and better.

It's been said that in negotiations of any kind the perfect solution is one in which neither party gets exactly what he or she wants. And that makes good sense: negotiations are about compromise and finding alternative solutions to seemingly intractable problems. Unfortunately, not everyone is comfortable with this notion; some people are only satisfied with winning, while others seem to expect to lose. That can make the challenge even greater: not only do you have to tiptoe through the delicate minefields of negotiations, you may also find it necessary to negotiate over the issue of negotiating itself!

Negotiations, even successful ones, are only the beginning. To cement the deal you'll need some kind of contract. Don't worry: we're not talking about lawyers here, or even putting anything in writing, although sometimes that's not a bad idea. This is about turning the results of your negotiations into a few specifics: who's going to be responsible for doing what, when does it begin and end, how do you measure success, and so on. In short, you need a plan that both parties can sign on to, verbally or otherwise.

◆

How the Eight Preferences Negotiate and Contract

Before we offer specific tips on how to successfully negotiate and contract, here is some advice for each of the eight preferences on how to approach these matters:

◆ **Extraverts: Remember that talk is cheap.** Sometimes you simply have to close your mouth and open your ears. When negotiating, it may be helpful to say, "Let me ramble on for a bit so I can sort things through. Don't hold me to what I'm saying quite yet. All I need is three or four minutes to think out loud." When your ramble time is up, make sure that you listen closely to the feedback. *Try not to always get in the last word.*

◆ **Introverts: If you don't say it, it won't be heard.** This will not come as news to some Introverts, who often assume that no one's interested in what they have to say. For a negotiation to happen, it takes two people, and both parties must be involved. *So take the time to reflect and think through what you want to say and then say it and even jot down some notes.* It can be helpful occasionally to have a temporary contract in which an Introvert agrees to blurt out the first words that come to his or her mind without necessarily being accountable. It's difficult to do this, but worth every effort.

* **Sensors: Look on the bright side.** Your natural tendency is to assume that the unknown holds more bad than good. Sensors have a tendency to pop the balloons of enthusiasm by interjecting the harsh realities of the situation. Such behavior quashes the negotiating and contracting processes. *Allow yourself the luxury of pretending that whatever the situation, it will work out for the best.* Try to restrain your tendency to look at the dark side of things.

* **iNtuitives: Just do it.** The toughest part for iNtuitives is getting to a bottom line. Whatever decisions you come to, they must be in a form that is reachable, deliverable, and doable. No matter how much you want to amend the contract and revisit the negotiations one more time, don't do it. *Stick to your original, specific agreement.*

* **Thinkers: Don't try to beat the system.** You naturally view negotiations as a game to be won or lost. Relationships are not chessboards to be manipulated and conquered. Resist the temptation to push beyond the limits to see what you can get away with. Be ready, willing, and able to give in for the good of the relationship, even if it doesn't make perfect sense to do so.

* **Feelers: Bite the bullet.** During negotiations you have a tendency to give in easily simply to avoid further conflict. When this happens, you can end up holding a grudge or may use guilt as a lever in future negotiations. Instead, try to stick to your guns. *Don't be afraid to state your needs and stand up for them.*

* **Judgers: You're not always right.** This may come as a

shock, but you must face facts: Though you may be convinced that your point of view is right, you must recognize the possibility that other perspectives may be equally valid. However difficult, try to hang loose. *Don't push for closure or force your point of view.*

◆ **Perceivers: Make a commitment and keep it.** No matter how tempting it is to modify yesterday's commitment in the light of new information, it is important that you fulfill your part of the contract as agreed. Any modifications can make future negotiations difficult because your credibility to live up to agreements will be in jeopardy. *Stick to your original, specific agreement.*

◆

Four Tips for Successful Negotiations

1. Know what you want and how far you are willing to go to get it. To begin any negotiation you have to have a set of demands, or at least "wants." If you're an Introvert, you'll probably want to sit and ponder such matters; if you're an Extravert, you'll want to talk them through, especially with the person involved. If you're a Judger, you may already have a list of things you'd like to see happen in the relationship; if you're a Perceiver, you also may have some ideas, but chances are they haven't yet jelled.

If you're really organized, it's probably best to have some sense of priorities: which items are most important and which can you live without. In a dispute over finances, for example, the issue of rounding off entries in the checkbook may be irritating, but far less important in the scheme of things than the fact that one party wants to quit working full-time to attend graduate school. What's key is to be able to understand the difference between the issues that are significant and those that are merely symbolic.

2. Know what's nonnegotiable. There are some things

about which you feel so strongly that there is little room for give and take. What's interesting is that often people don't recognize these areas until it's too late. For example, there's the all-too-frequent case of differing desires about having children. During dating, courtship, and even during the early years of marriage, the subject may be glossed over or avoided altogether. "Kids? We'll deal with that later. We've got a few years to decide." In reality, one party may be dead set against having children, while the other may think that it is an absolute necessity for the completeness of life. Unfortunately, because neither was up-front about the issue—"Kids? I don't believe in bringing a child into such a dangerous world" or "Kids? I can't imagine life without them. Why else get married?"—two people can enter into a union only to find themselves at polar ends of a nonnegotiable issue. Had they known that, they might not have even gotten married.

Obviously, the more these nonnegotiables can be discussed early on in a relationship, the better. But when they do arise, it's vital that each of you recognizes the seriousness of the issue. It may be more resolvable than it appears on the surface if you can sort out what's important to each of you. This isn't a time for name-calling, blaming, or reminding one another of conversations held long ago.

3. Remember that the only constant thing in a relationship is change. The more dynamic the relationship, the more open it will be to change. As a result nonnegotiables can become negotiable, and new issues can surface that can threaten to jeopardize the relationship. So the woman for whom children was an absolute, nonnegotiable necessity may find herself so caught up in her career that having children no longer seems so important. In the meantime her husband, who earlier in the relationship wasn't particularly interested in being a father, may find that his masculinity and sense of mortality have stirred up stronger parental desires. The result is that this couple finds itself in a nonnegotiable stance, but with a different perspective than that of a few years before. This is a perfectly natural result of change over time.

Once again, this is serious stuff; it's no time for name-calling. Nor is it a time to replay the other's arguments as your own. ("You used to say that having children is the ultimate expression of love. Are you now saying you don't really love me?") If you truly believe in the capacity of people to evolve and change, it is neither fair nor appropriate to hold them to beliefs stated long ago under different circumstances.

4. Understand that the negotiating process is not a scorecard or a win-lose game. It is a process of mutual respect and interdependence. What's important is to have each negotiation or transaction produce a positive result, or at least something with which the two of you can live. Even if one or

---

◆ CHROME AND PUNISHMENT

There are certain things you don't find out about someone until you marry them, or at least live with them. In our case it was how much Otto prizes polished faucets in the bathroom and shower. You can't imagine how much this means to him—and how stressful it is for him when someone emerges from the bath without having taken the time to buff up the faucet with a towel.

Janet, of course, saw things differently. Shining spigots was something left for the weekly (or whenever) cleaning chores. She couldn't believe that her own husband was such a fanatic about something so seemingly trivial.

Still, she wanted to please. And it occurred to her that the process of cleaning up after a shower or bath took less than ten seconds. That, she figured, was a small price to pay for her husband's happiness. For Janet it was a matter of saying, "I'll make you a deal. I'll polish the faucets whenever I use them if you will promise never to leave the bed unmade if you're the last one up."

It was a done deal. We had a contract, and it's never been broken.

both of you is left unsatisfied, the event can still be seen as positive if you are both open to the process. You will be better off because you were able to communicate with each other about the situation, you were able to support one another in recognizing your frustrations, and as a couple you've learned that there's more to your relationship than simply scoring points or chalking up victories.

◆

Three Contracting Success Stories

There's no better way to explain the process of contracting than to tell a few stories of how others have done it. These tales come from our couples' workshop, a weekend program during which couples end up negotiating and contracting about a specific problem area.

1. **"Help me loosen up."** Sam was an off-the-charts Perceiver. His wife, Ella, was a highly structured and rigid Judger. Both were aware of this strong difference and asked us for help: Sam wanted some structure and organization, and Ella wanted to loosen up a bit. Their discussions allowed them to admit a number of important things. For example, Ella recognized that she loved Sam very much, but his indecisiveness drove her crazy. She viewed the situation as right versus wrong; she considered herself right, of course, and felt strongly that Sam should be the one to shape up. And though she tried to back off a bit, she recognized that it would be very difficult.

In the meantime Sam realized that while he appreciated her management skills, he rebelled at organizing for the sake of organizing. Moreover, he felt as "right" about his behavior as Ella felt about hers, though he had less desire to fight every issue tooth and nail. He was willing to go halfway, meeting some of her demands to get organized, if she would meet some of his about loosening up.

Having gotten to this point, contracting was relatively easy. The goal: Sam would be very structured about one thing a week; for example, he would come home for dinner at the same time each night, or complete a particular project. Ella, for her part, was allowed to pick, or at least help Sam pick, that one structured event for the week. That forced her to choose what was really important to her and what wasn't, rather than the usual approach of strong Js, which is to make everything a life-and-death issue. The contract would start seven days from the agreement and would end, or at least be reassessed, three months later. At Sunday brunch each week they would have a checkup and progress report. There would be no exceptions or changes to the plan during that period.

The point of the contract was not to turn Sam into a J, but simply to give Ella one thing upon which she could depend. By the end of ninety days Ella had learned to let go of her control a bit and trust Sam's word, and Sam had learned to view life with at least a modicum of organization. That gave both Sam and Ella a great deal of satisfaction.

2. "I can't make a commitment." That was the constant refrain of Arnold, an INTP, who had been living with Margaret, an ISTJ, for a number of years. Margaret very much wanted to tie the knot, believing very strongly in the stabilizing influence of marriage. Arnold, on the other hand, didn't see how a ring and a vow would improve the very solid relationship they already enjoyed.

Looking at their types, you can see how sharp their differences were. As an ISTJ, Margaret had a high need to do the right thing in the eyes of society, and especially of her parents. Her guilt over not meeting those expectations was **beginning to outweigh** the satisfaction of the relationship **itself. It was also important** for her to have children, and she simply wasn't about to have them out of wedlock.

Arnold could understand Margaret's needs, although he didn't share them. He felt these were things he could be flexible about. And Arnold had his own needs too. As an INTP, he wanted independence, and was concerned that being a father would impinge on his freedom. Margaret, who had less need for independence, understood Arnold and felt she could help accommodate him.

The negotiation process that followed helped each to clarify their different values on this subject and led them to contract about seeking an outside, objective third party to sort through the issues. So they agreed to see a counselor together for three months, then assess whether it was helping them determine one direction or another. They further agreed that each would prepare for the counseling sessions by writing out their points of view, including what was negotiable and what was not. By limiting the number of sessions it would also keep them focused on the subject. Finally, they contracted not to discuss it with anyone else, or with each other without being in the presence of the counselor.

Through the negotiation Margaret and Arnold were able to come to terms on the big items by giving in on some smaller ones. For starters Arnold agreed to get married. Margaret agreed to heed his wishes by having a small ceremony with just a few close friends and family. They agreed they would plan to have at least two children in the first five years of marriage. When that happened, Margaret would quit her job and become a full-time mother, resuming her career when the youngest child turned five. They also agreed that Arnold could have one night each week to himself, to go out with friends or do whatever else he wanted. In addition he could plan two weekends a year to go fishing with his best friend.

One of the things they learned through the negotiating process was that some of these things were already happening. For example, Arnold already had been going fishing with his friend, although he always seemed to get into a fight with

Margaret over these events. The negotiation put it up front, gave it legitimacy, and allowed both of them to feel invested in the process.

In the end, the time constraints, as well as the stringent focus, allowed them to resolve their differences and move toward a total marital commitment. However, that, too, could not be achieved until the full term of the contract had run its course. This allowed them ample time with the counselor to examine all the related issues surrounding their imminent betrothal.

3. "Where will we spend Thanksgiving?" Julia, an ESFJ, and Paul, an INTP, had been married for nearly a decade, but they were still struggling over where they would celebrate Thanksgiving each year. Each of them had a fairly tight-knit family, and both felt pressures to spend the weekend with their respective clans. Unfortunately, the two families lived nearly two thousand miles apart, making it difficult for all of them to celebrate as one giant group. On top of all this Julia and Paul were expecting their first child, and knew that travel would be difficult for a while.

Over the years, as the holiday approached, the tension mounted. Each set of parents, though aware of the difficulty they were having, nonetheless began subtly jockeying to lure Julia and Paul to their respective homes. This simply added to the stress and guilt Julia and Paul were already experiencing.

The obvious solution would be for them to alternate years—one year with her family, the following year at his. But things just weren't that simple. For one thing, Paul's father was having serious health problems, and Paul felt strongly that he wanted to spend as many Thanksgivings as possible with his dad while he could. Julia understood this and was sympathetic, but she didn't relish spending every Thanksgiving with her mother-in-law, who she felt was rather overbearing and at times obnoxious.

As the situation became intolerable, Julia and Paul came to us for help. We began by helping them sort out which areas were negotiable and which were not—the basic first step of any negotiation process. We learned that Paul's father's failing health was an overriding concern for them both—for Paul for obvious reasons, for Julia because she couldn't bear the guilt of denying him his request. It also emerged from our talk that both had a very strong desire to start their own Thanksgiving tradition, a fact they had not previously discussed with each other.

From the discussions Paul and Julia agreed on several things:

• Though Paul's father's illness was an overriding factor, there were other times of the year he could spend with his father. They would visit his father four times in the next year, more than they had been doing up to now.

• With their first child on the way it was a perfect time for them to inform both families that they would be starting their own Thanksgiving tradition. Each year Julia and Paul would invite both of their families to their home, welcoming any or all members who were willing to come.

• Paul agreed to talk with his mother about giving Julia and him more space when they got together instead of constantly being around them and determining how they would spend their time together. He also agreed that he would pay more attention to Julia's needs, rather than follow his usual habit of deferring to his mother's requests.

• They would make an effort to spend some time with Julia's family. When their baby turned two, Julia and Paul would take a vacation with her parents, something she had been pushing them to do for years.

• Both agreed they would put this agreement on paper and would each inform their respective families of the new arrangement.

◆ THE GIFT OF LOVE

It can be helpful to view the negotiating and contracting processes as asking one another for a gift.

If you were to ask a gift of your lover, what would that look like and what would be your expectations? Is it a one-time gift, or a gift that keeps on giving? Should you be direct or indirect in making the request? Would it be more effective to be seductive, playful, or something else? How do you get what you want?

For example, if an Introvert would like some quiet time during the day, you need to think the process through, the more specifics the better: For exactly how long? At what point in the day? Does it go on forever or just for a specific period? Does it apply to weekends? And so on.

Consider an experience we had a few years ago. We had just completed an extremely extraverted week of training and socializing. We were beginning our six-hour drive home when Janet said, "I would like my birthday gift a little early this year."

Eager to please, Otto responded, "Great! What is it?"

"I would like absolute silence in the car from here to home," she responded. "No conversation unless I initiate it."

Otto replied, "Can't I even play the radio?"

"No," answered Janet. The gift she wanted was absolute silence.

It was a challenge to someone as Extraverted as Otto, and yet Janet was so grateful and refreshed when we got home that it seemed worth all the effort. It was not an easy gift to give, but it was a meaningful one, and it was received with great appreciation.

It was all very simple: a request (making your needs known), a little stretching and giving, and ultimately a great sense of accomplishment and satisfaction for both parties.

It wasn't easy at first. Neither felt comfortable informing their parents, and the first Thanksgiving seemed a little awkward. However, what became very clear from the process was their mutual commitment and the importance of having their own family traditions. It was this awareness that gave them the confidence and sustenance to accomplish this difficult task with satisfaction on everyone's part.

What is apparent in each of these three stories is that if the contract is clear and both parties agree to it, the conflict can be tolerated—at least for a while. There will be plenty of opportunity to share insights and feelings before moving on to a new phase.

In each case it was the vagueness of the other's actions and intentions, and the lack of prospect for change, that created so much stress for the parties involved. Contracting is one way to gently promote behavioral changes and modifications that can be beneficial to the relationship.

◆

Four Tips for Successful Contracting

1. **Agree on when to begin and when to end.** Whatever you agree to do, don't put it on a back burner or say you'll "get around to it." Good intentions alone won't cut it; you must have a specific plan, with a specific starting date and some planned duration. For example, you might contract to say "I love you" to each other once a week for the next three months. After that you may decide to renew or renegotiate the contract. Even if it's your intent to do these things forever, you're better off keeping your contractual periods shorter. That keeps whatever you promised tangible and alive.

2. **Have some means of measurement.** If you agree to say "I love you" once a week, there needs to be some periodic checkpoints in order to determine that the contract is being fulfilled. It's a way of keeping both parties actively involved. Depending on the specific contract there needs to be time set aside where each of you shares how things are going, and decides whether or not your efforts are actually accomplishing what you set out to do.

3. Set attainable goals. Nothing breeds success like success, and nothing is more frustrating than setting your sights too high. If you were to contract to say "I love you" every day, or even every Thursday, it might be impractical, perhaps impossible, to pull off. That would set each of you up for disappointment. We've known couples who have contracted never to remove their wedding rings. But life inevitably gets in the way, causing some accident, weight gain, or other unforeseen event that forces a ring to be removed temporarily or permanently.

4. Make sure it's something to which you both can commit. If one person can't live with the contract, then it's doomed to fail. So it needs to be talked through thoroughly, written down and signed if necessary, so that both of you are crystal clear about the commitment. If you're vague, there will inevitably be wiggle room for one or both of you to violate or skirt the agreement. That can be worse than having no contract at all, because it can breed contempt and distrust rather than support and encouragement.

◆

When All Else Fails

Unfortunately, things don't always go according to plan. Sometimes negotiations fail and contracts are violated. Sometimes resentments run so deep that no contract could possibly resolve them. Whatever the cause—from unfaithfulness to two people growing apart due to natural changes over time—some relationships are simply beyond repair.

When that is the case, it is our conviction that the most constructive thing to do for everyone involved is to call it a day.

Please understand: We don't take this step lightly. And we believe that over the past quarter century, the institution of marriage (and committed relationships in general) have been taken too lightly. It seems as though we marry for better, for richer, and in health. And when "worse," "poorer," or "sickness" set in, we're out the door faster than you can say "I don't." We've seen far too many people run away from relationships that we believe had potential for mutual fulfillment.

Still, if you have done all of the above, and it's clear that things are not likely to get better, you owe it to yourself, and possibly to your mate, to find a humane and civil means to end the relationship.

As much as we discourage divorce, we'd be remiss if we didn't proclaim how much Typewatching can be helpful even in these situations. In fact, as trained and certified divorce mediators, both of us have found Typewatching to be extremely helpful in coming to grips with the personality issues that can drive separations and divorces.

For example, knowing that Thinking-Judgers can get frozen in their positions gives us the freedom to confront that in a mediation setting. They'll view the proceedings as a win-lose proposition rather than a give-and-take process. And knowing that Feeling-Perceivers have a tendency to sell out in the name of harmony and expediency can help us head off a situation that will inevitably lead to guilt and resentment that can take years of therapy to remedy. "Here, take the family pictures," the FP might say to an estranged spouse, "I don't need them." And for a decade or more the FP may resent having made that impulsive move.

Even in a situation as negative as divorce Typewatching can help us manage ourselves by allowing us to understand our strengths and weaknesses. Of course, that is exactly how Typewatching can help keep us out of Divorce Court too.

But even Typewatching doesn't do it every time. Nor is it the answer to every relationship problem. There are other resources worth considering, including professional counselors, clergy, and friends who know you well, value their relationship with you, and will be honest with you. Until you've explored all of the alternatives available and secured as much objective advice as possible, it may be premature to call it quits.

We can't state strongly enough the importance of giving a relationship everything you've got. That's why we believe completely in Typewatching: it provides a means for resolving tough issues in a way that can leave both parties feeling encouraged, energized, and positive about their future.

◆

When Relationships Are Over

There's no "right" or easy way to get out of a relationship, but there certainly are some wrong and difficult ones.

Just as there is a tendency for some of us to get into relationships for the wrong reasons—we're pushing forty and

---

◆ IF YOU LOVED THE BOOK . . .

We were at a book signing in Boulder, Colorado, a few years ago for one of our previous books, when a sixtysomething woman approached Janet and said, "Your book saved my marriage."

Flattered, Janet responded with a heartfelt thank-you. But the woman persisted: "You don't understand. It *really* saved our marriage."

She went on. "You see, my husband and I were already separated when I heard you talking on a local radio show. I purchased your book and in no time determined my type and my husband's type, which was very different from mine.

"I laughed, I cried, and mostly I saw so much of our marital struggles through the years that I finished the book and sent it to him, saying, 'Read this before we go any farther, and then let's talk.'

"He did, we did, and this year we will be celebrating our forty-sixth anniversary."

haven't yet married; we're pregnant and feel obligated to the unborn child; the invitations have been sent and it's too late to call things off—it is just as common for some of us to remain in relationships long after they're dead.

For example:

* **Feeling** types, and especially **iNtuitive-Feelers,** can be reluctant to say good-bye, prodding themselves, "Where have I failed? What have I done wrong? If only I try a little harder, maybe this relationship can turn around." They frequently become defensive of their ne'er-do-well mate, taking upon themselves the total failure of the relationship. Shrouded with guilt, they are too paralyzed to do anything constructive.

* **Thinkers,** and especially **iNtuitive-Thinkers,** can be reluctant to declare a relationship ended because they believe there is still more to be learned—if nothing else, about why the relationship failed. As a result they see the failed relationship as a paradigm that needs to be redesigned and reinvented. Surely, they say, if we can only understand the root causes that produced the failure, it will be a simple matter to restructure the relationship in a way that will engender future success.

* **Judgers,** and especially **Sensing-Judgers,** can hang on to a relationship long after it's dead because they are reluctant to break what they consider to be an irrevocable vow. They may sleep in separate bedrooms, barely speak, and generally avoid one another, but they'll keep up a good front for the sake of the kids, the community, all in the name of family values.

* **Perceivers,** and especially **Sensing-Perceivers,** are the least likely to stick around once the music stops. Their tolerance for a failed relationship is minimal. "Why stick around if we keep turning in the same old circles and there's little likelihood of change?" they might ask. "Life's too short to stay in a bad relationship." In their continual quest to live

for the moment they are the most likely of all types to give their best, and failing that, to simply get out of the way.

◆

Nothing Succeeds Like Success

Suffice it to say, we truly hope your relationship never comes to this point. And with Typewatching we believe it's far more likely to succeed. That's especially true when you consider the amount of time and energy (not to mention money) that can be expended in trying to end a relationship. If only a fraction of those resources were put into keeping it alive, fun, and dynamic, there'd be no need to call in the lawyers.

Relationships give each of us meaning and fulfill our growth. All of us are better off for the impact of our partner, our children, and our extended families. The fun, the laughter, the moments of intimacy, seem to make it all worthwhile. In their later years couples repeatedly give testimony to how much their partner keeps them young and—even after forty or fifty years—keeps them learning.

To get to this point requires undeniably hard work and a lot of give and take. That's why we bother with all of this negotiating and contracting. The process helps us clear out the interpersonal cobwebs that can mess up an otherwise tidy relationship. It is these seemingly trivial matters—the ones we shove off into the corner and forget about—that can build up over time and present themselves when we least expect it.

With Typewatching you'll be ready to take them on, and turn them into positive, life-affirming experiences.

◆

How to Be an Artful Negotiator

ESTP: Think long-term. Because you are good with details, keep your options specific and rooted in the here and now. Remember that the agreement you will reach will probably last longer than your interest in it. Make sure you agree to things you can live with.

ESFP: Take one thing at a time. Your easygoing manner can be read as insincere. So try to be more earnest and state clearly what's important to you. Above all, don't muddle the process with endless options.

ISTP: Express your concerns. You are good at listening and remaining open, so try to help draw out your partner's positions and needs. But don't be so objective so as to appear uninvested in the process.

ISFP: Take care of yourself. While you don't care much about winning, don't let your natural concern for others get in the way of your own needs. Pleasing your partner is important, but it will be of little use if you don't please yourself as well.

ESTJ: Let the other person win. You are objective, capable, and committed to the process, but it isn't imperative that you win every time. By doing so you risk coming off as abrasive and argumentative, even if that's not how you feel.

ESFJ: Stick with it. Your genuine need for harmony and your gracious style can lead you to grasp at any solution, regardless of whether it meets your needs. It's important for you to see the process through to completion, however painful that may be. Otherwise you'll end up feeling guilty.

ISTJ: Keep an open mind. It is important for you to see negotiation as a process, rather than as a win-lose event. Use your naturally good listening skills to stay open, rather than coming to closure before all points of view have been expressed.

ISFJ: Remember your own needs. You feel a sense of duty to make your partner happy, often at your own expense. State your position and don't personalize it if your partner disagrees with you. The tension is natural, and seeing it through will inevitably get you both to a better place.

ENTJ: Say something nice. The world won't come to an end if you give in a little, so don't be afraid to bend. Keep in mind that your natural directness and clarity with words can intimidate your partner. Your objectivity is a powerful asset, but remember to express your emotional side too.

ENTP: Try not to compete. You like to wheel and deal, but be careful not to turn everything into a game. Your creativity with options can be very helpful during negotiations, but it's important to know when to stop generating new ideas and settle on something.

INTJ: Show your interest. Don't let your naturally good listening skills make you appear aloof. Express your support for the other person's idea along with your disagreements. Be careful that your need to win doesn't get in the way of seeing the big picture.

INTP: Keep it simple. You embrace the negotiation process, but don't get so caught up in it that you forget the important issues at hand. Some solutions are relatively simple; try not to make them more complex than necessary.

ENFJ: Stay objective. Your natural smooth-talking persuasiveness can be effective in small doses, but smothering if overdone. Try to resist the temptation to affirm every new idea and stance lest it sound phony. Make the most of your desire to create win-win solutions.

ENFP: Stop and listen. Your concern for both the people and the process makes you a natural negotiator. In your enthusiasm, though, you can be a poor listener, constantly jumping in with your ideas, which your partner may interpret as competitive. Try to hear your partner out.

INFJ: Keep things guilt free. You like to be helpful however you can, but you risk muddying the process by making your own needs secondary. Try to keep guilt out of the negotiating process; resist the temptation to give it or get it. By remaining objective you'll be better able to be inspirational when needed.

INFP: Be direct. Don't be self-effacing in order to move things along. Remember, your needs are important and if you don't give them their due, they'll come back to haunt you. Your genuine concern for your partner is your most precious asset during negotiations.

10

MAKING LOVE
LAST FOREVER

*"Is the trouble with me,
or with the 'me' I see in you?"*

When it comes to relationships, hope springs eternal. Practically everyone enters into a relationship with the best of intentions that it will last forever. They think their relationship is unique, and though they have seen other relationships experience a variety of problems, every couple firmly believes their relationship is better. They feel they have talked through their differences and settled them in such a way that will enable them to live happily ever after.

Obviously that's not always the case. And when the honeymoon is over, even the most capable of couples discover that there are many, many things yet to be learned and untold hurdles to overcome.

It is our conviction that Typewatching is one of the greatest keys to living happily ever after. With such a set of skills and tools each couple can become more capable of dealing with their differences creatively and strengthening the foundation upon which the relationship has been built. Typewatching is a refreshing and positive way to prevent ourselves from repeating self-defeating behaviors—behaviors that haven't worked in the past and aren't likely to work in the future.

◆

Five Easy Pieces

Speaking in generalities is a risky business. General comments often are overstated for one half of the population and understated for the other half, without accurate substantiation for either. Still, there is a kernel of truth in most such statements that can be of value.

When it comes to intimate relationships, we'd like to pose five generalities that point up areas in which Typewatching can be a lifesaver:

1. Intimate relationships involve two people who must be responsible for their own actions. Relationships are not made in heaven, they are made on Earth by fallible humans. Because we're human, we need as much help as possible, and Typewatching, more than anything else we know, provides a positive frame of reference with which to help a couple at every stage of their relationship. Typewatching provides a positive explanation of why we behave the way we do so we can own up to our responsibilities. It provides helpful hints to smooth the rough edges that are a part of any relationship. And through the self-knowledge Typewatching brings, both parties are better equipped to handle conflict, negotiate, and get the most out of each moment.

2. There are no easy relationships. It takes a great deal of understanding, hard work, and effort to keep a relationship strong and vital. Strength and vitality come from knowing what's important to you and your partner—learning how to please as well as meet your own needs. The difference between what takes work in a relationship and what comes naturally is all part of the wisdom upon which relationships rely to remain positive and growthful.

The more you know about yourself, the greater the freedom to negotiate, appreciate, facilitate, and respond to a variety of needs, both yours and your mate's. For example, if you are an Extravert, you can say, "I need to hear you say 'I love you' more often." If your mate is an Introvert, he or she can do a little stretching to meet that need. If your mate needs more time and space alone, you can learn to allow for introverted time and even protect your mate from being tempted by all the extraverted demands and enticements the world offers.

3. There is attraction in opposites. We've said it before, but it's worth repeating: We are naturally drawn to qualities in others that reflect the parts of ourselves we feel are lacking or underdeveloped. So we often choose partners who are very different from us, at least in their personalities.

However, too much similarity in preferences between two people can also be problematic. In fact, if you are drawn to someone who shares all four of your preferences, we believe it will be a heaven-or-hell relationship, with very little in between. When things are going well, they go *very* well, because you are at psychological peace with yourself. When things go badly, they go *very* badly, because you *know* there is something wrong, but don't know what it is. "Is the trouble with me, or with the 'me' I see in you (because you're just like me)? I can see it in you ten times more quickly than I can see it in me, and I don't like it in you."

By the way, even a single preference similarity can lead to some version of this inner conversation. So, for example, when two Js, or two Es, or two of anything, get into a tiff, sometimes the source of the problem is something about themselves that they are experiencing in the other person. A J might become impatient with another J's rigidity and complain, "Why can't you loosen up?" Or an Extravert might complain that another E never listens. In both cases they may actually be talking to themselves.

If you've been drawn to a four-preference opposite, there's good news and bad news. The good news is that the two of you cover both psychological halves of the relationship. The bad news is that every time you look at each other, you are looking at that part of your personality you rejected when you had the chance to make the choice. (Remember that each of us is born with a leaning toward a set of preferences, then makes choices about those preferences as we grow and develop.) No doubt this can make for a complex existence.

In our workshops we always ask couples to identify what aspects of their partner's personality they find most attractive. We also ask them to attach a preference letter to it, if possible. After some discussion we then ask the couples to identify those aspects of their mates' personality that are least attractive, or a source of interpersonal heartburn. Again, we ask them to attach a preference letter to it.

Repeatedly the same preferences surface as both the attraction and the stress. People in intimate relationships frequently report that what they find most exciting and stimulating about their mate has to do with the same part of their own personality that causes them stress. For example, someone might state that they love their mate's structure and organization. And in the next breath will describe how confining and rigid their mate can be. Both behaviors, of course, come from being a Judger.

If there's one thing we want you to understand about all this, it's that those things that are most exciting and attractive to you about your mate, will also cause grief galore in the natural course of events. The heightened awareness that comes from Typewatching can be a source of perspective when the relationship becomes frustrating, and a source of satisfaction and joy when things are working.

4. There is a reason you chose the person you did. For some people their mate represents the parts of themselves they were missing—an Introvert who becomes involved with an Extravert in order to gain a more outgoing life-style, for example. Others link up with someone who represents that part of themselves they like best. Most of us probably do a little of each, picking someone who shares some things we like about ourselves and some things that fill in the gaps.

It is only when we get into an intimate relationship with someone who is typologically different from ourselves that we can appreciate the fullest dimensions of those differences. Through Typewatching the attraction of those differences can become a way in which each of you grows and supports the other. For example, if you're an Introvert, instead of being intimidated by an Extravert you can come to appreciate the beauty of this preference and become free to embrace it within your life. Rather than complaining about your Extraverted mate being a busybody, you can use Typewatching to understand and appreciate the virtue in his or her taking charge of your social calendar.

If you chose someone who shares most of your personality preferences, then Typewatching allows you to become aware of your foibles and your mutual "blind spots" and to deal with them in more constructive ways. For example, if you are both Perceivers, you may be able to remind each other that you have been putting off an important decision for weeks, rather than feeling guilty or blaming each other over the procrastination. And two Judgers can recognize that their "blind spot" comes from being so persnickety about the cleanliness and order of their home that they panic over the impending visit of relatives. Through Typewatching they can learn to laugh at how structured and rigid they've become, and perhaps develop a plan to cope with the familial invasion.

5. Intimate relationships require a commitment to lifelong learning and growth. As we said in Chapter 2, most of us come to appreciate our nonpreferences as we get older. That means that over the years couples may find themselves relating very differently to each other. In the extreme, the result can be a lifelong situation of continually growing or developing in an opposite direction.

For example, the period of life when the Extravert is more reflective and contemplative will be the same period of time that an Introverted partner may be more gregarious and outwardly oriented. As a result these two people may find themselves unhelpful and unsupportive of their mate. When the Extravert says, "I think we need to think about this for a while," the Introvert's comeback may be "Hey, I've been telling you that for years. It's time to quit thinking and start doing."

Typewatching can keep couples from beating up on each other—emotionally, that is. Their natural course of development will lead them to be in opposite states of mind. Instead of criticizing each other for being different, it might be more constructive to simply allow the differences to emerge and learn to appreciate them.

You can never learn too much about yourself and your mate. As a relationship grows, this ongoing self-discovery is a vital component of a successful and wholesome union. It's an ongoing movement away from "my way" to an excitement and respect for "our way."

◆

Turning Differences into Strengths

As we've said throughout this book, your strength maximized can become a liability. Now we'd like to offer another thought: The differences in your relationships can become its strengths.

How can something that causes so much heartache be such an asset? That's where Typewatching can be a real relationship lifesaver.

Keep in mind, as we said earlier, that your differences were part of the initial attraction that brought you together.

As you get more intimate, you can turn those very same differences into vulnerabilities. So the rock-solid groundedness of the Sensor may be very attractive to an iNtuitive who's always lost in the clouds. But as their intimacy grows, so can the sniping—in this case, over S-N issues. "You are such a nitpicker," says the N. Replies the S: "I get really tired of your glossing over what actually exists and not seeing things as they really are."

If, through Typewatching, you can remember the attraction of that difference, your mate can become the key to your own growth in that same area.

To illustrate, we'll use a J-P example that's very close to home. A few years ago the two of us had a hard time communicating when we had disagreements. Otto, an Extraverted-Judger, would talk louder, and in his determination would sound angrier and angrier. Janet, an Introverted-Perceiver, would close down, refusing to discuss the situation with such an angry person. To which Otto would exclaim, "I'm not angry, damn it. If that's how you hear it, it's your problem!" And the conversation would usually end with no resolution.

After years of hard work we've managed to recast this frequent discussion to the point where the following conversation can take place:

> Janet: "I know that you are not angry, but you sure sound that way. Listen to what you're saying."
> Otto: "I hear that and you're right. Let me rephrase what I'm trying to say."

And with those two simple statements we find ourselves in a much better place to continue whatever issue we were discussing. There's a much greater chance that we'll come to some resolution on it, usually to the satisfaction of both.

To an outsider this conversation snippet may sound so simple as to be obvious. But it wasn't obvious to us, and it took us several years of frustration and hard work to reach this milestone.

It was a classic case of turning attractions into differences, and back into attractions. In this case Janet was attracted to Otto's gregarious determination (EJ). And Otto appreciated Janet's reflective flexibility (IP). But in the heat of the moment Janet would chide Otto for being loud, abrasive, and closed—in other words, for being an EJ. And Otto would get extremely frustrated with Janet's being so quiet and unable to come to the point—classic traits of an IP. It made each of us very defensive, exacerbating our inability to deal constructively with the issue at hand.

How did we turn that around? We did it by cashing in on our strengths. Janet helped Otto use his Extraversion more constructively by saying something like "Don't stop talking, but try to say it differently, and try not to sound so angry." ("And by the way," she might add, "I'm standing next to you. You don't need to shout.") In other words she asked Otto to more constructively focus his EJ preferences by turning down the volume and sounding more open to discussion. She doesn't ask him to become an Introvert or a Perceiver; Otto can still be his EJ self in the process.

As he does this, Otto gives Janet more room to counter her IP tendencies by letting her express herself at her own pace. Moreover, rather than her simply raising questions about the issues ("Do you really have to take care of this today?" "Why do I have to give you a definite answer now?"), he encourages her to state her opinions. ("It would help a lot if I knew your opinion on the subject. You can change it later on if you want, but I need to know where you stand right now.") Janet being an Introvert, Otto knows that the answers may take some time before being expressed. (In the past he might have prodded her with "So, what do you think? Just say something so I know you're still with me.")

This same process works with any preference difference. There are two key things to remember:

* ◆ Making jabs at differences makes people defensive.
* ◆ Supporting differences encourages constructive dialogue.

Let's see how this works with each of the eight preferences:

TO EXTRAVERTS
* ◆ **Jab:** "You're not going to get anywhere by shouting at me!"
* ◆ **Support:** "I want to hear what you're trying to say. I would appreciate it if you would say it more softly."

TO INTROVERTS
* ◆ **Jab:** "Don't just sit there. Say something!"
* ◆ **Support:** "I would like to hear your point of view. Would you like some time to think things over?"

TO SENSORS
* ◆ **Jab:** "You're missing the point because you're hung up on the details."
* ◆ **Support:** "I agree with your points. Let's try to put things in perspective."

TO INTUITIVES
* ◆ **Jab:** "As usual, you're not dealing with reality."
* ◆ **Support:** "I like your perspective. I also think it's important to review the facts."

TO THINKERS
* ◆ **Jab:** "You obviously don't give a damn about anybody but yourself."
* ◆ **Support:** "What you're saying makes sense. I think it would help to consider the feelings of everyone involved."

TO FEELERS
- **Jab:** "Stop taking things so personally."
- **Support:** "I understand your feelings. Let's try to stay objective about the situation."

TO JUDGERS
- **Jab:** "Stop being so rigid about this!"
- **Support:** "I understand your point. Are you closed on this or is there room for discussion?"

TO PERCEIVERS
- **Jab:** "We'll never get anywhere if you can't make a simple decision."
- **Support:** "I'd like to help you sort things out so we can move toward a decision."

If you examine the above statements, you'll notice two things:

- The "jab" statements tend to be direct and highly judgmental—in other words, TJ.
- The "support" statements tend to be more empathic and flexible—in other words, FP.

That would follow with our theory that the TJs are the types that tend to take charge and be in control, while the FPs are the types that tend to move through life more supportively and adaptively.

You'll also notice that the "jab" statements more typically use the word *you*, while the "support" statements all contain the pronoun *I*. That makes good sense. By moving the conversation from the other person's faults ("you") to your own judgments and perceptions ("I"), you declare your investment in resolving the conflict while stating your own position.

◆ A WORD TO THE "WHY'S"

When raising a question during an argument, try not to begin a question with the word *why.* The very nature of the word tends to put people on the defensive and often the question is unanswerable. "Why are you late?" will likely be heard as an accusation, whereas "I was concerned about you. What happened?" is more likely to be heard as both supportive and inquiring. In the process you're more likely to avoid leaving the person without room to move in the conversation.

That removes the conversation from a harsh, accusatory mode and places it in a more constructive context.

All of the above can be helpful during any conflict, of course, but it is a survival tool in the special dynamics that accompany intimate relationships. There, like nowhere else, are there likely to be typological differences between two people. And through the closeness of day-to-day living we become far more skilled at using those differences to push each other's buttons—for better or for worse.

◆

Two for One

Couples who are lucky enough to celebrate twentieth, thirtieth, fortieth wedding anniversaries and beyond often enjoy an element of richness that can be experienced only by the give-and-take of marriage.

You've no doubt heard the expression "They've been together so long, they're beginning to look alike." That can also happen typologically, because over time two people can help each other "round off" their rough edges. That means a hard-core Extravert married to an Introvert will inevitably become a better listener, if only as a marriage survival skill.

And an overly empathic Feeler married to a Thinker can over time learn to not take everything so personally.

What is important to remember is that neither party's personality has changed. But in a constructive manner both are able to appreciate and learn from their mate's opposite preferences.

In a way that's what marriage is all about. For an intimate relationship to work over the long term, it has to go beyond sex, procreation, financial security, and other such tangible criteria upon which we frequently measure success. The real measure is the degree to which two people can give up some of their selves in exchange for gaining an appreciation of their mate. And in the process both become more complete individuals.

As a couple you're still two—but you're truly one.

♦ HOW TO BE AN ENCHANTING SPOUSE

ESTP: Settle down. You love excitement, surprise, and variety, but that is not always comforting for a mate. Give more attention to "settling" events. Once in a while be on time, hang around when things are boring, show respect for family traditions by doing things just the way they were done before.

ESFP: Stay on track. You are very good at meeting the needs of many people at once, but that means that you may be sidetracked in so many directions, you don't meet the "routine" needs of your mate. An example is the parent who agrees at the last minute to take one kid to Little League at six, and another to the gym at seven, while his or her mate is at home waiting for dinner that was scheduled for six-thirty.

ISTP: Be impractical. Lots of exciting ideas for expressing affection pass through your mind, like building your spouse a coffee table, or entering "I love you" into the data disk. But you put the ideas down as being impractical or stupid or flighty. Don't argue with yourself. Go ahead and act on your affectionate impulses sometimes.

ISFP: Use words. You think words are cheap and would rather express your affection in more tangible ways, like baking muffins (nothin' says lovin' like somethin' from the oven), or bringing home a huge bouquet. But once in a while use the written or spoken word. Stick a note in the muffin or on the flowers that says, "I love you, dummy."

ESTJ: Don't take it back. You like to show affection in a "macho" way; the slap on the back is a classic example, or saying something abrasive, like "You're all right for an old coot." Try not to give affection with one hand and take it back with the other. Just come out and say, "I love you."

ESFJ: Show anger. Your desire to mother/smother means you may sweep problems under the carpet rather than face them. You reach too soon for the chicken soup; the world is not going to come to an end if you show anger. Don't be afraid to fight.

ISTJ: Praise good behavior. You tend not to praise good behavior because it's expected. But you should train yourself to add overt pats on the head and words of appreciation, for big or small things, to your list of things to do. And make it a rule to say "I love you" at least once a week. It's part of your duty toward your spouse.

ISFJ: Be more assertive. Your mate would probably like to tell you, "I appreciate your twenty years of loyalty, but I wish you'd get mad once in a while." Getting angry with you is like eating cotton candy: you bite into it and it disappears. That's not constructive for anyone. Try to be more assertive and less committed to duty at any price.

ENTJ: Share your softness. You have the same temptation as the ESTJ, to give affection with one hand and take it back with the other, but you do it through sarcasm rather than macho remarks. Try to share your softness by itself, without caustic wit.

ENTP: Just do it! You see that details in the house need attending to, but instead of doing them, you try to design a system that will attend to them. Then when your spouse confronts you with the unfinished work, you get self-righteous and won't give in and do it. For the good of the relationship don't worry about beating the system. Just do what needs to be done—right away.

INTJ: Give a hand. You're very independent, but please don't demand the same thing from your mate. Give mates support and assistance. Don't let them sink three times in order to learn how to swim.

INTP: Speak from the heart. When you try to use your thinking to express your love, the meaning can get lost in translation. Share the fact that you *feel* love, not only *understand* it.

ENFJ: Allow disagreement. You usually assume that your mate is in complete agreement, but if your mate raises a few normal questions, you overpersonalize it and get very hurt. Allow your mate some room to disagree.

ENFP: Face today's problems. Rather than face a disagreement part of the relationship, you'll seduce yourself and your spouse into a happier place. Don't escape so quickly into your imagination or the future. Try to solve your present problems.

INFJ: Show that you know. You're very aware of people's feelings; you seldom need an explanation of interpersonal dynamics, but you don't always do something about them. You know very well that your mate needs a stroke or an "I love you," but it's not your day to give strokes so you clam up. Push yourself to give when your mate needs it, not only when you feel "inspired."

INFP: Offer advice. You have a great gift for helping people understand their feelings and feel better about themselves, but you have no confidence that you're being of any help. Don't be so tentative in offering advice, consolation, and appreciation to your mate.

We started this book by proclaiming that there are no easy relationships. And we'd like to close this section by underscoring that same point. Whatever it was that brought you together in the first place—even if it seems to have been an "accident"—there was some spark, some attraction, something magic between the two of you. It's rare when that happens, and it shouldn't be taken lightly. In fact, during your darkest moments it's often helpful to return to that beginning, recalling and trying to recapture that spark, attraction, and magic. Though it may seem elusive, there's a good chance it's still there, waiting to be rekindled.

Over the past two decades understanding personality differences has proven over and over to be the spark that ignites and reignites couples—from teenage attractions to marriages nearing their golden anniversaries. Its positive, affirming approach can cut through the clutter and the barriers of day-to-day living, creating opportunities for constructive and fulfilling relationships.

◆ WHAT'S YOUR STORY?

Got a good story about how Typewatching helped your relationship? We'd love to hear it. Tell us in as much detail as possible, including the types of the people involved, if known. We promise not to reveal your name without your permission.

Send them to us at Otto Kroeger Associates, 3605 Chain Bridge Road, Fairfax, VA 22030.

APPENDIX

THE 16 RELATIONSHIP PROFILES

We must warn you that there is danger in creating typological profiles because they can be viewed as rigid boxes encompassing a varying and static set of characteristics. That can make them more confining than liberating, ironically defeating the whole point of Typewatching, which is to allow room for you to be yourself and others to be themselves. We do not intend these profiles to be the final statements; rather, they are intended as points of reference for insight into yourself and others.

Please keep in mind that profiles are *general descriptions* of the behavior of the various types. There are many things that are not covered in these brief sketches.

First and foremost, there are gender differences: the male version of any given type is likely to be markedly different from the female of the same type. This is due to a number of factors, including societal scriptings (men are breadwinners and in charge of finances; women are in charge of the home and nurturing the children), family values (the role models provided by parents and others), and religion (formal training, or the lack of it, can be a very powerful agent in shaping personalities).

237

Second, because our personalities are continually developing and evolving over time, these profiles don't reflect age differences—the way any given type might appear over the course of the age spectrum. For example, as we grow and mature, most of us come to appreciate that our nonpreferences can add richness to our lives. However, that maturing process can take a great deal of time. As a result, a twenty-year-old of a given type may seem very different from a fifty-year-old of the same type. But when you examine their basic personality styles and drives, one would conclude that they share the same four letters.

◆

How to Use the Profiles

What's important about these profiles is how you use them. Here are some tips:

◆ Use them where they apply to you and your lover— where they are insightful and helpful, and give you confidence to manage yourself more effectively in your relationship.

◆ The profiles may be especially helpful in understanding some particular thing that bothers you about someone. Recognizing that a particularly bothersome trait is a natural part of someone's personality type may help reduce the concern that that person is out to get you.

◆ Avoid using the profiles to defend your own personality quirks. Remember: Typewatching offers only an explanation, never an excuse. Recognizing that a particular personality trait is bothersome to others, though a natural part of who you are, doesn't give you license to continue the behavior, but may help you to manage it more effectively.

◆ Above all, avoid using the profiles to bash someone. It is so easy to play "See, I told you. Now, shape up." That's just not helpful for anyone, and it's a serious misuse of these profiles, and of Typewatching.

ISTJ

Love Is a Goal Worth Achieving

GENERAL STATEMENT: Responsibility is their driving force, and after God they are most responsible to their mate, children, parents, in-laws, and friends, in that order. Fun—like work, sex, money, and everything else—is usually a part of their to-do list. If a successful relationship is not on the list, it simply won't happen. If it is, you can count on them to work hard to achieve that goal.

FIRST IMPRESSIONS: Neat, trim, crisp, and always appropriate, whatever the situation. Sharp dressers, who speak with precision. At times they may seem too crisp and even appear somewhat critical.

COMMUNICATIONS: They are good with words and always willing to assume responsibility for making sure communication takes place clearly and effectively. If not careful, ISTJs can transform a conversation into a win-lose proposition, prematurely curtailing further discussion.

SEX AND INTIMACY: They are slow to express their feelings and while their intimacies may run very, very deep, little of that depth is likely to be shared. Physical intimacy will be scheduled with attention paid to gender appropriateness: who initiates it, who's aggressive, who assumes the dominant role, and who's on top.

FINANCE: These are the financiers of the world—actuaries, accountants, brokers, bankers, and so on. As the guardians of money they are experts at handling it, and are pleased to do so. Though somewhat conservative, they are most forthright in their financial dealings.

CONFLICT: In general they don't believe in the concept. The only conflict is when someone disagrees with their point of view, which they assume to be correct. Therefore, conflict resolution can become an exercise in converting the other person over to their point of view.

COMMITMENT: Their word is their bond. A commitment made is forever, and they expect the same in return. Having once committed to something, only the fulfillment of this obligation or death is satisfactory.

PARENTING: The ISTJ's motto: A place for everything, and everything in its place; a role for everyone, and everyone in his or her role. Children should behave like children, mommies like mommies, and daddies like daddies. Don't change God's order.

CONTRACTING: Such an exercise seems unnecessary to ISTJs, because they and everyone else should be bound by their original commitments. However, if any contract is deemed appropriate, then it becomes the law.

ENDING RELATIONSHIPS: The ISTJ is slow to break any commitment, no matter how unpleasant it may be. However, if the ISTJ feels the relationship should be over, then the best thing to do is to accept that reality and get to work doing what must be done.

ISFJ
Service Before Self

GENERAL STATEMENT: They are the embodiment of home and hearth. Duty to mate and children precedes all else. ISFJs have a phenomenal capacity to tend to the needs of everyone else around them before they bother to take care of themselves. The danger is that others are likely to take advantage of their generosity and dependability; they can become the family door-mat. But they are dependable nonetheless, making them a stabilizing factor in a relationship.

FIRST IMPRESSIONS: Their quietness belies their rock-solidness. They dress and act appropriately, usually offering the correct word for any situation. Their presence is felt, but it is not invading. After an initial encounter one is likely to say, "What a pleasant person to be around."

COMMUNICATIONS: Though slow to express their own needs, they are straightforward and precise when they do speak. They are not given to argument, and expect others to act similarly. They can spot phoniness at a glance; they recognize when they are being snowed by a mate, child, or anyone else. For them communication is a simple matter: Say what you mean and mean what you say.

FINANCE: They are very good with facts and figures, though they tend to be conservative in money matters. Though they often underestimate their math abilities, they are masters at handling the family checkbook. They are not likely to go into debt; for them you can't spend money until you have it. Credit cards are the bane of their existence because they know cards can entice people to spend money they don't yet have, causing them to lose control of their finances.

CONFLICT: As with other Feelers, conflict can be difficult. They must be pushed to the limit before they will bother to openly disagree. When they do, it can be like a dam that has burst: They may unleash a pent-up laundry list of faults, slights, and wrongdoings. Though they may feel guilty after such an outburst, they will likely view it as a purging and refreshing experience.

SEX AND INTIMACY: Their intimacy is more an act of duty than a free, open expression of love. However, it is through such duty that a relationship can deepen and grow, thereby making intimacy itself more satisfying and meaningful. ISFJs see intimacy as an opportunity to say "I love you" in a very physical and tangible way. It is the ISFJ who is most likely to say, "I have never refused him/her."

COMMITMENT: Life, for ISFJs, is about commitment, and so life's ultimate pleasure is a commitment to a lifelong relationship. It is abhorrent to even consider breaking a relationship commitment. If a relationship seems off course, an ISFJ will likely feel he or she isn't working hard enough to keep the commitment. They will work extremely hard to get things on the right track, even if that goal remains ever elusive.

PARENTHOOD: It is a responsibility and a duty. The ISFJs' mission is to impose obligations and appropriateness so that children grow into wise and responsible adults.

CONTRACTING: This is another goal and another duty for ISFJs, which one moves toward fulfilling. Reaching the goal will result in a better or clearer relationship. You set your sights, reach them, cross them off the list, then move on to the next important relationship concern. ISFJs are bound by their contracts, and expect others to be too.

ENDING RELATIONSHIPS: They will hang on to a relationship long after it ends. Even after the death of a spouse they will resist dating, or even certain kinds of socializing, if it means they may be untrue to their beloved. The end of a relationship can be crushing and stressful to ISFJs. Having fulfilled their duty and remained true to their vows, they can't imagine how things went awry.

INFJ
Heart, Mind, and Spirit

GENERAL STATEMENT: Driven by a rich imagination and a deep concern for others, they are a source of unending inspiration and enjoyment to the people in their lives. Their inner life is their driving power, and a possible weakness is their slowness to share some of their inner richness. However, this is overcome by the sensitivity and concern shown toward their mate and children.

FIRST IMPRESSIONS: Tenderhearted and caring. Others come away mindful of their gentleness. They exhibit a marked concern for others and a desire to be pleasant and helpful in any situation. Low-key as they are, others find it pleasant to be in the INFJs' domain, and readily return for more.

COMMUNICATIONS: The real finesse of their communication is through the written word. They are clear, eloquent, and magnificent in their ability to use the perfect word for any situation. However, this is dependent on their having ample introverted time. Without it they can be somewhat slow to affirm to others or express themselves effectively.

FINANCE: Details, practicality, and precision are the banes of their existence. It is difficult for them to find anything inspirational about something so mundane as money. As a result they tend to be poor money-handlers. Often aware of this weakness, they can be conservative and cautious with their money.

CONFLICT: The word, and all it stands for, is abhorrent to INFJs. Death itself is probably faced more readily than anything that even resembles conflict. It is contrary to their nature and they believe that nothing good can come from it. When they must face conflict situations, they do so reluctantly, and with a heavy heart.

SEX AND INTIMACY: This is the confluence of heart, mind, and spirit. It is a giving of self in the meeting of the mate, so that the two individuals become one entity. Intimacy, for INFJs, represents the loss of self in favor of their lover's needs. Their inner inspiration reaches its fullest potential in the overt acting out of love, caring, and giving in such a physical and tangible way.

COMMITMENT: It is deep, abiding, permanent, and ultimately the fulfillment of all life's goals and purposes. Commitments are entered into with some caution and reserve, but once done, there's no turning back. Because INFJs are so determined about keeping commitments, they can be slow to forgive a lover who is less than 110 percent committed. They place high demands on themselves and their mates to give it all they've got.

PARENTHOOD: Children are the realization of much of the INFJ's purpose in life. After mate and God comes parenting, as the ultimate value of a relationship. For them it is an expression of the deepest meaning of a person's movement through life. The same inspiration that guides them is passed on to their children. As parents INFJs are remembered by their children as patient, goodwilled, tender, and inspirational.

CONTRACTING: They are heavily committed to interpersonal growth and development, so contracting is the thing that keeps the relationship vital. INFJs translate their various thoughts and visions into goals that, when achieved, are measurable accomplishments that reflect the energy invested in the relationship.

ENDING RELATIONSHIPS: Like other Feelers, INFJs tend to hang on after a relationship is over, wondering what might have made things work better. Guilt can also keep them "holding on," when "letting go" would be in everyone's best interest. Once the feelings of failing and guilt are resolved, INFJs deem a relationship over, and like many Judgers, put it behind them and move on to other relationships.

INTJ
Any Relationship Can Be Improved

GENERAL STATEMENT: Among the most visionary of the sixteen types, whose gift to the world is independence. They prize their independence, and wish it upon everyone in their lives—mate, children, friends, and associates. They face a constant challenge of reconciling the vision of a perfect relationship with reality. They are inclined to constantly improve every part of a relationship, no matter how good it may already be.

FIRST IMPRESSIONS: Deep, somewhat serious, intellectually engaging. May appear somewhat aloof; may need to have the fun pulled out of them if it is to happen at all. INTJs generally will appreciate others doing that for them. They appear to "see" through you, giving you the impression that there is little they don't or can't understand.

COMMUNICATIONS: Slow to share, think deeply about every word spoken. Given half a chance, they can make any conversation complex. They love a conceptual exchange or discussion. Their comments can seem biting to others, though they are not necessarily intended that way. Often unwilling or unable to see their responsibility in a negative situation.

SEX AND INTIMACY: Like much of life for INTJs, intimacy can be richer in its imagined state than in its actual experience. They need to think about intimacy, frame it, understand it, then work constantly at improving it and deepening it.

FINANCE: Inwardly they can have creative ideas and even develop iNtuitive schemes about money, but they tend to be conservative in the actual handling of it. As a general rule dealing with finances, especially the day-to-day stuff, is not one of their strengths.

CONFLICT: They typically respond to conflict with something like "I'll have to think about that." Though they do not shy away from a stressful encounter, they believe that if we better understood the words we speak, any conflict could easily be transformed into a learning experience with a positive outcome. They are often blamed by a more sensitive mate for intellectualizing or overanalyzing a situation when the mate only wanted support and understanding.

COMMITMENT: While they stand by their commitments, they may be occupied by reinterpretations of the original "contract." They believe a commitment is good as long as everybody involved understands the meaning of the word, all parties agree to that meaning, and it has not yet been redefined.

PARENTING: The greatest gift one can give children as a parent is independence. To teach them to think independently, to stand on their own two feet, to be their own person, is the essence of bringing up children. Not seen as a warm, snugly nurturer.

CONTRACTING: Contracts are seen as statements of intent. They are to be defined carefully, then redefined in the light of the emerging realities.

ENDING RELATIONSHIPS: Once a relationship is over it needs to be dropped so one can move on to new goals. One must learn from the experience now ending, but the mind may be slower to let go of a relationship than is evident in the INTJ's behavior.

They have an internal struggle over understanding the dynamics of the relationship's failure.

ISTP
Actions Speak Louder Than Words

GENERAL STATEMENT: The original Jacks and Janes of all trades. They are good at trying almost anything at least once; that's also the way they approach meaningful relationships. When a relationship is working, ISTPs will keep it going; when it is not working, they will fix it—or get out of it. They can become so engrossed in fixing or negotiating a relationship that they may occasionally mess things up just so they can fix them again.

FIRST IMPRESSIONS: Cool, yet very intense. Grounded and capable of many interests. They raise good questions and see most of life as a practical challenge. Though they can be somewhat informal, their self-confidence and ready capabilities carry them through most initial encounters.

COMMUNICATIONS: They speak little. In fact, they can become easily bored with lengthy dissertations or complex answers to simple questions. If a "Thanks!" says it, then "Thank you" is verbose. They are reluctant to share their own points of view, preferring to raise questions so as to involve others in the conversation.

FINANCE: Moderate risk-takers, they see money and finances as a challenge, another thing to be "fixed." ISTPs are precise and practical in financial matters, though never terribly bound by rules and procedures. Their motto: If you've got it, spend it or invest it; if not, go earn some.

CONFLICT: They are not ones to start conflicts, but neither are they likely to shy away from them. Because actions speak louder than words, they prefer not to waste time talking. And they resist starting anything, especially a conflict, unless they think it can be resolved. They get excited about negotiations, resolutions, and turning a difficult situation into something constructive.

SEX AND INTIMACY: Because ISTPs live in the moment, intimacy is meaningful and satisfying—as long as it lasts. Experiencing it through the five senses is what intimacy is all about. Talking about it will not make it better, and it could even ruin a good situation if someone says something he or she later regrets.

COMMITMENT: This, too, is of the moment. They can work hard at it, but will likely be mindful that things can change. So it is a matter of making the moment. Each new day is a renewal of the earlier commitment, and it is good only as long as both parties agree.

PARENTHOOD: Like other Introverted-Perceivers, ISTPs have little need to influence, let alone control, their children. In parenthood they do the best they can with what they have—and hope that it all works out.

CONTRACTING: The very word sounds psychological to them, and that makes it questionable to an ISTP. If they live by their commitments, they feel they don't need a contract. If a relationship is in trouble, get busy and fix it or forget it, says the ISTP. That's common sense, for which one needs no psychological training.

ENDING RELATIONSHIPS: When a relationship is over, it's over. Nothing brings the relationship back; that's just the way it is. So, says the ISTP, get on with your life, one day at a time.

Yesterday is dead and gone, and so is the relationship. So they make the most of each day as it comes.

ISFP

Can This Person Truly Be This Unassuming?

GENERAL STATEMENT: You can generally count on them for a listening ear, a tender touch, or a brief, supportive word. Their quiet, unassuming posture lends itself to being there for those who need them. Those who require continuous verbal feedback or affirmations may find this type frustrating, but for the ISFP, the kindly deed speaks for itself.

FIRST IMPRESSIONS: Warm, quietly friendly, easygoing, very unobtrusive. There is a sedate attraction that makes you want to be around them. They usually defer, regardless of what your type is. One can easily gravitate toward them, often wondering, "Can this person truly be this unassuming?"

COMMUNICATIONS: The other person generally must lead the way and the ISFP will be grateful. They can have many sharp insights to share about others, usually positive ones, but they need to be drawn out. Left to themselves, ISFPs can be self-effacing.

SEX AND INTIMACY: It is a here-and-now event, experienced at a very deep level, with little or no need to talk or say anything about it to anyone—including the ISFP's partner. Other tangible experiences, from cards and flowers to a gentle touch, may say it better than words.

FINANCE: They can be very good with money; however, their own self-doubt can undermine their capabilities. Though it's not something they relish doing, they still can take care of finances with precision when necessary. Their last letter, P, can make them a little more risky and frisky with investments. Long-term financial planning is rarely a strength.

CONFLICT: Without a great deal of support and encouragement, conflict is about the worst thing in the world with which an ISFP must deal. Anything is preferred to out-and-out disagreement. When finally pushed beyond their limits, ISFPs can become tenacious, and it can seem totally disproportionate to their regular demeanor.

COMMITMENT: Though their easygoing style may lead someone else to think the ISFP's commitment is fluid or changed, over the long haul it truly is inflexible and runs very deep.

PARENTING: They feel little need to control children though are usually aware of a great deal of the family's dynamics. They tend to express what is hoped for in the children. But beyond some gentle support they let the rest of the process take its own course.

CONTRACTING: Willing contractors, who live by their deals, albeit appearing somewhat flexible. A little late or slow to respond, but never disinterested, no matter how much others may be inclined to think so.

ENDING RELATIONSHIPS: In their unassuming way they may not only be taken advantage of but taken for granted. They may therefore be quite slow to let go of relationships.

INFP

Inspiring Idealists

GENERAL STATEMENT: Idealistic and inspirational, INFPs have a great capacity to nurture and encourage their mates. Though easygoing and affirming, they can be direct and even controlling when one of their personal values or ideals is challenged.

FIRST IMPRESSIONS: Easygoing, warm, gracious, very much aware of their space and yours. Fun and affirming, though a bit shy and removed. They can be slow to engage others, giving way to the inaccurate but common perception of being "stuck up."

COMMUNICATIONS: Though perhaps reserved in initiating a conversation, they can be deft in expressing themselves. Clear and precise with the written word, they can even be poetic when it comes to communicating about love and other relationship issues.

FINANCE: They usually have a low interest in these issues. However, when it confronts them, the INFP can be sharp, clever, and astute money managers. As with many other skills, they can underestimate themselves and their capabilities, yet prove to be very competent.

CONFLICT: Almost more than any other type, they shun and abhor conflict, doing anything to avoid it. When finally pushed to the brink, they can be tough, stubborn, persevering, confrontational, and downright unyielding.

SEX AND INTIMACY: Like other Introverts they can be slow to express their needs and affection. Nonetheless, personal needs and affection run very deep with this type. As they become freer to express themselves, sex and intimacy can turn into moments of unselfish giving.

COMMITMENT: It is deep and quite probably forever. They are slow to make commitments—cautious and questioning before the final signing on the bottom line. Right down to the end they ask, "Is this the right decision?" However, once a decision is made, it is a culmination of hopes, dreams, ideals, and it is good for a lifetime.

PARENTHOOD: This is generally an accepted responsibility that is relished. Children are a natural extension of the INFP's ideals, and parenting is the arena in which these ideals are nurtured and allowed to grow.

CONTRACTING: Because of their intense commitments, contracting can be a facilitative process that enhances the relationship. Though INFPs have a low need to be influential, they have a high need to be an integral part of those close to them. Whatever will help the relationship is worth doing.

ENDING RELATIONSHIPS: Their idealism makes it difficult for them to accept a relationship's demise. More than other types INFPs suffer great self-doubt, self-punishment, and other such self-rejecting feelings. Usually these are totally out of proportion to what has caused the relationship to end.

INTP

In Love, It's the Mind That Matters

GENERAL STATEMENT: The inner world of thoughts and ideas is endlessly rich for this type. Though they can be slow to communicate with their mates, it doesn't mean that things aren't churning in their minds. While appreciative of attention from their lovers, they can seem disinterested or unresponsive, but that's not the case. Special events, like anniversaries and birthdays, can be celebrated in a seemingly haphazard, last-minute way, not because of thoughtlessness but because the INTP had too many thoughts—and too little time to carry them out.

FIRST IMPRESSIONS: A bit aloof, maybe snobby, often intriguing. The intrigue changes to engaging as conversation ensues. Not good at small talk, but loves to talk or argue about nearly any concept.

COMMUNICATIONS: Until someone has proven themselves worthy of the INTP's mind, communication will be slow and somewhat awkward. Once challenged, the INTP will be engaging and confrontal over any exchange of ideas. Once disengaged or bored, however, they can walk away in a flash.

FINANCE: Generally not their area of expertise unless the INTP has made it so. If not, they dabble in these matters and can have great financial schemes or plans, but may be very slow to translate these thoughts into action. If they make it an area of expertise, they will become more interested in money systems than actual dollars and cents.

CONFLICT: Often intrigued by the concept of conflict but do not handle it personally very well. If it's unavoidable, they may connect it to something to be learned, objectifying it, riding it out, and process the results. INTPs can write mental word pictures of conflicts—what happens, who says what—and carry it out to infinite detail, but never move it much beyond their minds.

SEX AND INTIMACY: Often a rich imagination sets up rich imagery for exotic moments. There is no limit to the pictures they can paint in their minds. As those pictures develop, the INTP's intimate moments can turn into an inferno of explosive and expressive affections.

COMMITMENT: Though it is forever, "forever" is defined daily in the light of new information. If a mate does not keep up, the INTP can get lost in a world of new definitions and redefined expectations.

PARENTHOOD: Independence is the gift of the INTP parent. That is done by stimulating the children, exciting them to learn, and above all, giving the child's mind a chance to develop its own thoughts.

CONTRACTING: While appreciating the need for a contract, it's far more stimulating to write the contract, redesign the form, or interpret the contract than actually get down to the day-to-day nitty-gritty of carrying out the commitments.

ENDING RELATIONSHIPS: They have great difficulty doing this. But once an INTP says it's over, hell would freeze before the INTP would have a change of mind. If it's over, the INTP is rigid and unheeding in the resolve to let it stay over forever.

ESTP

Relationships Should Never Be Boring

GENERAL STATEMENT: Exciting, thrilling, and risk taking. They live in the present, driven by the philosophy that "what is" is always better than "what could be." It's a waste of time to cry over spilled milk, because the milk can't be recovered and the crying can get in the way of managing oneself. They try to make the most of every moment in a relationship, with the assumption that everything will fall into place. If it doesn't, it wasn't meant to be.

FIRST IMPRESSIONS: Savvy, witty, clever, and easy to be around. They are quick at repartee, they can be charming and delightful in an initial encounter. Very realistic and somewhat hard charging, they reflect the philosophy that "Doing something is better than doing nothing."

COMMUNICATIONS: They can be precise with words, very literal, usually speaking in present tense. When something is said, they are likely to respond to it because ignoring it will mean they have passed up a once-in-a-lifetime opportunity. They have little interest in philosophizing or rehashing what was just said, putting off the discussion for later. For them, if it doesn't have immediate meaning and impact, it's probably not worth pursuing.

FINANCE: They frequently can be clever in their handling of money, and are often viewed by others as high rollers and risk-takers. Their financial bravado can give them an edge in the financial world. Though sharp with figures, they can be a bit stressful to their mates, who often long for more financial stability.

CONFLICT: Much like the common cold, conflict is a fact of life that can't be cured. Resolving conflicts requires about the same amount of time and energy as it takes to ignore them, and the ESTP is equally capable doing either. When they do confront conflict, they tend to see it as a stepping-stone in the process of moving through life.

SEX AND INTIMACY: This is a very sensual event for ESTPs—touching, seeing, smelling, tasting, and hearing. It is best when all the senses are stimulated and there is ample time for expression, affirmation, and conversation about all that is happening. The act is most satisfying when the ESTP can make the most of the moment.

COMMITMENT: It is only as good as the present moment. They are not prone to make promises they cannot keep. For the ESTP the best-kept promises are simple, tangible, and specific. They work hard daily at the immediate parts of the relationship. Promises are not forever, says the ESTP. They are for the moment, and you discuss and renew them each day.

PARENTHOOD: Every day, parenting begins anew. Each moment of parenting is an experience in which the ESTP teaches and is taught—they grow with their kids, and help them grow. As with the rest of life, parenthood is an adventure that the ESTP enters—and often leaves—with more questions than answers.

CONTRACTING: The ESTP can see contracting as an unnecessary layer that is little more than good intentions. It's probably not even necessary, because if you're working daily at your relationship, the contracts will take care of themselves.

ENDING RELATIONSHIPS: A relationship can be over anytime either party fails to make the most of each moment. Driven by an awareness of not being able to undo what's happened—the past—they are more likely than any other type to sever strings to a relationship that has lost its meaning.

ESFP

Love Is Making the Most of Each Moment

GENERAL STATEMENT: Life is a thrill a moment, and they want everyone to share in the fun. But in their freewheeling, free-spirited excitement they can become somewhat tiring over time. They can become so immersed in a given moment that they can lose a sense of where the relationship is going—or not going.

FIRST IMPRESSIONS: Fun, upbeat, can seem a bit fuzzy headed, though usually delightful to be with. Quick spoken, perhaps even a bit abrupt or unintentionally direct. One is often drawn to be in their presence.

COMMUNICATIONS: Tend to be very literal and immediate. They hear precisely and speak exactly what they mean to say, almost always placing it in the present tense. They can misconstrue discussions of future events or even just thinking out loud as being immediate, concrete, and requiring action.

SEX AND INTIMACY: They experience it in the here and now, and with all five senses. Their goal is to hang on to the moment, not losing it by thinking too much about how good it may have been the last time—or how good it could be the next time. Very earthy and sensual, wanting the close physical experience of their mate.

FINANCE: Can be somewhat risky with money. They spend it when they have it, and don't worry about it when they're without it. While quite capable of handling day-to-day finances, they can get blind-sided as a result of their lack of long-term planning.

CONFLICT: Can't stand it, can't face it, can't believe that it's happening. They would prefer to whistle a happy tune in the hopes that it would just go away.

COMMITMENT: Though their intentions may be forever, the only "forever" is right now, and that's how the commitment must be defined. Every day, every moment, the ESFP lives that commitment—but every day is a new day.

PARENTING: As with most other things it's a go-with-the-flow experience, making the most of every encounter. The more people, the more events, the more of everything, the merrier for all. Unfortunately that can leave them scattered and overextended, trying to take care of so much at one time, though they handle this process better than any other type.

CONTRACTING: Any agreement is only as good as the moment. They make a contract, live with it, and are not likely to panic if the contract is bent or modified a bit. It's all in a day's work.

ENDING RELATIONSHIPS: They tend to define themselves as one part of "two," rather than as a loner, so they may have trouble believing the relationship is over. But once that's accepted, it is clear that crying won't bring the relationship back. They are likely to have a good emotional release, accept the reality, and get on with their lives.

ENFP
You Can Never Be Too Close

GENERAL STATEMENT: Their sphere of close personal relationships can include more than just a mate, extending to anyone from the Little League team to a community group, all of which are approached with intensity and affection. Their mate may feel it necessary to compete for the ENFP's prime-time affection with these and other individuals and entities.

FIRST IMPRESSIONS: Easygoing and engaging, upbeat and highly enthusiastic. They can be all over the place at once, wanting everyone to be involved and happy. As a result ENFPs can appear a bit touchy-feely and smothering at the outset.

COMMUNICATIONS: They are prone to blurting out expressions, and their words may seem charged with emotions. Often, they are very tuned in to other people, often taking on their emotions, even to the point of unconsciously miming them. While quite good with words, their enthusiasm can be given to overkill and become tiresome to listeners.

SEX AND INTIMACY: The ENFP's rich imagination can make intimacy a constant pursuit—even when a conquest has seemingly been achieved. Their pursuit of perfection in intimacy can keep them highly involved, energized, and focused in all aspects and moments of an intimate relationship.

FINANCE: Unless they have a knack for handling money, they will tend to go with the flow, doing whatever seems right at the time. For example, they may change banks or open new accounts rather than balance their checkbook. Where money is concerned, they tend to go in streaks—one week being very hot, seemingly psychic on investments, the next very cold and even uninterested in the process. More often than not they would prefer that someone else handled money matters.

CONFLICT: Often, their enthusiasm and spontaneity can unknowingly start a conflict, at which point the ENFP will immediately wish to be somewhere else. Unfortunately, their response to conflict doesn't often help the situation and can even compound it. For example, they may blurt out a harsh reaction, then be consumed with guilt or sorrow over their action.

COMMITMENT: It runs deep with an ENFP, though their imagination can provide a longing or searching for the "perfect" relationship. While being true to their vows, their natural tendency to fantasize can seduce them to consider other possibilities, though they may never act on them.

PARENTING: They are very affirming, creative, and dynamic parents. Children feel positive and are central to the family structure. ENFP parents turn "growing up" into a day-by-day adventure filled with many activities and lessons.

CONTRACTING: For ENFPs this is a process, not a goal. Hence, a contract is likely to be constantly revisited and redefined.

Though intense and meaningful, a contract always can be changed in light of new data.

ENDING RELATIONSHIPS: More than any other type they can have trouble ending relationships. Frequently they hang in long after the relationship is dead, wondering what went wrong and where they failed, saying, "If only I had tried harder . . ."

ENTP
Relationships Are Just Another Challenge

GENERAL STATEMENT: They are the idea people, constantly improving and innovating ways in which relationships can grow and mature. This happens not just daily, but hourly. There are new ways to grow, worlds to conquer, and things to do that will produce growth, excitement, and self-improvement. The danger is that their enthusiasm isn't always backed up with action.

FIRST IMPRESSIONS: Easy to get along with, refreshing to be around, though their constant use of puns, plays on words, and other bits of cleverness can become tiring to others. Generally, they are facile conversationalists who can speak on many subjects, often all at the same time.

COMMUNICATIONS: They are skilled with words, so communication becomes an art form for ENTPs. However, they can argue for the sake of arguing, which can make others wary of engaging them in any real depth. For ENTPs such engagements are opportunities to help others think as well as to clarify their own thinking.

FINANCE: They are big risk-takers, capable of winning and losing fortunes several times over in their lives. Finances are means, not ends, and so life with them can be a roller coaster. They always seem to be working some new scheme, investment, or idea that will not only end their financial troubles, but also make the world a better place for everyone.

CONFLICT: What is perceived by ENTPs as a simple exchange of clever words or ideas can be viewed by others as a fight-provoking comment. But ENTPs aren't necessarily committed to what they've said; it's merely a matter of getting all the words and points of view out on the table, where they can be confronted. For them, what's important is not to take things personally so much as work things through in order to engender learning. Their need for constant improvement often results in wanting to get in the final word on a subject, even though they know they risk dragging out a conflict.

SEX AND INTIMACY: Like everything else, this is a learning process subject to continual improvement. So everything from conversations to body movements can be constantly monitored in order to ensure that each intimate moment brings growth and satisfaction to both parties.

COMMITMENT: They view it as meaningful and deep, but it can be constantly reviewed in light of unfolding developments in the relationship. By revisiting their commitments on a regular basis they are able to redefine and reorder their commitment based on whatever growth has taken place—or hasn't.

PARENTHOOD: This is an opportunity to challenge, encourage, and improve young minds. Children, for ENTPs, can be an excuse not only to teach, but to learn themselves. They can turn any chore, event, or family matter into an exercise in self-mastery for their children, their spouse, and themselves. Their goal is to make everyone an independent thinker, regardless of whether this is appropriate for each individual.

CONTRACTING: It is a process by which the relationship will grow. For them contracting is a journey, not a destination. Consequently arguing, reframing ideas, and exchanging opinions are all part of contracting. Nothing is in concrete; everything is up for constant redefinition, and the ENTP knows the relationship will be better because of the process.

ENDING RELATIONSHIPS: Generally a relationship's end is a time for ENTPs to examine their competencies, failures, satisfactions, and successes. For them the relationship isn't really over—even if their mate has left or died—until they have reviewed and resolved such matters. This gives them one more chance to fit the relationship into the scheme of their lives, and extract whatever learning there is to be had. At that point the relationship is over, and not likely to be revisited.

ESTJ
Lean on Me

GENERAL STATEMENT: Their gift to a relationship is stability and organization. They tend to be dependable, gregarious, and generally optimistic. Their capability and thoroughness can make them appear impatient and at times short-tempered. Rarely at a loss for words, they move through relationships convinced that they are right and that the world would be a better place if everyone else would conform.

FIRST IMPRESSIONS: Appropriate and well mannered, they give an aura of being in charge of themselves and able to be in charge of the situation whenever necessary. They are engaging and easily engaged, rather robust and quick to share opinions of anything if moderately encouraged. Enjoy wit in others and are quick to be witty.

COMMUNICATIONS: They are sharp with words and very easy to talk to, always conveying the right words for the situation. Will be initially friendly and involving; however, as communication continues they can appear impatient and opinionated. They have a high need to be heard and to be influential. Can also be status conscious.

FINANCE: Conservative but concerned about money. Good at long-term investing. They tend to have money and keep it. Responsible to causes if institutions (church, company, community, family) expect them to be. They can be very guarded and unwilling to take risks, always seeking to maximize security in the name of the family.

CONFLICT: It is a reality of life. Responsibility includes finishing what you start, and that includes conflicts. In other words, if you start a conflict, you must finish it, and if you can't take it, then stay away. Don't open your mouth with any inflammatory words if you are not ready for the consequences.

SEX AND INTIMACY: Intimacy is tangible and objective in terms of measured promises and obligations. For an ESTJ the mere act of providing for a family, and the stability that comes with such providence, are proof of their love. If it can't be measured and predicted, then intimacy probably doesn't exist. When you've got it, you know it; there's no need to blab it in sentimental inappropriateness.

COMMITMENT: It's forever. They took the vow and remain true to their word. If the relationship gets into trouble, you may sleep in separate beds, barely speak, but never split up. ESTJs may prefer to get lost in their work, hobbies, or other pursuits as means of avoiding a bad relationship. But to the outside world the commitment is intact, and that's important.

PARENTHOOD: For ESTJs this is a never-ending responsibility, accepted as a fact of life. They can meddle when the kids go astray, work hard at shaping them up, even cut them off when things go badly. But when they show up at the door, an ESTJ parent will always take them back because they are their children forever. It's a duty that the ESTJ accepts gladly.

CONTRACTING: Contracts are one more goal that can be measured and quantified. If satisfaction is not realized, one must redo the contract or consider it null and void. So a contract is binding, but if you break your word or the contract, then all is up for grabs.

ENDING RELATIONSHIPS: It's not over until it's over, but when it's over, cut the cord and get on with life. Relationships, like anything else, are measurable and have certain goals. Without them you've got no relationship; without another person you've got no need for a goal. Of course, goals change or are redefined. It's just another fact of life.

ESFJ
Stand By Your Lover

GENERAL STATEMENT: They are bound by duty and responsibility in a relationship. They act appropriately and expect the same from their partners. Though somewhat ruled by "what other people think," which can bog them down in a number of ways, they are still true-blue lovers committed to making everyone happy—according to their rules.

FIRST IMPRESSIONS: Formal, impeccable, gracious, maybe a bit plastic, yet fun. You are at ease in a moment.

COMMUNICATIONS: The ESFJ takes charge, talking easily (and often excessively) about many things. They feel a responsibility for keeping a conversation going, so they are quick to fill silences. If there is a communication problem or mix-up, the ESFJ may be quick to accept the blame.

FINANCE: Male ESFJs often have a high need to be in charge of money matters, while female ESFJs usually defer to their male mates. Both will tend to be frugal, spending according to a schedule, only rarely engaging in self-indulgent pleasures; an overdose of such pleasures will surely lead to guilt.

CONFLICT: They shun conflict, are intimidated by it, and prefer to sweep it under the rug. They would just as soon feed chicken soup to warring parties in the hopes that all will come together in harmony. When they do occasionally sound abrasive, their harsh words will be quickly followed by syrupy ones, so as to quell any possibility of strife.

SEX AND INTIMACY: ESFJ males may have some need to assume a dominant/leader role and will be put off or intimidated if the female doesn't assume *her* "traditional" role. Female ESFJs may prefer permission from some authoritative source—within or outside themselves—to temper their tendency to be scheduled and formal. Beyond those obstacles they are warm, loving, and self-sacrificing lovers.

COMMITMENT: It is forever and ever. And if anything goes wrong, they tend to think of the relationship's demise as their own fault.

PARENTHOOD: They can be very formal and structured. They expect children to behave and can inflict guilt upon them if they don't. They can be almost smothering in their love and very sacrificing on behalf of their children. But these are not "free" sacrifices. The ESFJ expects obedience and commitment in return.

CONTRACTING: They stick by any contract. Their word is as good as gold. They are likely to sell out or subjugate their own needs in the name of harmony.

ENDING RELATIONSHIPS: They have trouble accepting relationship failure. Even death is easier than a relationship gone awry. But after they get past the guilt and the thought that they were responsible for the ending, they can wrap it up and walk away.

ENFJ
The Relationship Is Everything

GENERAL STATEMENT: The relationship junkies. Generally skilled at interpersonal dynamics, they are an inspiration to, and are inspired by, others. They do well motivating those closest to them and generally are happiest when a mate responds to their affirmations. The ENFJ also loves to rescue and take care of his or her mate and children. Though such caretaking can at times be smothering, ENFJs are generally appreciated for warmth and affection.

FIRST IMPRESSIONS: Fun and delightful. Not overly aware of protocol and appropriateness. ENFJs' facility with the spoken word, as well as their sensitivity to others, usually leaves positive first impressions. They are generally affirming and sensitive toward others, which is initially very evident in deeds and words.

COMMUNICATIONS: As a rule they are good with words, though in an effort to be diplomatic in difficult situations they may hem and haw. Generous in their approval of others, they are quick to put people at ease and make them feel worthwhile.

FINANCE: Their need for closure, coupled with a high concern for others, makes them use finances to serve some ideal. So while they may be somewhat conservative with money, they are generally responsible and effective in financial matters.

CONFLICT: This is troublesome for ENFJs, something to be avoided. With such a positive approach to people, they use a great deal of time and energy to keep negative thoughts and actions from surfacing in the hopes that they will simply go away. There is no conflict so big that it cannot be swept under a rug with a few affirming words.

SEX AND INTIMACY: As with other areas of life, intimacy is a chance to express caring and concern, so the mate's happiness and satisfaction is foremost in any intimate encounter. As with other Feelers, part of the ENFJs' need is to meet others' needs. Intimacy is a scheduled, affirming opportunity for sweet talk.

COMMITMENT: Not only is it lifelong, but ENFJs especially can be undone with guilt and self-blame if a relationship fails. They are more self-critical than some other types because they assume that much of the commitment's success is on their shoulders.

PARENTHOOD: Because ENFJs have an unusually high need to impose their values on others, children are in the direct line of fire. So the ENFJ sees parenting as an awesome task in which he or she must be a role model, responsible for shaping the kids up. Parenthood is the vehicle to pass on goals and ideals.

CONTRACTING: Like any other interpersonal enhancement, contracting is a positive experience. If it will help a couple grow, strengthen their relationship, or help them through a stressful situation, then a contract is by all means a good thing. The overriding force is the relationship, and anything that helps it is a plus.

ENDING RELATIONSHIPS: Though they may resist a relationship's end because of the fear of hurting someone, or not wanting to face the reality of the situation, once it becomes clear the relationship is over, they will end it and find a new mate relatively quickly. A poor relationship is better than none; after all, it still can be rescued and improved.

ENTJ
Good Relationships Require Leadership

GENERAL STATEMENT: Their gusto and enthusiasm can make them seem somewhat argumentative in an intimate relationship. They appreciate the excitement of every encounter, especially from a mate who is willing to challenge them on their ideas. Such hearty exchanges are gateways to genuine affection and deepening commitment.

FIRST IMPRESSIONS: Robust, in charge, and proud to let the world know about it. They can appear a bit arrogant, maybe even impatient when things seem listless. They love verbal exchanges and can quickly move a conversation to a win-lose argument.

COMMUNICATIONS: Often quite clear and articulate, reflecting a good command of the language. They like to engage any and all in spirited banter and appreciate people who are willing to take them on. They can be stunned when their enthusiasm for a point of view is interpreted as anger or argumentativeness. It's as if they're saying, "If you can't stand the heat, stay out of the conversation."

SEX AND INTIMACY: Like everything else, this is an opportunity for leading and learning. Leave it to this type to convert the most intimate of moments into an opportunity for joint learning through creative leadership.

FINANCE: Often very effective with their money. They can often be geniuses to manipulate finances to accomplish goals. All phases of finances are just another system to measure life—and the ENTJ's success. Effective financial success for them is sufficient proof of competency.

CONFLICT: They can be dynamic and creative. In fact, what most others call a conflict is only a "healthy discussion" to an ENTJ, and it is likely to produce a number of creative and powerful lessons for both people.

COMMITMENT: Though an ENTJ may try to redefine it through clever use of words, generally, commitment is seen as a very objective act into which one enters with great seriousness. The ENTJ can assume personal responsibility for fulfilling the commitment.

PARENTING: This is an opportunity for joint learning and leading. The children are challenged daily so that growth and development are never-ending. The gift of the ENTJ parent to children is that they grow into independent adults, having been challenged and confronted at every turn.

CONTRACTING: They are often more excited by the form than the content of a contract. What does it say? What does it mean? How will it be accomplished? What benchmarks are built in to measure progress? What next steps are there when the contract is satisfied? These are among the many queries an ENTJ will pose in the process of refining, arguing, and ultimately fulfilling the contract.

ENDING RELATIONSHIPS: They are clear that a relationship is over if all of the opportunities for learning are past or complete. It's time to move on to the next situation. When this happens, the ENTJ can be seen as uncaring, unloving, or uninterested because of the objectivity with which they discuss the relationship's demise.

About Otto Kroeger Associates

Otto Kroeger Associates (OKA) is a psychological and management consulting firm located in Fairfax, Virginia. It uses the Myers-Briggs Type Indicator to help people understand themselves and others and communicate better—in their personal lives as well as in the workplace. OKA provides consulting and training to individuals, couples, and companies, helping them set goals, build teams, and resolve conflicts—all through heightened awareness of personality type. Among its clients are AT&T, Cigna Corporation, Equitable, General Electric, McDonnell Douglas, SmithKline Beecham, NationsBank, Westinghouse Corporation, and the war colleges of the United States Army, Navy, Air Force, and Defense Department. OKA also offers Couples Workshops, which use type as a way for couples to gain new understanding and appreciation of their similarities and differences. In addition, it offers a variety of Typewatching-related products, including books, audiotapes, jewelry, and a series of sixteen T-shirts.

For more information write or call:

Otto Kroeger Associates
3605 Chain Bridge Road
Fairfax, VA 22030
703-591-6284